Text Classics

T0358010

RUTH PARK was born in Auckland, New Zealand in 1917. After moving to Australia in 1942 she married fellow journalist and author D'Arcy Niland. They travelled the outback, then settled in Sydney's Surry Hills to write. Park came to fame in 1946, when her novel *The Harp in the South* won the inaugural *Sydney Morning Herald* literary competition. The book was published in 1948 and translated into thirty-seven languages; the following year the equally popular sequel, *Poor Man's Orange*, appeared. Again, Park had captured the mood of Depression-era Australia.

After Niland died, in 1967, Park visited London before moving to Norfolk Island, where she lived for seven years before returning to Sydney.

Equally adept at writing for children, she created the Muddleheaded Wombat radio series in the 1950s, followed by fifteen Wombat books in the 1960s and '70s. The most famous of her other books for young readers, *Playing Beatie Bow*, was published in 1980 after *Swords and Crowns and Rings*, a return to writing for adults, had won the 1977 Miles Franklin Award. *A Fence Around the Cuckoo* (1992), her first volume of autobiography, was the *Age* Book of the Year.

In 1994 Park received an honorary D.Litt from the University of New South Wales. One of Australia's most loved authors, she died in 2010, having published more than fifty books.

TEGAN BENNETT DAYLIGHT is the author of three novels: *Bombora*, *What Falls Away* and *Safety*, as well as several books for children and teenagers and a collection of short stories, *Six Bedrooms*. She works as a lecturer in English and Creative Writing, and lives in the Blue Mountains.

ALSO BY RUTH PARK

Novels
The Harp in the South
Poor Man's Orange
The Witch's Thorn
A Power of Roses
Serpent's Delight
Pink Flannel
One-a-Pecker, Two-a-Pecker
Missus

Non-Fiction
The Drums Go Bang (with D'Arcy Niland)
The Companion Guide to Sydney
The Sydney We Love
The Tasmania We Love
Fishing in the Styx
Home Before Dark (with Rafe Champion)
Ruth Park's Sydney

Thirty-eight books for children

Fishing in the Styx
Ruth Park

Text Publishing Melbourne Australia

textclassics.com.au
textpublishing.com.au

The Text Publishing Company
Swann House
22 William Street
Melbourne Victoria 3000
Australia

First published in Viking by Penguin Books Australia 1993
This edition published by The Text Publishing Company 2019

Cover design by W. H. Chong
Page design by Text
Typeset by Midland Typesetters

Printed in Australia by Griffin Press, an Accredited ISO AS/NZS 14001:2004 Environmental Management System printer

ISBN: 9781925773392 (paperback)
ISBN: 9781925774214 (ebook)

This book is printed on paper certified against the Forest Stewardship Council® Standards. Griffin Press holds FSC chain-of-custody certification SGS-COC-005088. FSC promotes environmentally responsible, socially beneficial and economically viable management of the world's forests.

CONTENTS

Standing on Nothing in the Middle of Nothing
by *Tegan Bennett Daylight*

FOR much of my life I've had a nightmare—intermittent, generally occurring when I feel overwhelmed. It's night, and I'm in a room in a house next to the sea. I am woken by a sound, a roaring that fills the air, louder than anything I have ever heard. I leap up and switch the light on, and through the window, instead of the sky or the garden, I see water. Green water: a wave, rearing high over the house, about to crash down and destroy everything in it.

Returning to Ruth Park's *Fishing in the Styx,* I found that my dream was not original. I didn't 'write' it. I read it: it first appears in *The Drums Go Bang,* which Park wrote with husband D'Arcy Niland, and almost four decades later, in 1993, in this book, her second volume of autobiography.

In 1945, Park and Niland, desperate to find accommodation beyond their rat-ridden slum in Surry Hills, had rented part of an old house in Collaroy, then an outpost of Sydney. It was a release from the cramped, dirty inner city, where their daughter Anne, frail and asthmatic, was not thriving, where the rats were the size of small cats, and the two writers, sitting up late to work after the baby had gone to bed, had nearly died from the leaking fumes of their old stove, the only source of warmth in the house. Moving to Collaroy was meant to be an escape to the seaside, to a place where they could breathe fresh air.

But it was not to be as easy as they had hoped. First, Collaroy was such a long way from the city that Niland, traipsing around the offices of publishers and newspapers, often had to stay overnight, leaving Park alone with a collection of deeply idiosyncratic fellow lodgers. Like most women of her era, she had many Barbara Baynton moments, one occurring when 'a strange man' crept along the verandah and into her bathroom. Park stood listening at the door, a 'frying pan in my trembling hand, resolved to emulate my bold cousin Helga who had fractured a man's skull with a similar weapon'. This man (unlike others) did not attack her—he contented himself with pissing in her bathtub and disappearing into the night, leaving her rigidly sleepless.

The autumn of 1945 was cold and brutal on the Northern Beaches, with an easterly wind that 'blew for days, weeks, on end, with all the urgency and muscularity of a river... At night the sea was black, edged with luminous foam; the clamour of the huge surf on the headlands was deafening'. The two writers were in bed when:

an appalling crash shook the house, followed by explosions, fizzes and spitting sparks as the electric power died. But before darkness covered us D'Arcy saw one of the most fearsome sights of his life—the light shining through the window into the depths of a huge green wave. The next moment the room was dark, the window blew in, and in poured a cascade of seawater. The waves broke on the roof, two, three, four, then with a hideous sucking sound withdrew.

This scene has become part of my inner landscape, imprinted ever deeper by my many re-readings of *The Drums Go Bang,* and my subsequent reading of Park's two autobiographies when I was in my early twenties. It shares space with images from *The Muddle-Headed Wombat* (1962), *The Harp in the South* (1948), and, my early favourite from Park's oeuvre, *A Power of Roses* (1953), whose heroine, the teenaged Miriam, takes care of her old and destitute Uncle Puss in the slums of Surry Hills. Park's writing, her bold, glittering descriptions and her vigorously alive characters, is forever lodged in my consciousness.

Ruth Park's story is, or should be, well known to Australian readers. Born the daughter of a truck driver in rural New Zealand, she met the Irish-Australian writer D'Arcy Niland first through correspondence—they were introduced by their teachers, nuns who had known each other in earlier life. Park met Niland only once before she emigrated to Sydney in 1942 and married him three weeks later—after the attack on Pearl Harbor scuttled her plans to move to San Francisco and take up a job on the *San Francisco Examiner*. Park's childhood in New Zealand is vividly recalled in her first volume of autobiography, *A Fence Around the Cuckoo*. *Fishing in the Styx*, published when its author was in her late seventies, turns its attention to the two great relationships of Park's life—with Niland, and with her writing.

Park and Niland would have five children together, and together they would remain committed to the early dream of their marriage—to support themselves through writing. Early on Niland quit a steady if backbreaking job on the railways to commit himself to the written word. The pair, along with Niland's adored and adoring brother Beresford, travelled and worked through the war—the men as shearers, Park as camp cook, as the assistant to a country taxi driver and, finally, as an opal miner—until Park fell pregnant with Anne. And then, having gathered material that would have a lasting effect on their work, the two settled, still accompanied by Beresford, into Surry Hills and the writing life.

The Drums Go Bang, published in 1956, is a vital, richly inflected piece of writing, a clear and striking demonstration of what worked in this partnership: a shared vision, a merging voice, a set of values doggedly stuck to through the hardest of times. It has the comic warmth and descriptive brilliance of other autobiographical classics like *My Family and Other Animals*; if its authors were British or American we would still be reading it. It describes the way Park and Niland observed the world together, taking notes, divvying up the material of their lives in a glorious battle for certain scenes, certain descriptions. 'That metaphor I thought of,'

says Niland, '"The cat stropped itself against my legs"...
how do you like it?' Park protests immediately: 'That's mine.
I wrote it down with eyebrow pencil on my grocery list
and you jolly well know it.' It is a joyful, funny, rich book,
while also feeling—when one knows Park's and Niland's
future—almost dangerously optimistic.

Fishing in the Styx completes the picture of the Niland–
Park marriage. Park's writing never shied away from poverty,
from violence, cruelty and prejudice, but in *Fishing* she turns
to some of the injustices of her own life. Niland was, in
many senses, a wonderful man—a loving partner and father,
a loyal son and brother, committed to ideals of hard work
and honesty in all things. He was kind and generous and
good-tempered. He was also

> self-absorbed to a degree that frequently made me
> think he was wrong in the head. His own purposes
> and requirements dazzled on his horizon like an
> all-consuming sun. If his attention were drawn to
> the ineluctable fact that other human beings, such
> as myself, had needs and desires different from his
> own he blinked as if I had suddenly stuck out a
> foot and tripped him.

Anne-Marie Priest, in her excellent, thoughtful book *A Free
Flame: Australian Women Writers and Vocation in the
Twentieth Century* (2018), notes that Park was the main
breadwinner in the partnership. Niland was more difficult, less flexible than Park—liable to alienate editors and
publishers, less willing to shape his work to the demands
of Australian publishing. While his output was still varied
and prolific, Park outstripped him, writing radio serials,

children's books, novels, scripts, short stories and newspaper features. And of course, she was a woman, and this was the twentieth century. Guess who did all the housework and most of the child rearing.

Add to this the precariousness of Niland's health. In 1959 he suffered a heart attack that, in hindsight, they had seen coming. 'Is it the same thing that makes him grab his chest sometimes when we're kicking a football about?' asked their oldest son. It was, and after Niland's hospitalisation the doctor said other, possibly fatal heart attacks were imminent—adding that it was lucky Mr Niland was engaged in the 'peaceful business' of writing. After this Park was so stressed that she had a short but terrifying spell of total amnesia while travelling in a taxi:

> I looked at my shoes and realised I had never seen them before. This seemed a mild curiosity, and I stared at them for some time before I became aware that I did not know who I was, where I was going, whence I had come...In such an experience, all the boundaries of one's little life are gone. One is standing on nothing in the middle of nothing.

Park's material was always and ever suffering and the stoicism of the suffering. Her childhood was spent in the lee of the Great Depression, seeing her beloved father succumb to psychosomatic illness after the collapse of his truck-driving business. She worked twice the hours for half a man's pay as a journalist in Auckland, and then she married a loving but self-absorbed man, and had five children. This marriage brought with it deep love, comradeship and laughter, but also endless work, illness and the ever-present threat of eviction from a series of run-down houses.

Fishing in the Styx teaches us that Park herself was called upon to be stoic in ways it is hard to imagine today. Reading her, I find myself thinking about the electric washing machine, perhaps the most important invention in the emancipation of women, at least until the arrival of the pill. Electric washers were not in widespread use in Australia until the 1950s. And Park's first child was born in the early 1940s. It is no surprise that she did not sleep a great deal.

D'Arcy Niland died in 1967, in Park's fiftieth year. By this time she had published some of the defining literature of Australia, but *Playing Beatie Bow* (1980), *Callie's Castle* (1974) and these two superb volumes of autobiography were still to come, along with the Miles Franklin-winning *Swords and Crowns and Rings* (1977). Literature is a kind of well, ceaselessly renewing our idea of ourselves and of the place we live in. Almost more than other writer, Ruth Park can bring an older Sydney to life before my eyes. My experience of having my dream life colonised by one of her images is surely not unique.

I met Park once, early in the millennium, at an event for writers, an event whose purpose I cannot remember. I do remember being uncharacteristically speechless, and glad of the presence of my illustrator sister-in-law, who peppered her with questions. Park, who must have been in her late eighties, was as beautiful as she appears in her many photographs. She spoke softly but emphatically, with no qualifying, no niceties or returned compliments. When my sister-in-law asked her how we were to manage the artist's life and the mother's life she said, 'By working hard.'

Fishing in the Styx tells us this. It contains riches and griefs. It is a life fully lived, bravely faced and superbly described.

Fishing in the Styx

For our children

The Styx is only *rumoured* to be a dark and terrifying river. Who has explored it? If you threw in a line, mightn't you pull out a golden fish?

PART ONE

One boiling day I was writing in my garret when the murderer knocked at the door below. I knew it was the murderer because I looked from the bedroom window of our landlady, Mrs Cardy. Her window surveyed Devonshire Street and the rowdy world, whereas mine was slapbang up against the sweating wall of the Chinese grocery next door.

As Mrs Cardy was at church, I went downstairs to see what he wanted. But it was merely to inquire if my landlady could put a few stitches in the torn lining of his coat pocket. His demeanour was as circumspect as his knock had been modest.

'Leave the coat with me, Mr Green,' I said, and we parted civilly. As he turned I observed on the back of his head the rubbly dent where some friend had once cracked him with a hatchet.

In Devonshire Street, Surry Hills, we were not short of murderers, no. We had Sweetpea, a child strangler, a musty old rapist who had inexplicably slid by on a manslaughter charge, served his time and been freed, but still had bottles and hard words thrown at him. We had rabbity women who had done in their newborns but got off on a plea of insanity. In those days of the second World War it was still widely believed that women who had just delivered could reasonably be expected to be off their heads.

'Yes, dear,' these meek women said, with a certain mournful importance. 'I was outa me mind. Terrible, really. All me milk went to the brain. I suppose it curdles, like.'

Being in a delicate condition at the time, though extraordinarily ignorant of the entire process, I plied my mother in New Zealand with nervous questions about these ladies with heads full of junket.

'Have I reared a looney?' she asked testily.

There were plenty of things about Devonshire Street that I did not mention to my mother, and I did not tell her about famous Frankie Green, either. He was *the* murderer, exalted above all others, a man of renown. He attracted obsequious attention from the drunks who yammered and fought outside the Shakespeare Hotel on Saturday afternoons, yet he wasn't even one of us in Surry Hills. He lived in foreign parts, Darlinghurst or Paddington, where he ran a few girls. His main business was frightening people. A standover man, what is currently called an enforcer, he made a living threatening illegal bookmakers, drug peddlers and shopkeepers with gun, razor, or anything else handy, such as tailor's shears, or half a brick. When he knocked

8

so gently on Mrs Cardy's door he was still the most feared underworld figure in Sydney.

'Fancy knowing a man like that!' I marvelled when Mrs Cardy returned.

'Know him me foot!' she retorted. 'My Ownie wouldn't let me *know* a man like that! Murdering no-good! I just do a bit of stitching and darning for him like I do for a dozen others. It stretches my pension, you see. No, 'course I don't know him. He comes over to visit his old mates here, like that Sally Bux, the Afghan with his face all minced up like a cat's dinner, you know the one. And he brings his mending for me to do,' she added with a little preen.

In the razor-gang days, in the 1920s and 1930s, Frankie began his career as a minder for the Palmer Street brothels of the gaudy old girl, Tilly Devine. Known as the Little Gunman, he was afraid of no one, and quickly became a notorious and dreaded figure.

'The fights there were over that Nellie!' recalled Mrs Cardy. 'Him and that Italian Calletti.'

Guido Calletti, in fact Australian born, was *capo* of the Darlinghurst push, and a formidable man with any weapon, as well as fists, boots and teeth. He was a celebrated biter. For years he and Frankie Green battled over the ownership of the fascinating prostitute, Helen Cameron. How much one would like to read a biography of this wayward charmer! A well-educated girl from a good family, she ran away from home at fifteen, leaving her own world behind forever in favour of the hazardous, dirty, vagabond life of gangsterism. A pretty redhead with a dancing step, she was bold enough for any adventure. There are many traditions

9

of her courage; she joined wholeheartedly in gang warfare, was three times shot, and was often thrashed by her brutal lovers. But there are no records of Nellie being mean or cruel.

'She was right off the lid of a chocolate-box,' said Mrs Cardy, referring to her youth when hand-tinted photographs of actresses and admired beauties were so to be found. 'Classy, like.'

Nellie left this world at forty-one years of age when she put her head in a gas oven.

Now and then I saw Frankie Green in Devonshire Street, looking older and glummer each time. He was a thickset man with strong regular features and wintry eyes. He never spoke to or looked at anyone, and the story was that if you bade him good morning he was likely to knock your block off. Mr Green was glum not only because he was a waning force, and knew that any day now some drunk outside the Shakespeare Hotel would be dared by his mates to stick out a foot and trip up the ex-king of the pushes, but because he was always in pain from four untended bullet wounds. One had created a large unhealed lesion at the bottom of his spine, and another was in his stomach wall, where it formed vile recurrent cysts. These made his belly swell like a pumpkin, and the Surry Hills residents would murmur, 'Poor bugger, eight months gone again.'

Until 1956 he was still pimping around King's Cross, still engaging in vicious fights, although by then he was well past middle age. He died in Paddington, stabbed through the chest with a breadknife by one of his women, a haggard creature whom he had beaten atrociously and twice cut with the same breadknife.

At her trial she pleaded self-defence and was acquitted. Those were not days when people thought of the criminal as a sick or misunderstood person and the victim as one who must have invited the crime.

No one knows how many people Green actually murdered; he had a remarkable facility for keeping out of the courtroom and gaol.

'At least eight,' said Mrs Cardy. 'Not counting the poor girls he kicked so bad they died later. Oh, yes, *we* know. But of course we aren't talking.'

How fortunate we were that Mrs Cardy of Devonshire Street had had a room to let! She lived behind and above an unoccupied barber's shop; the room we rented was twice the size of a single bed, with five walls and a fireplace four handspans across and decorated with Biblical tiles depicting the near-sacrifice of Isaac. There was one disturbing tile of the trussed boy kneeling meekly on a tidy pile of kindling, awaiting his papa's carving knife. I often cried over it, until my husband, exasperated, stuck a picture of a bulldog across it.

D'Arcy and his brother, Beres, knew Mrs Cardy quite well; she had come from the same New England town as their mother. Grace was her name, but never in a hundred years would we have thought of addressing her except by her proper style. She was a strong-built woman in her sixties, her handsome face unlined, her hair still brown, and her fine eyes speckled with green and yellow like a bird's egg.

I liked her the moment I met her. She had a grand gift of irony and a generous view of life.

'It'll be good to have a baby in the house again,' she said. After all the gruesome women we had interviewed in our search for a roof in overpopulated and houseless Sydney—drunks, psychotics, and ladies demanding fantastically large 'key money'—it was a wonderful relief to meet Mrs Cardy. Blunt-spoken, decent in her very bones, she was similar to the countrywomen I had known during my travels in the bush. She was also to be my only defender against the Niland family's incomprehensible hostility to the stranger who had joined the clan.

'And what about the boy?'

She knew my brother-in-law Beres was also without a roof.

'You could sleep in the shop,' she said. 'But I haven't another bed.'

'Oh, the barber's chair will do me,' he said, and he hopped into the chair, let his head fall to one side, blasted out a snore, and looked so exactly as if he had been hanged that Mrs Cardy fell into a hooting fit, banging her chest and gasping, 'You'll kill me!'

Mrs Cardy had a heart condition of some kind, but had so organised things that her life was serene and orderly. Her sister, a retired nurse, wanted Grace to live with her in a more pleasant environment, but she was content where she was.

'I don't need much from life,' she said. 'Here I'm near the church, and the picture show, and I have two or three good friends, and besides, there's Ownie, you see. He died in this house and I see signs of him everywhere.'

I have always been saddened that an unlikely and melodramatic fate decreed that because of me Mrs Cardy should lose her home and its comforting memories. But she was a strongminded woman, and survived the demolition of much of Devonshire Street that followed the publication of my first adult book. She lived, anyway, until she was in her nineties.

Mrs Cardy had a sorrow that followed her every step, ate away at her heart. How was I to know then, at my age, that some griefs never heal; they glaze over with the thinnest integument, so easily cracked by a chance odour, a word, a waifish memory from God knows where. But I was to learn.

She had lost her husband Owen, her cherished Ownie, and whenever she had a drink or two grief caught up with her and she wept for days. The boys had little concept of her pain. Puzzled, they said to each other, 'But he died two years ago. *Two years!* She ought to be over it.'

To them two years was a largish part of a lifetime. I, too, had little idea of what to say to her during these periods of inconsolable pain. Once I shyly put my arm around her, and she choked out, 'You've been brought up well. Not like some I could lay me tongue to.'

But in a kind of way I understood the boys as well. At their ages they were psychologically years younger than I, still self-absorbed in the manner of masculine youth, not yet come to the place where empathy with other people would mature them.

In the Depression years in New Zealand, my family had been forced to retreat to shabby neighbourhoods, forlorn and in decline. We had never lived in city slums such

13

as those which, in my persona as Wendy, children's editor of the *Auckland Star*, I had seen whilst accompanying the City Missioner on his rounds. And no matter where we had lived, my parents had made the place livable, mended leaks, painted the kitchen, hung curtains, put in a few vegetables. Surry Hills was not like that. No one repaired anything. If the kids playing in the street broke a window with a ball, someone scrounged a bit of cardboard and kept the rain out with that. Thirty years later the cardboard was still there.

Surry Hills was on the fringe of the criminal quarter, and in its own way notorious for minor crime and farouche social behaviour. Nowadays it has changed its character, but when I first saw it, it was a queer, disreputable little village, half hidden under the hem of a prosperous city. A port, rather, for Sydney was strongly maritime until the 1960s or 1970s of this century. Somehow Surry Hills, growing up higgledy-piggledy amongst the prehistoric sandhills that once made Sydney much smaller than it is now, had divided itself into the posh and the poor. There were some fine broad streets, carriage ways, lined with stately three-storey town houses once owned by rich merchants such as the original David Jones. But also there was a scramble of lanes and working-class streets—places of scrawny terraces; ruinous cottages far older than the terraces, sagging roofs; snaggletoothed fences and warped green shutters that always dangled idly from one rusty bolt. Such neglect, such disrepair! No one had cared for Surry Hills since Victoria was on the throne.

And as in a Victorian rookery, life was lived on the street, rowdily and often outrageously. It was what sociologists call a close community, but in truth the people were not as much close as closer together, mostly in each other's pockets and not wanting to be there. Overcrowding; dwellings dark and meagre as hutches; narrow streets and spindleshanked lanes were the major determinants of the manner of their lives. In later decades, in other countries, the anomalies of tower blocks and islanded council estates that related to humanity and its needs only on paper would similarly create misery, violence, and the extraordinary phenomenon of feral children.

Violence there was, in nearly all cases associated with the misuse of alcohol. Mrs Cardy's sister visited every Saturday to watch; she said it was as good as a show. As a nurse she probably recognised that much of it *was* a show— a version of the braying and ground-pawing indulged in by many animals. Some things were bizarrely amusing. One Saturday I saw a respectably dressed elderly lady take off her knickers, finickily fold them into a pillow, put it down on the footpath and lie down and go to sleep, her hands folded over her bosom. Another man liked to make his dog drunk; this was his party piece. The small creature, a Sydney silkie, lapped obediently, and in a moment its legs, all four, shot out at right angles. This caused great hilarity. The only disappointment, as far as I could see, was that the dog became drunk so quickly.

It was the street fights, the ferocious wife-beatings and the egregious female displays that raged up and down the street that devastated me. If I had not been so ill myself—I was one of those unfortunates who, like Charlotte Brontë, are intermittently nauseated for twenty-four hours in the day, and for six or seven months—I might have been able to adapt more tolerantly to people who scarcely knew any other way to behave. Later, of course, I realised that they had demonstrated convincingly that violence is indeed the theatre of the disenfranchised.

Many times I was ready to run away. Almost the first day I lived there, as I walked home with my shopping, I saw children throwing a litter of kittens, one at a time, from an upper-storey window. Their mother was below, heaving a stained mattress over her front railing.

'Ere!' was what she said, angrily. 'You bloody well nearly hit me with that one!'

As the kittens were dead as well as broken, I walked home, trying not to scream.

'What should I have done?' I asked my husband.

'If you'd said anything she'd have likely given you one over the chops.'

'But why?'

'Because her first priority is to defend *anything* her kids do. That's the way they are here.'

Still, after the kitten episode I was desperate. 'I can't stay here,' I said. 'I just can't.'

'There's nowhere else to go. We've tried everywhere, you know that.'

This was the truth. Every friend of D'Arcy's high or low, was looking out for a flat or even a room 'with conveniences'—a gas ring. Nearly every night, quite late, D'Arcy rang friends of his in the proofreading departments on the *Sydney Morning Herald* and the *Daily Telegraph*, to see whether they had proofread advertisements for any vacant accommodation. He would turn up before dawn at the addresses provided, but always there was a queue which had probably been there from the night before. The person offering the highest key money won the flat or room, no matter how appalling it was—and many were. D'Arcy would stump home from the city in the brightening day, gnashing his teeth.

'I feel like going out and bottle-fighting someone,' he growled after one of these fruitless vigils. It was the shamelessness of the greed exhibited that so disturbed him.

'And Australians, too!' he said sadly. He was the most innocent of patriots and remained so all his life. He deplored my native canniness and cynicism, believing correctly these were regrettable Kiwi characteristics.

'Music, man, music!' cried Beres, chassée-ing into the kitchen, and obediently D'Arcy took out the mouth organ he always carried in his back pocket and played some kind of cross between a jig and a dirge.

'Eeet ees opeless, opeless,' complained Beres, leaving. In between jobs he was forever trying out for the chorus in the Tivoli shows, but somehow his feet were never up to the work.

But these small distractions did not allay my frequent despair.

'I'll die,' I said. 'I can't stand it.'

But of course I could. I just did not want to stand it.

'There are plenty of good decent people in Surro,' said D'Arcy. 'You're a writer. Observe.'

'In between chucking up, I suppose.'

17

'At least there is a between,' he replied. I could have killed him then and there, but he was right, and I knew it.

And yet, you know, so strong is the literary vision, whether it lies in the conscious or that twilight region below it, I was already seeing beauty in this place I thought so odious. Each little 'front'—not a garden, just a space between the steps and the street—grew something. I had the impression that these shrubs had never been planted; they had burst spontaneously, in accordance with Divine law, from the exhausted, cement-like earth. Yet, look at them! Frangipanni—scented creamy flowers exploding from bare tumerous branches. Poinsettia, so spindly, so frail, climbed by cats, pissed on by kids and drunks, yet seasonally offering ragged blooms like handfuls of flames.

Some householders, very few, did try to grow something. That old friend of Frankie Green's, Salim Bux, the Afghan camelman with the face carved up like a cat's dinner, he had a row of old boots on his window-sill, each growing a leek, and one on the end sprouting a sickly rose.

The smell of those streets was compounded of leaking gas, decayed fruit, mouldy wood, a vegetative garbage odour and sometimes, only sometimes, a faint breath from the wondrous frangipanni. It was an old-fashioned smell, a Victorian smell.

On the elder cottages, where the spinach-green paint had flaked away, I glimpsed the sandstock bricks of which they were made—rubbly, uneven in shape and size, hand-moulded. Apricot and cinnabar flecked their mealy brown. These bricks were the very stuff of a Sydney not lost but built-over and hidden. I thought that if I could find a loose brick and prise it out I might see the thumb print of the convict who made it.

For I knew nothing about Sydney, though I had discovered the Public Library and was about to begin my long study of what was to be my own city. Like many overseas people, I thought early Sydney was populated by convicts alone; I didn't know of the hordes of greedy younger sons, exploiters and carpetbaggers, as well as the shiploads of frightened, hopeful immigrants. But my Sydney, my heart's Sydney, was to be older than that.

My Sydney sparkled and flashed with streams and little rivers, uncountable splashes that winkled through the ferns and grasses and tumbled into the nameless creek that flowed in the deepest crack of the Vale. There Captain Phillip, first Governor, pitched the first tents. It was a place of palms and creepers, orchids, water birds, and the sweet essence of damp soil and wet stones.

Captain Phillip knew his people, shackled or free, were not alone. In the thick and silent woods that grew as far as the eye could see, were black fays who appeared, stared and vanished, whispered around the tents at night. What they whispered was eventually understood.

'Go away! Go away!'

I was beginning consciously to observe. Each scalding summer day, about 4.30 p.m., the chimney pots above our ceiling made a sound like a child blowing on the lip of a bottle.

'What *is* that?'

19

'The southerly, of course,' replied D'Arcy, not even ceasing pounding at the typewriter. 'Would you use determinant or determinative as the noun? Both are correct.'

'What's the southerly?'

'Determinant then, it sounds better. The southerly comes every afternoon, don't you notice the room getting cooler? Oh, I don't know, determinative may *look* better.'

I was filled with wonder. A clockwork wind! Nowadays the southerly comes only rarely; they say the tall buildings deflect it. But it was one of Sydney's most idiosyncratic blessings, for in ten minutes the temperature would go down, five, ten degrees, and people would stop being cranky and fevered and feel like human beings again.

It was a swift something that rushed up the east coast, barging against the hills, sprinting across shoaly shores, no more than treetop high, agitating the forests into puffs of snatched leaves. Reaching civilisation, it split a thousand ways through the chimneys, gables and dormers of low, crouching outliers of the city, depositing on roofs and in streets twirls and whirligigs of burned leaves, a one-winged butterfly, a torn rag of teatowel. It scrubbed away the heat and tweaked up the sea, and in half an hour was gone.

In Surry Hills itself I looked for other things, such as the golden glaze of the sunset on the polluted air. Only industrial areas like Surry Hills had pollution then. And if I got up before dawn on Sunday mornings I heard in the distance the clopping of hoofs, unhurried and majestic. Running down to the street door, past the pseudo-hanged body in the barber's chair, I watched with joy the divine dignity of the brewery Clydesdales going off for their holiday, a green holiday in Centennial Park, each matched team with a couple of elderly stable lads.

'G'day, love. Ain't it a bottler of a day?'

Then I would go upstairs and cram in beside my husband, maybe just lying there staring at him, as newly weds do, marvelling at this new person in my life, his feathery black hair, the white skin, the strong square hands. I liked to put my hand on his heart and feel the steady regular beat, so different from the nervous skitter of my own. It never occurred to me that one day that heart would come to a stop.

The girls at my old newspaper in New Zealand wrote me letters for a year or so. Oh, you're so lucky, they said, to be away from dreary old here, to live a fascinating life!

'If you only knew,' I thought, for in my first six months in the Hills the blissful moments were few indeed.

Nevertheless the time would come when I could see under the dirt, the human detritus and the frequent wretchedness of Surry Hills the great kindness and loyalty and unornamented human durability of which I was largely ignorant when I was twenty-two.

Once more I would be able to read that wonderful letter of William Morris's to his stonyhearted lump of a wife: 'I entreat you to think that life is not empty, not made for nothing, and that the parts of it fit one into another in some way; and that the world goes on, beautiful and strange and dreadful and worshipful,' and know he spoke the truth.

But until that happened, many times I asked, or even shouted, 'How and why did I get into this place?'

D'Arcy Niland was not one to regard temperament in others in any way but impartially. He turned a tranquil blue gaze on me and said, 'It was me, or I, if you insist. You longed and longed to be close to I.'

'God!'

'You must face the truth,' he continued complacently. 'I was a lover wailing for a demon woman, and you answered the call of Fate.'

In fact, my reason for emigrating to Australia was primarily pragmatic. Though a well-qualified journalist with a small success as freelance in international news-paperdom, I had a fatal defect. I was a woman. In my native country I had ample evidence that I would never be allowed to hold a prestige position, or indeed be given a quality assignment. The most I could hope for was, at the age of fifty or so, an appointment as Lady Editor, when I would spend my time describing the dreadful 'frocking' at the Easter Racing Carnival.

Also I was deeply, permanently insulted by being paid what was called two-thirds of the male rate—though it was more like half—solely because I had ovaries.

'Bugger the lot of them,' I said to myself. Working on newspapers teaches even the convent-bred girl to swear. Then out of the blue I was offered a job on the *San Francisco Examiner*. However, my plans to sail on December 10, 1941 were wrecked by the Japanese assault on Pearl Harbour, after which all civilian travel was officially cancelled.

'Go to Australia,' said my father Mera, 'there's little for you here. Go!'

My law of life was an ancient Maori proverb: *He who climbs a cliff may die on the cliff. So what?* Still, I had enough Scots hard-headedness to obtain two firm offers of employment on Sydney newspapers before I departed with a capital of ten pounds for an unknown future. Many months passed before I secured official permission to travel between these two adjacent countries.

After one glance at the newspapers which had offered me jobs—they were tabloids—I took up neither offer. Besides, after seeing D'Arcy Niland again after a long separation, it became plain to me that I wanted more than anything to be close to he.

Let no one think that I was not clearly aware I was climbing a cliff.

2

How fortunate I was to have had six months of extensive Australian experience before the calamitous housing
shortage blew me willynilly into the disordered world of
Surry Hills. At least I had comparisons.

The huge golden continent and I had not met tran-
quilly; as with all immigrants I had reeled before that
abiding shock wrongly called cultural, but more intimately
related to climate, mores, language and personality.
There was in me the common resistance to difference,
based more on old loyalties and old loves than reason.
It did not help when D'Arcy remarked that I gave him a
cultural shock as well, but that he was prepared to weather
it out.

Neither of us had experienced a consummated love
affair; we had been too busy writing. We were stunned by
all the fighting, yelling and laughing that went on.

'This isn't like me,' he said, awed. 'And as for you, I've never met anything like you. You're like chain lightning in a billycan.'

'That's just what I feel like. I can't understand it,' I confessed. 'I suppose all my hormones are standing on end.'

In between tumultuous rages and blisses we spent much time curled up together like two possums, not saying a word.

'What are we doing this for?'

'Just to be close.'

Yet I was still afraid of marriage; I had seen it swallow women like a tide of mud.

'I need to be a writer, that's what I need from life.'

'I wouldn't want you if you weren't a writer, Tiger.'

So, three weeks after I had landed in Sydney, we married, to stay that way for almost twenty-five years.

My wedding gave me the pip. The ceremony was conducted in a workworn, dusky church by a priest with a face like a rock knocked into shape with another rock. At the other end of the building a curate struggled to turn a yapping infant into a Christian. In our little group there was not one person I knew. My dear brother-in-law-to-be, Beresford, was working late. D'Arcy's family stood in a huddled mass, staring grimly. Only the youngest child, sunny-faced and golden-haired, peeped from behind his mother and waved shyly. I did not, of course, realise that they were totally discomposed by this foreigner who had flown into their lives; they scarcely knew what to make of the situation.

I felt solitary, dismayed and homesick.

Two old women, of the kind that haunt churches, sat in the front seat and criticised my hat.

'Oh, Lord, I wish Beres would come!' I hissed to my loved one.

'Me, too, by crikey,' he hissed back.

My father-in-law, Frank Niland, turned up full to the gills, but behaved like any ordinary person during the ceremony. As I knew he was an alcoholic, I had often felt a certain subterranean unease about him, but found his personality engaging. I approved of his bold hand with the English language. A man who used words like addictified, fundamentacious and furiosity was worth any writer's attention. He almost won my friendship with his term for pregnant—spermatised.

Having seen his eldest son wedded, he did perhaps feel a need for attention, and kicked up a hullabaloo in the vestry. The old priest, who had preceded our nuptials with a funeral service, which he described as a long stand on short legs, roared, 'G'wout of here, you pestiferous thing!'

Frank made the sign of the Cross, as though against the evil eye, and stumbled out. All too clearly I saw that here was a family complication to which I had not given sufficient thought.

My new husband caught my eye. 'Ah, don't be hard on him,' he whispered. 'He's only a poor broken-down old tomtit.'

As we could not afford a honeymoon, Beres arranged a treat. This was a visit to the Chinese opera, somewhere up a lane of cabbage-leaves and old potato sacks in the

Haymarket. The performance went on for three days. The opera house must have been the top floor of a rickety warehouse, for even while the villain with the white-painted nose was howling and stamping, five or six hearty young Chinese carried some kegs of what smelled like salt fish to the very front of the auditorium and with satisfied smiles, sat on them.

The manner in which we sole westerners sat in one chair and cuddled must have alerted our fellow opera-goers, for we had many approving smiles, and several old ladies, with kind diamond-shaped eyes and scant white hair drawn tightly into buns the size of nutmegs, patted us both on the head.

In retrospect I tremble for those two cheerful young knuckleheads. For me the birdlike shouts of the actors are drowned by the murderous clamour of the pivotal Battle of the Coral Sea, fought that week.

But do they feel insecure, in that time of phenomenal insecurity? Such a thought never enters their heads, for insecurity is for older people to worry about.

'Nevertheless,' I said, 'you might be called up again.'

'Sure I shall, if the Japs invade us. And you too, don't forget. But in the meantime I'm an Army reject, one of Manpower Authority's nameless slaves.'

Early in the war he had been indignant and argumentative when an Army doctor excluded him from active service because of a cardiac malfunction.

'I'm as strong as a bull, I said. He just shrugged and said it was congenital and probably would never bother me and tossed me out on my ear. I bet he made a mistake.'

27

He was immediately drafted into essential industry, and had worked all over the country for nearly three years. Shortly after our marriage he was to be called up for another long period in the wool industry, but after that there was silence from Manpower. Perhaps his file had been mislaid.

But those wandering days were to come.

By a miracle we had managed to rent a minute flatlet in King's Cross, the converted back verandah of one of the wonderful old mansions that once lined Darlinghurst Road. In those days King's Cross was not the sleazy dump it is today. Maybe it was slowly on the way down to gimcrackery and crime, but in fact it was sunny, picturesque, and liberal-minded. Still the actors' and artists' quarter, it was crowded with European refugees with long haircuts, no money, and romantic manners.

'Oh, Mum,' I wrote excitedly. 'It's just so *glamorous*. The streets are packed with people all night, laughing and singing, and there are open-air cafés. A waiter *bowed* to me, imagine! D'Arcy is still doing the night shift at the Railway, and Beres takes me to the Minerva, a live theatre not far away. You may have read that Sydney was shelled by the Japanese, but it wasn't much, and of course nowhere near us.'

This was untrue, as the shells had whistled over our heads and landed a few streets away. I had the naive idea that my parents wouldn't have a map of Sydney. But it was true that we King's Cross-ites hadn't been alarmed. The streets were full of chattering laughing people, looking up into the sky (we thought it was an air raid), flashing torches and chiacking the hysterical wardens who ran amongst us, ordering us back inside and under tables.

The sounds of shells bursting, fire brigades setting up a screech, and a distant hubbub down at Elizabeth Bay were followed by an enormous whoomp as the moored ferry *Kuttabul* (we learned later) was torpedoed and blown up, drowning twenty or so Navy ratings.

'Get under cover, under cover!' howled the wardens, and reluctantly we went.

'Gee, I wanted to go to the Kardomah for a cup of coffee,' complained Beres.

From all over Sydney people came to frequent the dim and decadent little cafés at The Cross. Many were in cellars, others in attics or lofts, or courtyards once the kitchen gardens of fading Georgian mansions or urned and turreted Federation terraces. The flood of European refugees had brought not only cosmopolitan chic, but the correct method of making coffee. Hitherto I had tasted only that offence against the Lord, coffee essence. I went overboard with the new discovery.

D'Arcy thought coffee indefinably non-Australian. His family, like many others, regarded the teapot as an icon.

'Your eyeballs will turn yellow,' he threatened.

'I don't care. As long as I can stare with them.'

Staring was my favourite thing. I was capable of standing outside a fruitshop and staring dreamily at the grapes—red jewels and black jewels, little brown grapes, long green and round white frosted. I had never known such varieties existed.

The coffee shops were full of diverting people, artists, actors, producers, model girls groomed to enamel smoothness. They all had their hair up in the front and down at the back, and stood with one hip forward, maybe to make themselves look narrower. Poor things, like the rest of us they wore austerity garments with tight hems and mighty Joan Crawford shoulders.

'Why does every girl look carrot-shaped?' wondered my husband.

'Blame Mr Dedman!'

John Dedman, Minister for War Organisation of Industry, was the joke figure of the Battle for Australia. He had great power. Being allowed to make decisions on his own, he took on some of the mythos of Hitler. Certainly he made high-comedy judgments. Pillows were stuffed with grain huskings instead of kapok; dry cleaners were forbidden the cleaning of evening dresses or dinner jackets. He forbade pink icing on birthday cakes, and 'banned Santa Claus' by suggesting that Christmas be forgotten one year. Hotels were allotted a quota of beer. As the cry 'Beer's on!' often electrified the city from 4 to 6 p.m. some catastrophic guzzling took place. I shall not forget the rows and rows of men outside hotels, returning to the gutter what they had taken aboard in the pub.

Mr Dedman was also responsible for monstering clothing manufacturers into using a painful minimum of fabric for women's garments. We all developed an obsessive yearning for pleats and flares, but didn't get them.

There I was sitting in the Kardomah in my short tight skirt which I feared might show my tail-end as twin Christmas puddings. From the number of wolf whistles I got, it probably did, much to my chagrin. In those primitive days there was no popular interest in buttocks. They were for sitting on, to spare one's bones.

There I was, rhapsodising over the coffee, when a woman of distinction entered. She was very old, large, with a craggy face, and a hat the dog had brought home. She was accompanied by a slight, small young man, dark and sardonic.

'I know him!' I hissed. 'That's Douglas Stewart. He's a poet, and he's from New Zealand.'

'And I know her,' whispered D'Arcy. 'That's Dame Mary Gilmore, and she's from Australia.'

'Why was she made a Dame?'

'She writes. Poems. Journalism. Memoirs.'

She was unlike anyone else, drawing all eyes, tall, of monumental build still, though she was in her late seventies. Her face was alert, lively and rustic. She could never have been a beauty. She reminded me of Eleanor Roosevelt, and like Mrs Roosevelt, had a pair of wondrous eyes, dark auburn brown, as her hair was in her youth. In every respect she gave an impression of power.

'She's like a pioneer woman,' I said, 'who hewed out a home in some place no one has ever heard of.'

And indeed, when at last I became a friend of Dame Mary, almost her first words to me were, 'One day when I was cutting down a tree in Patagonia . . .'

As we watched, she fished in a bag that was half shopping basket and half brief case, and came up with a pot of jam, which she gave to Mr Stewart. I thought this mystery delightful. I noticed then that she was not drinking coffee, but had asked for hot water for a small teapot which had also come forth from the carryall. As I learned later, she always drank maté.

This powerful figure was in no way like the little mouse person she appeared to be in her nineties, though interiorly she was no mouse. However, that is the period of her life that most living people remember.

She lived at 99 Darlinghurst Road, King's Cross, and was there for all the years I knew her, which were fourteen. But she wrote to me for years before that.

Writing to my mother, I mentioned another famous person with whom I had done an interview to sell to the *Auckland Star*.

'Her name is Rosaleen Norton, and she's a New Zealander, too, and everyone seems to have heard of her. I'm just so lucky to have met her.'

Whoever had made Miss Norton known to me obviously had not mentioned that she was reputedly a Satanist, and that her fame rose largely from the obscenity of her paintings. The obscenity would seem marginal today, but Roie Norton had many trials, both legal and personal, because of them.

In those times Roie was not the queer person with electrified hair, teepee eyebrows and teeth apparently filed to sharp points, who hung around dubious bars in later years. She was pale and ill-fed, with a thready comeliness. Unable to make a living with her art, she often worked as a painter's model in the schools, and her sexless body, undershot jaw, and large hazy eyes are probably to be seen in many an amateur work.

She lived in the poorest circumstances, in a dank room, once a Victorian kitchen, on the garden side of another noble mansion broken up into flatlets and studios. The twilit room was crowded with canvases and painting paraphernalia. I saw an unmade rough bunk in one corner, and against a wall a small altar, unadorned but scattered with crumbs.

'For the mice,' she told me.

Though she had never seen me before, she lent me her scrapbooks.

'Bring them back when you're ready,' she said, carelessly generous. This trait was, I have heard, characteristic of her.

In fact D'Arcy took them back, and returned to me looking like a man who'd had a severe shock.

'Crikey, she scared me!'

He would never tell me what had happened. Maybe she had come on to him. Or maybe he was more sensitive to witches than I was. I had no bad reactions at all.

In later years, when she was celebrated as the Witch of King's Cross, a monster of depravity, magistrates revelled in admonishment, as they are wont to do. I attended one obscenity trial and recall a skinny old vulture, shooting his bald head in and out of his gown as if it were feathers, pouring forth the kind of vituperation that seems to come only from the committedly self-righteous. I felt a great deal sicker about the magistrate than I did about the painting which seemed to me to be as peculiarly lifeless as most of Rosaleen's work. But perhaps Satanism is not about life anyway.

*

33

She was undoubtedly involved with the earthshaking downfall of Sir Eugene Goossens in 1956. Sydney's cultural circles were shattered; lionhunting hostesses fled in all directions like frightened hens when it was revealed that the revered conductor, and indeed builder of the Sydney Symphony Orchestra, had been arrested for importing a huge amount of pornographic film and appurtenances such as masks, dildoes, and 'certain unnameable objects'.

As well as being patriarch of a brilliant family, and an internationally acclaimed musician, Goossens was a sober, distinguished personality. None of us could believe that he was a card-carrying member of Roie Norton's King's Cross coven, which was said to number nearly three hundred.

'But what do they *do*?'

Very soon everyone knew what they did, for the coven had been penetrated by a mole, a newspaper crime reporter. It was he who tipped off Customs officials that Sir Eugene's baggage would be worth examination when he flew back from Europe.

Few friends remained to Goossens. You could hear the rooster crowing thrice all over Sydney. A dishonoured man, he returned to Europe, and died a few years later, a waste of a great talent.

Rosaleen Norton never veered from her path. What the true inwardness of this woman was we do not know. But she must have been resolute. For Satan, if indeed she acknowledged him as master, never gifted her with riches or power or genius. Many years later, not long before she died unrepentant and unconverted in the care of the Sisters who conduct the Hospice for the Dying in Darlinghurst, I saw her stumbling along a street in King's Cross. I looked at the doughy old face that seemed to be painted on chicken-skin, and remembered that day long before when I came through her overgrown garden towards a symbol-painted door, and was assailed by a gander that scorched out of the shrubbery like a missile. That fierce creature was not to be beaten off. He pecked, used his whole head and neck as a weapon, whacked with his powerful wings. He was a watch-gander, I suppose.

Fortunately Rosaleen appeared, said a word or two, and he lay down on the grass with his neck stretched out like a dead swan's. I saw that she was one of those people with rapport with animals.

'He dreams wonderful dreams,' she said, and indeed I think that bird, even in his unnatural position, was asleep.

'Do you like snakes?' she asked.

'I've never been close to one, so I don't know.'

'One lives near the old rockery. I give him water.'

She poured water into a declivity where a rock had fallen away, and after a while a slim brown snake with a pink belly trickled out. It had a neat head crowned by a broken yellow band.

'What a beautiful creature!'

'Speak quietly, they hear by vibration. They are shy, precise beings, very clean and skilful.'

'Skilful?'

'At living.'

*

We had already made a vow that one day we would earn our living at writing. But in the meantime as directed by Manpower, D'Arcy laboured at Central Station, and I worked as a mail sorter at the long-demolished Darling-hurst post office in William Street. The post-office maps were an education to me, for Sydney was then a city of innu-merable lanes, dead ends, lost squares and 'jump-ups' or flights of stairs bordered by houses. But within two months the Manpower Authority transferred D'Arcy to the shearing circuit. He was not a shearer, but had often travelled with his father, a woolclasser, and done one or the other of the hundred jobs around a woolshed.

'First stop's Moree, and what do you think, Beres has applied for the same circuit.'

So for many months we three travelled around from the Queensland border to the Victorian. When the boys worked at distant sheds, I lived in tiny peppertree towns, where the main street is called Main Street. In all these places, and often far outside them, I worked as a fruit picker, opal noodler (picking over mullock dumps, like a hen, looking for crumbs of 'colour'), a hotel kitchenhand, a shearers' cook, a taxidriver's secretary and book-keeper, and an offsider to a Chinese chef on a wealthy station almost as big as an English county.

All the time I wrote, children's fantasies mostly, nothing about my environment at all. I was erecting a frail psycho-logical shelter from which I could peep surreptitiously at the kingly spaciousness to which I had come.

For all was awesome to me—the mighty-winged wedge-tailed eagles playing in the blinding noon sky, hooking their talons together and tumbling head over tail a thousand metres towards earth, disengaging at the last moment and spiralling up and up to do it again. The drumming of wallabies across wide clay pans; however near, these footfalls always sounded muffled and distant, like a knock-knocking in the hills. The astonishing spa bore at Moree, which feeds swimming baths to which I went every night in my Moree time—unstoppable, unchangeable water punching out of a pipe wider than my arm, clouded with steam, a fierce 41° celsius. For almost a century the bore has delivered more than thirteen million litres daily without a pump. Healing for skin and arthritic ailments, the water comes from a long way under the earth's skin, and tastes like it, bitter, alkaline and volcanic.

One night I heard a strange singing note, echoed and reechoed, across the huge stillness, and I asked the woman with whom I was boarding what it was. Was it a bird?

'It's the Koori women calling to each other,' she said. 'They can speak across such distances!'

The Kooris lived mostly in 'camps'—shanty towns outside the settlements. My landlady did sewing and mending for the womenfolk, who had no sewing machines. One day when she was going out she said, 'There's a parcel of children's clothing there. Will you give it to the lady with dark eyes when she calls?'

How pleasing! Instead of the clumsy, ugly word aborigine, she called them the people of the dark eyes. And what eyes they are, like black water, with eyelashes thick and sweeping as a doe's.

On the pastoral plains, fenced with stony hills ruffed with bush, smelling of cracked riverbeds and diminishing waterholes, the air was so clear I could see twice as far as I could in the cities.

D'Arcy Niland tells it best: 'In the morning . . . it was like walking through a house of glass. Then the sun came up like a dog to the whistle.'

When we returned to Sydney we found that the housing shortage had escalated to a famine. We could find nothing at all to rent. Then D'Arcy remembered Mrs Cardy, who lived in Surry Hills. This is how we had come to live in Devonshire Street, seven months after my arrival in Australia.

3

'So you're going to be writers,' said Mrs Cardy on that first day. She was impressed by the typewriter, and D'Arcy's several suitcases bound with rope and containing loads of manuscripts. He also had every letter, in its original envelope, that anyone had ever written to him from the time he was six and became aware that he was born to be a packrat.

I had the small suitcase I had brought from New Zealand and an insignificant folder of published work.

'And what will you be writing?' asked our landlady.

'Everything.'

D'Arcy Niland and I had many arguments over writing, but one thing we agreed upon was that if we wanted to make a living from writing we would have to be versatile. Everyone said a writer couldn't make an apprentice's wage in Australia.

'Who is this everyone?' asked D'Arcy.

This is what he wrote later, after years of experience:

Versatility is the greatest asset of the freelance. He was born to be a writer, not born to be a writer of some specialised type of literature. He was, perhaps, born to write that specialised type best, but if he is going to make a living he will have to cultivate versatility. Investigate the history of those who, from the beginning, wrote exactly what they wanted to write, and you will find in the background a grant, a patron, or a sucker. The latter two are hard to find nowadays, and the first provides too fertile a field for discrimination.

So we worked, early and late, and at everything that came our way. We submitted story outlines to radio stations and had them stolen; ideas for articles and fictions to newspapers and magazines. Sometimes the person on the other end said, 'Yes, wouldn't mind looking at that' and we fired ahead and wrote whatever it was and had it turned down.

'Still working?' Mrs Cardy would say, taking off her church hat and looking amazed.

'Yes, the darned thing won't come out.'

'Come out of *where*?'

But who can say?

We lived for the postman's twice daily round. The faint chirp of his whistle as he turned the corner from Crown Street made our blood fizz.

'Alight somewhere, will you, you two?' demanded Mrs Cardy. 'Running back and forth to the door—you give me the willies.'

But there was always the chance of an acceptance, or a thin thrilling letter containing a cheque, even if a meagre one.

The postman must have hated us and all those thick, heavy envelopes he had to carry. One morning, nine such letters fell through the slit in the door. Woebegone we watched. Nine! Then the flap banged up, a reddish nose poked through and a voice bawled, 'Fair go, willya?'

We went back to our work like the man in the Lost Chord, weary and ill at ease. And often if there wasn't a letter from home I wept privately in the dunny, because I didn't want D'Arcy to know how much I fretted about my father, my good friend Mera, whose heart condition had at last been diagnosed. Now he often suffered severe angina. The impossibility of my seeing him, even of receiving frequent news, gnawed at my heart. Sometimes I received four letters at once, held up for lack of transport, and several times for random censorship. I always tore open the one with the latest date, trembling in case there was bad news.

'You are ever in my heart, though seas divide,' says a long-ago emigrant song, and that was the way it was with my father and me. He wrote to me almost every week until he died, not mentioning the war, or his health, or the thundercloud of Japanese invasion that hung over the Pacific, but how the old cat was faring, the great crop of plums on the yellowgage tree, and the latest chat about the aunts and uncles. And always something specifically New Zealand—'the tuis are back in the flaxbush' or 'I heard the shining cuckoo yesterday, but saw not a speckle of him.'

D'Arcy had no idea of what my father meant to me. He, who later was to write one of the great novels of fatherhood, *The Shiralee*, at that time could not comprehend my love and anxiety for an ageing man who had once opened for me the world of knowledge, shown me that stories must be stories; shaped, I suppose, my idea of a man. He had had none of that experience.

'But you must have some feeling for your father,' I said. In his perplexed gaze I read none of the expected things one sees in the eyes of children of men who, for one reason or another, cannot stand up under the responsibilities of fatherhood. No regret or deprivation, anger or resentment. He was merely thinking the question over.

'You have to make the best of a bloke like Dad,' he said at last.

Frank Niland's younger girl, a kindly, rosy child of thirteen, crying in Mrs Cardy's kitchen after she had been drunkenly abused for something not her fault, wiped off her tears and said, 'I try to offer him up, but it's real hard.'

Offer him up! That ancient Catholic phrase that means far more than the words say—accept the will of God, agree that you will suffer cheerfully this pain, problem, deprivation, if God wishes it. A richly generous phrase, possibly Irish, and one totally maddening to the person offered up. My mother-in-law offered me up, and told me so, so I know.

My mother wrote too, trying to hide her anxiety. When I told her I was to have a baby she went on as if I were a chambermaid seduced by the bad Lord Byron. She was a great worrier, a loving woman with the empathy of an angel, so I kept from her many aspects of my life—anything at all that would cause her to fret, speculate, live on the rack that is so often the bed of the parent with an absent child.

And I had many letters from soldiers overseas, two or three of whom, enchanted by distance, expanded working acquaintanceships at the newspaper into emotional friendships. Very well did I know that this is an occupational hazard with lonely soldiers, especially prisoners-of-war, but I wished my husband would show a livelier interest.

'Can't you even be a little bit jealous?' I complained.

'No.'

I suppose I loved that man. There was an inexplicable affinity between us that never wavered during his lifetime and indeed is unchanged even now. When I am asked why I have not remarried, my impulse is to riposte, 'Why do you think I love my husband less because he lives in another country?' I don't say that, of course. Sometimes when I experience a sudden certainty, an awareness that is brief, so brief, a dragonfly flight, I see him in other places, other guises; once in Rome I seemed to be present at a death, not in the Forum or any awesome place, but in a dirty street in Trastevere. I don't know much about these things, so shall say no more. But without doubt there are times in our lives when destiny blazes forth. This was one of them. I felt I had spent my young days talking to myself, and out of nowhere someone answered.

Nevertheless, I actually liked his young brother Beresford more. He was the brother I never had, the funniest boy. Too young to be called up, he spent his time going from one preposterous job to another. My grist, he called it. It was grist for his mill when he became an actor. During our first six months at Surry Hills he was first a singing waiter, an eccentric specialty of that time. He sang Italian songs of the *O Sole Mio* variety, and was modestly popular until some officious person reported him as an enemy alien. He was carted off and interrogated by the police.

For the younger generation, I realise, the come and go of our gallant allies during the second World War may well be baffling. First Russia was a neutral nothing, an unknown quantity, then became the enemy when she attacked Finland. Then Finland was the enemy when that hard-pressed nation accepted the assistance of Germany. After that Russia was a gallant ally, although she did not seem to help us in any way except by keeping the German army occupied during the worst years of the war. The Italian question was even more complex. Mussolini, a journalist elevated to the position of a Caesar, had dreams of European domination, and precipitated the obviously reluctant Italian nation into a marriage with Germany. He was even shorter than Herr Hitler, and it was saddening to see him standing on his toes and wearing higher hats. Still, he, and consequently Italy, became the other end of the Axis.

Thus Italians, of whom there were many in Australia, mostly in Queensland and the vine country, became the enemy. Later, of course, the Italians divorced themselves from the dreaded Axis and sensibly became our gallant allies. But alas, they were then the enemy of Germany, which dealt out appalling punishment.

When Beres was marched off, Italy was the enemy.

Though he spoke Italian much as Man Friday spoke English, he could chatter fluently in an Italianate gibberish, and now, scared silly by this alarming occurrence, couldn't stop himself.

'*Non e vero, illustrissimo!*' he protested, when replaying the interview for us in the kitchen that night. '*Lasagna, tortoni! Signori, signori, quattrocento! Ah, Dio, il mio stomacho!*'

He also carried rosary beads in his pocket, a damning indication of his foreign and Papist origin.

However, an interpreter was called in, who pronounced him probably retarded.

'It was touch and go for a while,' said Beres, kindly banging Mrs Cardy on the back. She had this tendency to lose her breath when laughing.

He always considered he had had a narrow escape from internment, and was fidgety about police thereafter. Once when we were walking along a street in Sydney—well, I was lumbering, and he was being very tender about it— he suddenly grabbed me around what had been my waist, reversed me deftly and walked me off the other way.

'What on earth did you do that for?'

'There was a dirty big blue thing coming towards us,' he hissed.

He ceased being a singing waiter and took a job in a pickle factory, where he had to wade around all day in gumboots on a floor awash with spices and vinegar. I didn't care to ask whether the pickles were down there, too. One night he came home with a tragic face and two nameless black rubber tubes.

'What on earth are those?'

'They're my gumsocks. The vinegar ate off the feet.'

45

Then he joined an Ur-type film advertising company, which produced brief films to be shown during that mysterious interlude when theatre owners open and close the curtains several times for no discernible reason. The film company was extremely cynical about youthful would-be actors who joined their staff. Long before, they had been irremediably wounded when young Errol Flynn, marching around in some advertiser's newly fashionable all-wool spring suiting, had flashed his moustache at the camera for the last time and then marched off in the suit, never to be seen again until *Captain Blood* appeared upon the screen.

Beres thought Charles Blanks Advertising Studio might be his start. Although most of the time he was setting up flats, borrowing props, getting advertisers cups of tea and quick snorts, sometimes portions of him actually appeared in these promotion films.

'Look, look, there's my Adam's apple!'

'That's my hand giving the girl the ice cream. Ah, you weren't quick enough!'

'Now, watch carefully, here come my feet. No, they're in the shoes, dope. Striding through the park, nonchalant like. Gee, I wish I had a pair of shoes like that.'

For he was a dandy, carefully cleaning and pressing his few clothes, shining his shoes, burnishing his teeth—all to be ready for that big moment. And indeed he did many unpaid bit parts between being arrested for being an enemy alien and wading in pickles. Because of this he often received free tickets to plays and so I saw a great deal of little theatre work, all of which enthralled me.

Sunny tempered, ever-hopeful, always ready to play the comic and make someone laugh, he was also an excellent cook and taught me a great deal.

I missed him greatly when he was at last manpowered, and sent off to do jobs which were called essential but didn't seem so to me. He was a cook's offsider in a timber camp, a deckhand on a Murray River paddle steamer, and a worker in a fruit and vegetable cannery. The US Army in the Pacific used an astronomical amount of canned vegetables. Just before the war began Australia's output was 4.5 million kilos. In 1944 it was 45 million kilos. Beres canned so much beetroot he could not even mention its name. Thenceforth he always referred to it, if there was some horrid necessity, as rhubarb, which he loathed almost as much.

Dear Beres. He never made it as an actor, but at his too early death was a respected senior journalist with the news division of the New Zealand Broadcasting Corporation. He died of the same ailment that killed his brother and later the elder of his sisters. When I visited him in hospital a few days before he died, he said, 'When I'm better I'd like to come and stay with you on the Island.' (I was living on Norfolk Island in the Pacific at that time.) He said, 'There's so many things I can tell you about your old man. When he was about twelve he fancied himself as a pharmacist. Used to send me to the chemist's for the ingredients—tuppence worth of nux vomica and a bob's worth of strychnine, that kind of thing. He made up miracle pills of extraordinary shapes, like lumps of coke, really. We all revered him so much we swallowed them like lambs. After *his* dose Dad coughed for three days.'

I wish I could have heard those stories. After he died I felt very dark for a long time; his was one of those fleeting, glancing spirits, not very strong, unable to stand firm against cruel and unjust people, but in the end someone to recall with love. I always smile when I think of him.

Like most young couples my husband and I spent the first months of marriage trying diligently to change each other in both subtle and explosive ways. D'Arcy said I required him to become a person halfway between my father and Gary Cooper, and he was damned if he would. He did not want much; only that I should transmute quick smart into someone his mother would tolerate if not like. Like so many sons of alcoholics he was very protective of his mother and longed for her to be happy with his choice of wife. Still, our affection was such, and remained so steadfast, that very shortly we both accepted the exasperating for the sake of the good, which was manifold.

We were, in a literary sense, obsessively industrious, partly because we had to work like demons in order to make the most basic of incomes, and mostly because writing was life itself.

When I wasn't chucking up I was electric with energy. This may have been pregnancy, but more likely was because for the first time in my life I was living intimately with someone whose entire psyche was directed towards writing and the study of writing. We were an immensely literary trio, for Beres, the ambitious actor, studied plays constantly, pulling them to pieces, dissecting motivation, proclaiming dialogue, until Mrs Cardy, majestically ascending her stairs

48

with a candlestick in one hand and her chamberpot in the other, declared, 'You're all as mad as meataxes,' and to me 'Don't keep that baby of ours up all night, dear.'

Even when we did retire, Beres to his barber's chair and D'Arcy and I to our jampacked pink garret, we used to lie in that single bed—and as our baby grew it became ever more single—writing ideas for stories on each other's palms and rubbing them out and writing others. We also wrote personal messages: 'Of course we'll have our own home one day' and 'you'll become a famous writer, I just know you will' or 'well, we did have six rejections yesterday, but tomorrow will be lucky'.

Did he ever say 'I love you'? Of course not. He was an Australian. But I did, because I wasn't.

In that bedroom we rarely spoke aloud because although the century-old sandstock walls were thick and soundproof, the tiny fireplace opened directly into the flue of the larger one in Mrs Cardy's bedroom. Although we did not suspect that good woman of eavesdropping, we tried to be private, speaking in whispers and making love decorously, usually with my man's hand over my mouth, for I was a giggler.

Sometimes I was tremendously happy, for I believed in the goodness of God and His plans for us. And D'Arcy believed even more simply and firmly than I did. His background was entirely Irish, devout and trusting. He even wore a tattered example of my *bête noire*, the scapular.

'Take off that awful piece of superstition!'

'No, I won't. Sister Roche gave it to me when I left Glen Innes,' he explained.

49

'It's only a dirty piece of brown wool. I can't even *read* what's written on it. Ugh!'

'What matters, you heathen islander from the Antarctic Ocean, is not the brown wool or what's written on it. It's to remind me that Sister Roche believes in me, and is always praying for her errant lad.'

'Oh, God!'

'And mind your mouth.'

How young and innocent we were. Fearless, too, for I can see now that the ambition we had set ourselves, to make a living as writers, particularly in wartime, was a dream for children. Yet, two people of a single mind can bring prodigious energy to a project, and ours was dual. We had determined to become good writers, and to build a good marriage. There was, anyway, a perverse delight in us both to fight against the wind.

An old school exercise book is still in existence; it contains dated lists inscribed, alas, in pencil. Those were the days before the ballpoint pen, and if you did not possess a fountain pen, casual notes and memoranda were written in pencil. On the first page, faint and rubbed though it is, there can be discerned a record of fourteen submissions from January 3 to 9. Of these stories, articles, radio-play outlines, verse, thirteen were rejected. The survivor, a short story, sold to a classy little magazine called *Australia*, which paid D'Arcy £2.15.0, but not for three months. The tradition for publishers of journals and newspapers to hang on to contributors' money for unstated periods was the greatest bane of a freelance's life. Some of them did not pay at all unless you sent in a claim. Only the Australian Broadcasting Corporation, which was then called the Australian Broadcasting Commission, paid promptly, not always on acceptance but at least on broadcast.

Some terrible knuckleheads worked for the ABC, but its charter had plainly been formed on professional lines. Upon acceptance of any work, the writer was immediately sent a contract which plainly stated which rights the Commission wished to buy, and what it was prepared to pay. The rights were just, modest and strictly within the scope of broadcasting. Not so other magazine and newspaper firms. Some editors engaged in demeaning badinage: 'How much do you think it's worth? Oh, come now, you do have a big opinion of yourself!'

This kind of power play, frequently sexist as well, must have killed off many a promising writer. It was not peculiar to Australia but it was in that country that we suffered it. Fortunately, as both of us had cut our teeth on this attitude when youngsters, we had sworn to each other we would never accept it, even if starving.

But ah, we were tempted to give in sometimes.

D'Arcy still displayed a fatal combativeness towards editors. You could see hate coming into their eyes when they looked at him.

'What's the matter with it?'

No amount of argument from me would convince him that a good editor has a bell in his head that goes ping! when he reads a manuscript suitable for his market.

'And he doesn't have to tell *you* why or why not.'

'Bullshit!'

51

'Suit yourself.'

It was my custom, when a story of mine was rejected, to smilingly ask for it back. In fact I didn't care why, or why not. Rejected was rejected. Interestingly, this calm attitude often led to a request for some small compromise, which usually I agreed to do. Early I learned that it never hurts to give your opponent a way out. My husband, a much franker character, at first thought this duplicity rather than diplomacy.

'Are all girls like you?' he demanded.

'Yep.'

He was a slow learner, but the *Australian Women's Weekly* presented him with the ultimate lesson. When the *Weekly* accepted a story he was delighted, for its circulation was then as now, enormous. Even the cheque was for a sum fair if not extravagant. Turning over the cheque to endorse it, he discovered that his endorsement was an agreement to the relinquishment of *all copyright, worldwide*. In other words, if you did not agree to this piracy of radio, audio, film, reprint, translation and anthology rights, you could not cash that cheque.

'Cunning bastards!'

We were very much in need of money that day, as we were most of the time, but D'Arcy returned that cheque to the *Weekly* with a civil request that his story be sent back. Happily, the story later sold to an American journal, the *Saturday Evening Post*, and has since been anthologised in eight or nine languages.

This type of indefensible editorial and publishing behaviour dwindled and almost died when literary agencies appeared and societies of authors gathered some clout. But the possibility of rip-off for the writer who prefers to work independently of these valuable protectors remains as it was.

The foundation, the absolute rockbottom of our financial affairs, was the weekly script I wrote for the ABC, *The Wideawake Bunyip*. For this I received a guinea and a half. In real terms one cannot define what this was worth. Did half a guinea equate with ten or twenty dollars?

Let me say only that the cost of travel by public transport, at least on the popular trams, was calculated on twopence for the first section and a penny each for those succeeding. On the same scale I could do the entire weekend shopping for the three of us for ten shillings. Mind you, it was not luxury shopping; almost everything was in short supply. But Surry Hills, like all working-class suburbs, was cheap, and I was cheaper still, hunting around to save threepence here and a shilling there. Not for nothing had I done all that snagging in the Depression.

But still, after paying our fifteen shillings rent and contributing half the bill for coal and wood, there was not much left.

My Irish Grandma, who had all her life lived so closely with poverty that she treated it with a haughty kick in the pants, held to the tradition of always giving away the last coin in her purse. Of course she took care it was a small coin; *she* was no dummo.

Frequently faced with the question of where the next bite was coming from—or the next stamp, far more important—I began to do the same thing. It worked like magic. The minute my change purse was as empty as a boot, some dilatory editor paid up. We thought it might have been because nature abhors a vacuum.

To save postage we delivered most manuscripts, and my weekly enormous treat was to take my ABC script to town to the *Children's Session* and spend half an hour with the delightful people who worked there. For one of the many things I was homesick for was working with and for children, which I had so expansively enjoyed when I was Wendy of the *Auckland Star*. Never did I have any ambitions to teach children; what I wanted was to find out what gave them fun, and to do my best to supply it. This aim was exactly that of the ABC's *Children's Session*, and of the people who ran it—or should I say galloped it—Elizabeth, Mac and Joe.

These weekly visits with my scripts brought back the enthusiastic and inventive days of what in my more disheartened moments I called my girlhood—the years before I was twenty.

The ABC had the disturbing habit of renting premises all over the city and suburbs, which led to whimsical dispersions of its possessions. Once, I recall, Dick Parry, the *Children's Session* producer, said apologetically, 'I'm sorry but you can't have a harp. It's out at Burwood. But the glockenspiel is at Darlinghurst, so much nearer. Would that do instead?'

Drama and Talks, and the *Children's Session*, were at 96 Market Street, in a glamorously ratty building long since demolished to make way for the serpentine magnificence of the shopping complex Centrepoint. The building had once been His Majesty's Theatre; the old auditorium was an immense Woolworths' store, and the warren of dressing rooms above it the ABC offices and studios. Oh, I loved that building, and the creaky lift which one was likely to share with some celebrated actress or overseas producer. Once, I remember, with a rotund, melancholy-faced gentleman in a superlative waistcoat. At first I thought he was Oscar Wilde, then realised he was Britain's Robert Morley, whose work I esteemed highly. I was so overcome my feet shrank and when I left the lift one of my shoes fell off.

'Surely,' he said gravely as he handed it back to me, 'it cannot be midnight yet?'

The very idea of entering the *Children's Session* offices delighted me. I never knew whom I might find there, maybe an admired actor or that other imponder-able, *'a personality'*. For radio was the only alternative to theatre work, and sooner or later all the stars played radio. Once I found a young man with his face muffled in a curtain, practising being a crow. Peter Finch his name was. At the time he was as yellow as a smoked fish with atabrin, the anti-malarial drug. He was either going to Darwin to be bombed by the Japanese or had just returned. Later D'Arcy became close to him. Peter always said they had been copyboys at the *Sun* together, but this was not true. Peter had long preceded D'Arcy there; he was several years older than he admitted. I wouldn't say we were all good friends; I find it difficult to know who an actor actually is. Peter Finch was a complex, secretive character with whom one had to be careful. He was adept at the old actor's habit of inviting one to lunch and then leaving one with the bill. (Robert Helpmann did it to me once, and at a costly restaurant too. But that mischievous little troll had been so entertaining, told so many outrageous tales of his dancing life it was worth it.)

Peter Finch was multi-talented. His was the most heart-stopping Mercutio I ever witnessed, and Laurence Olivier said the same. He could also write well, and his painting was said to be excellent. He was supposed to have had a bizarre childhood, but who could say when the sinister tales came from such a fantasiser?

When he was playing radio his face could change eerily; so could his body. Within a year or so he played the lead in a play I had written about Abel Tasman, the brutal cattleboat captain who preceded James Cook round and about the Australian coasts.

'I played him as a big man,' Peter said.

'How did you do that on radio?' I asked with a smile.

'I made myself a foot taller.'

Now I could say I knew Elizabeth, Mac and Joe, whose voices I had first heard on the north-west plains of New South Wales, while I dried dishes for the Chinese cook, in a smoky homestead kitchen. Those laughing voices had laughing faces to go with them. Mac looked like a youngish Ronald Colman. Dear tubby Joe had survived the same Napier earthquake in which my runaway Auntie Willy had so sadly been banged on the head with a bit of cathedral. I felt this a great bond.

Then there was Elizabeth—Ida Osbourne—whom I admired more than words can tell. When I looked at her I always thought of the goddess or nymph in one of the classic Greek tales—'a fair and lightly-sparkling girl'.

She was capable and composed, her clothes always perfect. I imagined her living in some heavenly apartment overlooking the Harbour, probably with a housekeeper. As it happened she, too, had had a struggle to find lodgings in houseless Sydney, and her salary was adequate and nothing more, for the ABC was never princely in its remunerations to employees. But her delight in her work, her friends, in life itself made her golden, and I longed and longed to be exactly like her.

I dreaded her finding out that we were living on the lick of a fish bone, in a place where rats looked in the bedroom window and murderers came to the street door to ask that their coats be mended. These things, I felt, did not add to the persona I wished to present, that of the successful young writer.

It was a great shock to me years later when Elizabeth published some reminiscences of her work at the ABC and I found out she had known all along.

Nevertheless, my instinct was correct, though it did not apply to people like Elizabeth. Long before we married, D'Arcy had written a gag script for Jack Davey, a famously successful radio personality for two decades.

Jack Davey was originally a New Zealander; he had comedic wit, a remarkable voice, and all the hubris in the world. In times when self-promotion was considered lowlife, Mr Davey excelled at it. He did spectacular things and was forever in the headlines. He drove fabulous cars; bought a city building and painted it bright red; was constantly arrested for illegal gambling in the various underground baccarat clubs and was as mean as catsmeat.

For three months D'Arcy chased Jack Davey for payment. He stood outside his office door, he telephoned him, he accosted him in the street.

'That cow owed me five guineas, which was the arrangement, and I was determined to get him if it took two years.'

At last he managed, this threadbare kid of seventeen, to catch the great man as he was getting out of his Porsche (a car then scarcely heard of in Australia) and said, 'You owe me five guineas, Mr Davey, and I want it.'

He added, fatally, 'I've just lost my job at the *Sun* and I really need it.'

Jack Davey put his hand in his pocket and pulled out a pound note. 'That's all you're getting. But here's four quids' worth of good advice—never cry a poor mouth, it ruins your chances.'

'He threw the pound note at me, and strode off, the lousy bastard. And he was wearing a *silk suit*!'

Nevertheless, Jack Davey's advice was worth a great deal more than four pounds, five shillings, and I pass it on to all those in a tight corner. In need, which so often translates as defencelessness, there is some mysterious component which brings out the worst in many people; regrettably too, in all races. It is as if defencelessness, no matter the cause—poverty, age, gender, physical weakness or anything else—instantly marks you out as an appropriate victim.

Jack Davey had it right. Never appear in need of what the other person owes you. I think that Christ's statement that 'the meek shall inherit the earth' is a mistranslation slavishly followed. The meek inherit nothing. They get rocks dropped on them from a great height. Unless, of course, human nature changes, which it shows no sign of doing.

It was after one of these lifesaving half hours with the *Children's Session* staff that I came close to being filleted by a plate-glass window. Happily hurrying down to Pitt Street to wait for a tram, an Austro-American riot broke out under my very nose. One second there was a street full of traffic, shoppers, lunchtime dawdlers, and the next Pitt Street from Market to King was a roaring berserk mass of people, all, in the recognised manner of crowd madness, struggling violently to reach the centre. The noise was deafening—police whistles, rebel yells, cooees, screeches, barracking, and frenzied bell-ringing from trams caught embattled in the middle of it all.

Having been in other wartime riots, I knew what to do. Get out fast. I scurried for Woolworths' front entrance, which, had I but known it, the well-drilled staff had already locked and barred. But in a second the crush of panicky people charging from both directions pushed me up in the air against the window. My feet were at least a metre off the pavement. Certainly from up there I had a remarkable view. Over the heaving mass of combatants I noticed the frenzied staff of Farmer and Co. (now Grace Bros), struggling to put up wooden bomb shutters to protect their expansive windows. Shutters and staff were borne away like flotsam.

One huge US military policeman leaped to the top of a tumble of sandbags—there were sandbags all over Sydney—and in an orderly manner hit every head that passed him. Crash, crunch, yelp! Then he too was dragged down, and there was a short dogfight, all fists and boots and hoarse caterwauls. I often wondered whether he survived.

All at once the Woolworths' windows pressed against my back began to give, bulging and trembling. At the same time the steel frames that supported them emitted a long thin yawp. One of the upper corners had given way.

'My God, my God, the windows!' someone shrieked, and the crowd shoved all the harder, in all directions, in the mindless rage of panic. I was pushed so far up in the air that a man's head was level with my waist. I suppose I screamed 'Let me out! Let me out!' Heaven knows what one screams in these circumstances. And suddenly he collapsed. For a moment I thought I'd murdered him, but I think he had already fainted or lost his footing with some tidal eddy of the crowd.

Did I care? I jumped on his prostrate torso—his legs were already being trampled upon—scrambled into a fleeting clear space and around the corner into Market Street. There I pressed into a doorway, convinced I was going to have that baby on the spot.

Later I heard that the Woolworths' window had cracked but not fallen. Still, it was a formidable few minutes. I much preferred another inter-ally riot I saw on Manly Wharf when a large group of wandering Australian soldiers, out of money and things to do (the Australian troops received approximately half the pay of the Americans), met a carefree band of US sailors and marines, plus girls, as they disembarked from the Sydney ferry. Again firepoint was reached as suddenly as a flash of lightning. People were tossed off the wharf like fleas; the air was full of flying

60

servicemen. As for me, I jumped down on the beach and was away to the bus stop like a champion.

However, the impression one had of these affrays was that both sides had the time of their lives.

Sydney was never as openly violent as Brisbane, Perth or Townsville. Many an old digger have I heard speak nostalgically of the Battle of Townsville, when two troop trains, going in different directions, carrying Aussies one way and 'Yanks' the other, stopped at the same station.

'Ah, she was a bobby dazzler, love. She was a bloody beaut. Me mate had his nose broken twice.'

The Battle of Brisbane was even more spectacular, beginning at a United States canteen, which was besieged by drunken Australians, and spreading in an uncontrollable rampage throughout the city. Some deaths occurred in that engagement. In the interest of international relations, no publicity was given to these events.

It was obvious to all that no racial hatred, not even dislike, was involved. In a tense, unfamiliar atmosphere, with invasion or death always tomorrow's possibility, it is no wonder that men of both armies trailed their coats from both mischief and nervous aggressiveness. They were young, fit, and toey. The marvel is that there were not more punch-ups than there were.

As a civilian I found the Americans courteous, friendly, generous to the children, and more easy-mannered than our own boys. One of D'Arcy's young brothers owed his life to a G.I. He was ill with pneumonia, the family kneeling around saying the Rosary, when the elder girl came in with her American boyfriend. In a moment he had sized up the situation, wrapped the sick boy in a blanket, and carried him out to a taxi and the hospital.

The poor mother ran after him, weeping and tugging at the blanket. Perhaps she thought her boy was being abducted.

Even after D'Arcy arrived and explained how grateful they all should be to the quick-thinking young American, she was resentful and indignant.

'The cheek of that fellow, interfering like that! We were saying the Rosary—God would have looked after Joe.'

'He did,' said D'Arcy. 'So he sent an angel. In a uniform.'

She didn't see this at once. She was Irish but differently Irish from my grandmother and her family. Unlike them she could not snatch a flying word like a butterfly, comprehend it and its ramifications in a flash, pull off its wings and flick it back towards its originator. She seemed to come to any resolution ponderously and passively, like an old heavy tree settling defensively into its roots at the twitch of a breeze.

I came from a family of lively, romantic thinkers, full of passionate likes and dislikes and brief though noisy enmities, so I couldn't get the hang of her at all. Equally, she could not find any common ground with me. I didn't look right, 'sort of foreign'; I talked 'like a Pom'. Certainly the New Zealand accent of fifty years ago did not resemble today's, but my speech was not that of an Englishwoman. I think my non-Australian speech and manners flustered her. She felt she had to bite someone and the stranger seemed the logical person.

The name of this woman, large, low-voiced, soft-faced, with a skin like yesterday's rose, was Barbara. She gave me eighteen months of what was effectively a groundswell of loneliness and unhappiness. Nevertheless, in many significant ways, she was one of the best women I have known.

4

At Mrs Cardy's house began my lifelong habit of insomnia. I have often wondered whether sleeplessness, discontinuous but prolonged, frequently total, has a significant effect upon the creative faculty. It seems that a certain degree and quality of dreamtime is essential for the mental stability of humans, but this is not available to the habitually sleepless. Certainly when one is deeply involved in writing, curious mental states are observable. Is it possible that the dreaming of the sleepless is done in the daytime, and translated into literary material? I do not even know whether insomnia is a common burden of writers and other creative people. D'Arcy Niland did not know what it was until his last few months of life when he was very ill.

He often worked all night, but invariably he compensated for it next day, his head on the typewriter. Inkstains from the ribbon often decorated his forehead. Or he would fall down for five minutes upon the sofa. 'Resting my eyes,' he called it, but he was as soundly asleep as an exhausted dog. During these periods he liked to have something on his stomach, usually a sleeping baby, his fingers hooked in the back of its pants. In later years when we had dogs, it was often a puppy.

My husband originated my curse of insomnia. Until I married I slept as soundly as any other young girl. He changed my sleep style. No matter what time of night it was, he would creep up the stairs from Mrs Cardy's kitchen where he had been writing in longhand, for we had a typewriter curfew of nine o'clock. More likely he had just returned from his mother's house, which he visited several times a week to try to solve the family's myriad insignificant problems. He still felt responsible for his family, and of course they loved to see him.

Arrived in the bedroom, he shook me awake. He wanted to talk right that moment about an idea for a new radio play, or how his Dad had thrown his dinner at the wall, and the hilarious way the sausages had slid majestically down the wallpaper. Or he wanted me awake for what he called a bit of a cuddle.

What he really needed was company. He could not bear being alone. Also he had no idea that other people, once they have gone to sleep, like to stay that way. I had trouble enough with broken sleep, having to get up four or five times a night to trail downstairs to the lavatory to be sick.

One morning at 1 a.m., after he had made a lightning dash to the post office to get some hopeful manuscript on its way, he shook me awake with the excited announcement that he had just seen the most extraordinary Chinaman. There was nothing nearby with which I could murder him, so I seized his shaving mirror and threw it at the fireplace with such force it not only shattered into crumbs but scarified a tile.

'What did you do that for?'

He was absolutely, innocently shocked. Not a whisper from his rich imagination suggested a reason. Years afterwards he confessed he thought I had gone dotty; expectant women sometimes did, his mother said.

'If you ever, ever wake me up again to tell me about a weirdo Chinese or anything else for that matter, I shall kill you.'

'But I thought you'd like to know.'

As I became sicker and sicker in the months before my child's birth, the kitchen became my night refuge. There was no point in returning to bed, to be sick again in another half hour. So I sat there, wrapped in a blanket before the cooling stove, where nightly Mrs Cardy 'smoored' the coals with the little prayer to Sts Michael and mighty Gabriel her grandmother and mother had recited long before. In New Zealand we had called this nightly ritual banking—placing a lump of hardwood at the back of the firebox, and carefully covering the red embers with fine ash; lightly, lightly, don't smother them, fire needs oxygen.

In the morning, with any luck, all one had to do was to blow up the embers, feed them with kindling, and put on the kettle for the tea.

I remember the kitchen very well; it was a comfort against the hardships of that time—'the narrow anxious bed, the brief apprehensive sleep, invocations frequent and early,' as the Irish poem says. I sat there half drowsing, wondering now and then what was in store for myself and my daughter. For I was sure my child was a girl.

Sometimes, while I was crossing the backyard, always watching for rats, I looked up at the sky. The yard was the size of a bedsheet; it was like peering up through a chimney or from the bottom of a well. Often I saw the scissor blades of searchlights clipping at the darkness. Sometimes I perceived a star or two, which might well break into fiery splinters through my tears.

Yet I would not have the reader think that I had any regrets about leaving my home and country, my dearly beloved family, to enter upon a life I knew very well would be difficult. My tears were because of physical discomfort, the animosity of my husband's people, whom I wanted to be my people too, and the times. Australia was under siege. I emigrated in the worst and most dangerous year in its history, and though in this story I do not mention the war overmuch, it is because the abnormal had become the norm, so to speak. We took it for granted that times were bad, and were grateful that for us they were not as terrible as for others.

Somewhere I have read that sin is falling short of one's own totality. With love, one rises above it. Certainly, in the moments of awareness I have had, whether through my ancestral occasional second sight, or the awareness I was sometimes to attain in later years through the practice of Zen, I recognise that this is so. To rise above one's own totality is to realise that there are no boundaries to one's own totality; one is not separated from the whole, the gestalt, whatever that may be. And I had always been a child rich in love, both giving and taking. As a writer, love is what I have always written about. Not man-woman love alone, for that is but a small thing compared with love of life, or love of the planet. It is love itself that matters, that lifts the spirit above totality—the capacity to give it, and take it. That was what made my world one I had not only chosen, but could make golden.

I knew that when I went back up the narrow stairs my daughter and I would squeeze in beside a very unusual man, a Stone Age man in many ways, a person with self-knowledge and self-respect who knew nothing about role-playing but who possessed the greatest love of all, of humanity at large. The opposite of love is not hate but indifference. What D'Arcy Niland had was complete absence of indifference towards mankind. It is the rarest of all virtues and one I have never attained.

Night in Surry Hills was unquiet. There was the distant thin wail of a baby, the scutter of rats on neighbouring roofs, harsh bellows from Kate Leigh's grog shop, which was only four or five doors away. What I liked best were the unidentifiable sounds from John Curtin Hing's Chinese grocery next door. The wall of this three-storey building was also the south wall of Mrs Cardy's house and shop, so we heard much thready soprano music, laughter and creaking beds. In the night our yard filled with pungent gusts from the Hing house; pink fuzz drifted above its chimney, Chinese curses sounded *sotto voce* as unseen people wrestled unknown objects out on the flat roof. The family was making pickles at 3 a.m. From my bedroom window in the daytime I often saw tiny wooden casks scrubbed and laid out to dry on the roof. Sometimes, also, the black-clad grandmother or great-grandmother would appear at the parapet, smile a toothless smile, and with many nods and jigs of head hold up the family's youngest for me to admire. He was a perfect little buddha, with azalea-red cheeks. She had spotted I was pregnant, rubbed her stomach, pointed to her chest, indicating that if I breastfed my baby I too would bear a jolly buddha like Winston Churchill Hing.

Occasionally this old lady dropped a little parcel of rice into the yard; it was unprocurable for us foreign devils. Expired crackers also rained down on the slimy bricks whenever the Japanese were forced to retreat. Later I heard that the old grandmother was the family's sole China-based survivor of the fearful massacre in Nanking. Her grandson had spent a lifetime's savings to bribe her way out of China.

Beres used to send Mrs Cardy into gasping fits by postulating what this ancestor had rechristened herself. As is obvious, it was customary for our Chinese to give themselves new names. At last they settled on Betty Grable Hing, though Marlene Dietrich was a strong contender.

Mrs Cardy's house was astir with ghosts. Exhaustion brings curious creative breakthroughs. I have heard this described as a disturbance of sequential progressions in the brain's activity. I would simplify it; I would say it is a sweeping away of intellectual white noise. Many years later, as I served hot tea to advanced students and Buddhist monks emerging from the terrifying *sesshin*, I was to see the same thing. They were pallid, gaunt, but their faces carried an unfamiliar radiance or exaltation. *Sesshin*, an attempt to crash through into awareness or enlightenment, is a rigorous Zen exercise in intensive meditation—*zazen*—lasting several days, the practitioner sitting in the one place, eating and sleeping minimally, still in the same place. When these people spoke, sometimes poetry came out. They had dipped water and nourishment from wells which they had not known existed within themselves.

Alone in the cooling kitchen I often found my mind swept along on a whirlwind of incandescent dust motes, or so it seemed—a hurricane of ideas, words, memories, even titles. The title of this book was one of them, when it came to me that although many, we are told, cross the tumultuous river of the dead, nobody fishes in it. Who knows but that one might bring up a golden fish?

The ghosts that watched in Mrs Cardy's house seemed comfortable and many. In the early 1950s when much of the street was demolished, I pondered guiltily over the wasteland of crumbled brick and plaster and wondered whether the house and its ghosts would still exist, had I not spent so many sleepless hours in the kitchen in the dead of night.

Come with me through Mrs Cardy's house, for it was here that I conceived the consuming interest in Victorian social history that has been the backbone of so many of my books. It is quiet; the baby asleep in its distant cot padded with newspapers; the police have cleared out the drunks from Kate Leigh's. Some have crept thankfully into the paddy wagon; others have stuffed themselves into any cranny or rubbish tin they can find. We can hear the nightmen running up and down the meagre lanes behind the shops and houses, for this part of Surry Hills is unsewered. But they are fairly quiet, not clanking cans over-much; their boots are covered with felt buskins.

Mrs Cardy's house has worn itself into the ways of human beings—five or six generations in time, and small changes occurring with each generation.

Its 'front room', not much more than two metres wide, and opening flat-faced on to Devonshire Street, was in the late 1860s converted into a shop. First it served as a grog shop for the soldiers from the Paddington Barracks, then as a chandlery, a harness-maker's, a gunsmithy, and at last a barber shop. During the catastrophic depression of the 1890s it was closed for many years, then rented as a dosshouse for a charitable society. All these permutations left their mark on the walls, the stairs; made this lopsided, that wry; a door or window swollen, shrunken or intractable so that it never shuts or never opens.

People have died in it and their coffins have gone out the front window in a sling because of the scarcely more than hip-wide stairs. Our landlady's husband, Owen, went out that window, hurting her feelings something terrible. To see this loved man going through his own bedroom window like a piano was not a thing you got over in a wink.

Behind the shop, closed and empty since Owen's death, for he was the barber, is a living room two and a half metres by three. Out of it elbows the steep staircase, making the small room smaller. All is in twilight, for the only light or ventilation comes from a handspan window at the foot of the stairs. It is propped open by a tomato-sauce bottle, black of glass and antique in design.

'It was there when Ownie and I came and it'll be there when they carry me out,' said Mrs Cardy.

In earlier times the parlour was the kitchen. Once when the grate was removed from the fireplace so that the chimney could be swept I lit a candle, shone it up into the sooty darkness and saw rusted nubs of huge bolts and hooks that long before had carried a jack and the suspension chains for cast-iron cauldrons and Dutch ovens. Here women for generations cooked by candlelight, or the soft illumination of kerosene or whale-oil lamps.

'Hoisting around those iron pots that weighed a ton even when they were empty! No wonder they had miscarriages by the dozen,' said Mrs Cardy.

She looked around contentedly. 'Me and Ownie made it a picture, though, didn't we?'

So it is. An etched-glass globe on the gaslight, waxed furniture, and a floorcloth of Euclidean design, washed and polished twice a week, for she is a meticulous housewife. On the wall are Our Lady of Lourdes; Owen wearing a narrow-brimmed phallic-looking hard-hitter; and Mrs Cardy herself, also in a hat though this one resembles a casserole full of pansies. Her cheeks are soft and round and her remarkable eyes beautiful with youth.

'Wasn't bad, was I?' said Mrs Cardy in honest admiration when I first saw that picture. 'People said I painted, but I didn't.'

The houses around here do not have bathrooms. Mrs Cardy's bedroom is furnished with many things, all wedding presents of forty years ago, a rosewood dressing table, a huge bed with a marcella quilt, and a wash stand and 'set'—jug, basin and chamberpot, the chinaware deeply embossed with tall leaves and white irises. In the corner stands a midget oil stove; nightly she boils up a kettle of water and has a thorough all-over. Besides being sagacious and firm of manner, she is an admirably clean and tidy old woman, and her house reflects her personal principles.

The boys and I make do with piecemeal washing in the kitchen. There is a splintery wooden sink in the corner, the water draining into a bucket underneath. The rule is to wash dishes in an enamel basin on the little table. Thus the sink is kept sacrosanct for what Mrs Cardy, in the Irish manner, calls 'a rench'.

She has many old Irish songs, many of which I am never to hear again. One of them begins with a long doglike yip, 'There was an old prophecy found in a bog'. Sometimes I think it refers to me, that I'll never have a proper bath again as long as I live. But it is four o'clock, time to leave the ghosts and go to bed. I know it is 4 a.m., not because I hear a clock striking somewhere in the snoozing city. All bells and chimes have been silenced, and indeed some steeples and towers taken down for the duration. What I hear is a cyclist coming up Devonshire Street, slowly and laboriously, for the street is steep at the eastern end, and he is an elderly man, one of the many who took over their sons' jobs while the latter served in the Forces. Every morning before dawn he fires up the boilers at Playfair's Smallgoods Factory, just across the road.

I often think of him entering the shadowy factory, the shrouded machines and benches, the air choking with the stinks of brine, spice, smoke, unacknowledged chemicals. Does he look up at 'the watchman'—the long carpet snake, two or three metres of sulphur yellow, black and chocolate in an aboriginal design? It is said it has a cold hard nose like a dog, and will sometimes unfurl behind a workman and tickle his neck in a snakish joke. Playfair's keep it to frighten away rats.

'It's a calm old bugger,' I heard one of the men say. 'Quiet, too. There's something about a quiet snake . . . peaceful.'

The rats worried me greatly; several children had been bitten in their beds, and a paralytic drunk had one side of his face laid bare almost to the bone before he was found. The municipal rat catcher came and ineffectually laid poison.

'They're wise to poison,' he said. 'Very artful, rats.'

Rat traps were unobtainable because of the metal spring—almost everything made of metal had vanished during the war. There was even a motor vehicle made largely of wood, incredible as this sounds. We set mouse traps, they caught mice, and the rats sneaked in and ate the mice.

One day, as I sat typing at the little table by the bedroom window, I saw a rat sitting at his ease in the sunshine, watching me. He was an old warrior, bald blue scars all over him; his eyes were little garnets ringed with scales like those of certain birds. This was a composed, leisurely rat, taking my shouts and gestures for what they were. He was like an Egyptian granary-rat, murderous as Set, a kitten-eater.

D'Arcy scavenged a piece of fine chicken netting from some dump, and nailed it on the outside of the window. The rat, returning, showed me his fine brown teeth in a grin; he could bite through that stuff like shears.

All municipal services had been cut for lack of men; women swept the streets and some even collected the garbage, which was thrown pellmell on the backs of trucks in huge stinking heaps.

'It's like when the plague was here,' said Mrs Cardy. 'Millions of rats there were.'

'What plague?' I cried.

'Bubonic.' She went on rattling the clinkers through the stove's firebox into the ashpan. Riddling, she called it. 'Some of the old people around here remember it. Being evicted, and all that. Having to live in tents on the Common and in the parks. The rats brought the bubonic and the cesspits brought the typhoid and cholera.'

She had told me before about the cesspits that pre-dated the nightsoil collection, barbarous civic cloacae where people often threw murder victims and unwanted babies.

'Crikey!' said my husband, 'what an article, what a talk for the ABC!'

He was all the more enthusiastic when he discovered that the plague almost coincided with Federation. What a perfect paradox! However, when I did the research at the Public Library, reading old newspapers of the time until my eyes almost dropped out, I found that bubonic plague had once been almost endemic to Sydney, as it was to so many ports.

An appalling epidemic in South China in 1893 was the genesis of Sydney's Great Plague in the midsummer of 1900. The scourge crossed to Hong Kong, ploughed vast furrows through the populations of India and Africa and reached the Pacific in New Caledonia in 1899.

The Sydney I found in the old photographs could have come from the writings of Hippolyte Taine—'stifling alleys thick with human effluvia, troops of pale children crouching on filthy staircases' and 'in the Haymarket the abject miserable poverty of the streetwalkers; it seemed as if I were watching a march past of dead women.'

Taine wrote of the London of the 1840s and 1850s; but the odd and valuable journalist of Sydney's 1870s and 1880s known as Vagabond told the same tales of a new green land so many thousands of miles away from London, and yet already fallen into identical dark pits of ignorance and corruption.

The photographs were fearful. During a vast rat drive some 30,000 rats were exterminated. People with fox terriers hired them out by the day. At the same time a general sanitary cleansing of the city took place.

'Do you know what they fished out of the Harbour, just the main Harbour?' I demanded at the dinner table. 'A thousand dead dogs and cats, and dozens of cows and horses. And human corpses . . .'

'Oh, shut up!' said Mrs Cardy. 'You're almost as bad as Beres was when he was working for the St John's Ambulance.'

This referred to a time when Beres, overcome by enthusiasm for his new essential job, insisted on telling us at breakfast about a motor-cycle accident.

'His liver was wrapped around *a post fifty feet away*,' he marvelled.

I had always been interested in housing, partly because of my observations in New Zealand when I accompanied the City Missioner, the Reverend Jasper Calder, on his rounds, and partly because of our own difficulties.

Needless to say the ABC didn't want any talk on the Federation Plague.

'Rats,' they said faintly. 'Cesspits. Buboes. No, really, ABC listeners wouldn't care . . . imagine the letters to the G.M. . . . Buboes, dear me.'

Talks Department didn't know I lived in Surry Hills; they thought I lived in a box at the G.P.O., which we had prudently rented the moment we had some money to spare.

The early governors had left Sydney prosperous in a modest way, speckled with grassy open spaces, a decent village. Fifty years after Macquarie, the best of them all, left for home, photographs show it to be a city of half a million people, certainly with green and leafy suburbs, gardens and mansions to the east, where the wealthy lived, but in general a scrubby old dockside town. It was a chaos of roofs, dunnies, fetid alleys, stairways, old limepits, quarries now filled with lean-tos of turf, and doss-downs of iron and old sacks.

The Commissioners in charge of sanitation rid Sydney of many of these squalid lanes, especially around Darling Harbour and The Rocks. Many houses were pulled down, others forcibly scrubbed with lime and carbolic, white-washed and repaired. Of the plague cases, 38 per cent occurred in the Surry Hills area, that is, around Liverpool Street, Elizabeth Street and Devonshire Street. At that time the latter bisected the vast drear treeless cemetery that lay where Central Railway Station now stands. Its original name was The Sandhills graveyard; many of the poor old brown bones hidden there had already been moved once, from another horrid, vagrant-haunted cemetery in the area where Sydney's Town Hall now prinks in glorious High Victoriana.

These photographs fascinated me, particularly those of The Rocks. I sometimes had the feeling they were three dimensional and I had fallen in amongst the shanties stuck in coigns of sandstone, or on ledges reached by ladders, or narrow jump-ups hacked in the rock itself. Some were of snaggletoothed timber, propped against a natural cave or cranny; others of stone blocks pockmarked with age and weather. Here and there, in a deep natural crankle was a dwelling like a martin's nest, all spit and mud, with an elbow chimney breathing out smoke.

Though I studied Hogarth's drawings of London's evil slums, the people in those were remote. But in the local photographs the people were real, eyeing the camera with excitement or resentment, the kids poking out their tongues. Maybe their descendants still lived in Sydney. The children looked well-fed, but they were scruffy little rapscallions. One could see little boys wearing the sloppy clothes of an older brother, the girls already with a hip slightly out of whack through carrying the youngest baby a-straddle across that little hip all day. The girls mostly had their hair chopped close to the scalp; to keep down the nits, I expect. But there was one, pale, sharp-faced, with slitted tiger eyes, to whom I returned again and again with my big magnifying glass. Watch it, you, that kid was saying. Don't take me for less than I am, or I'll punch yer yeller and green. She stayed in my head for thirty years, emerging in the end as a member of a family of decent immigrants called Bow, trying to keep up their standards in a decrepit slummocky antipodean city. They'd been told there was gold in the streets, but the only gold was the sunshine. And, of course, their own courage and durability.

No one can truly tell how novels are written, least of all myself. Structure, plot, storyline, creation of many characters who must, absolutely must, walk, talk and think for themselves—all that can be explained. But the primordium cannot be defined. True, I gazed for hours at a little girl in a photograph of 1899, but why that child; how did I know her name was Beatie Bow? Some sorcery in the subconscious was operating in the trackless, wordless dark.

And yet the most commonly asked question of all writers is: 'where do you get your ideas from?'

No wonder many writers, in their inability to explain, fire off facetious remarks. I know because a reader once seriously asked me, 'Do you also get your ideas from the Idea Factory in Wagga, like so-and-so always does?'

On a freezing day in June, just before daybreak, my daughter was born in Crown Street's Women's Hospital, in the public wards. Because of my constant sickness I suppose little food

79

had ever remained long in my stomach, so she was small and fragile. I did not care for the experience and even in my direst agonies was aware that this natural process was being forced by the medical profession to proceed in an unnatural way. My youngest children, twins, were delivered by a midwife. This was altogether on another level of insight.

My husband fought and defeated me on the name Brigid, which I wanted to call this little girl. We both fought off his mother, who was profoundly disappointed when we would not call her Eileen, after an infant of hers who had died at birth. In the end she became Anne.

5

The day of my daughter's birth I sat up in bed in Crown Street Women's Hospital and swore by God I would never again bear a child in a public hospital. I do not criticise the medical care exercised, but the curt, rough, dictatorial way it was exercised. Communication with the patients on a human level was nil. The women around me, in severe pain, exhausted, mostly with too many children already (and no family-planning clinics), were treated as units in a vast, though probably competent system. They, like me, were 'on the free', and that makes a difference.

We did not have names. We were addressed as 'mother' even before we were mothers.

'Stop screeching. It has to come out the way it went in,' I heard a nursing sister say, coarsely impatient, to a woman in the ultimate throes. I myself was slapped by a nurse on a painful swollen breast because I was awkward in feeding my child.

'But I don't know anything about babies yet!'

'Your worry, mother.'

During my four days in hospital I distracted myself by mapping out a seven-part adventure serial for the ABC *Children's Session*. On the fifth day I walked home. Taxis were unprocurable. They whizzed past by the dozen bearing US servicemen and their girls. It seemed a very long way to Devonshire Street. I carried the baby and D'Arcy carried my suitcase. I was bleeding like a stuck pig. There was something amiss with my reproductive system, though no one at the hospital had mentioned it.

'You get into bed this very moment!' said Mrs Cardy. 'Let me have the baby. Ah, the little duck, she has a complexion like a sweetpea!'

Thank God for that kind woman, for I had kindness from no one else except the girls at the ABC and my brother-in-law, Beres. I remember weeping woebegone because the baby's grandmother had not come to see her, and I knew very well why.

'It's because Anne is *my* daughter. And I don't understand any of it.'

The child's father sighed. He had no understanding of the matter either.

This little girl of mine was deliberately invited into life so that I would have a friend of my own. This is not a good reason to conceive another human being, but it was so with me. For D'Arcy still belonged halfway to his own family, and once Beres went off on manpower jobs there was no one for me except the girls at the *Children's Session*, and of necessity, they had to be business-hours friends.

'How homesick you must be, darling,' wrote my mother, she who had pined so bitterly when marriage had taken her far away from her mother and sisters. 'But D'Arcy's mother will do her best to make you feel at home, I know.'

As I have said, there were many things I did not tell my mother, for life during wartime was stressful enough without added apprehension for an absent child. So I had told her nothing about that poor woman who did not understand homesickness because she had never had a home, but had fled helplessly like a lost hen from one corner to another, as the winds of circumstance blew. Her only home was her children, as she was their home, patient and faithful, the static centre of turmoil and disorder. Perhaps this is why she could not come to terms with my very existence; she feared that in some undefined manner I would disturb the small cell of security that her ardent maternal love had built.

There seemed no subtext to her dislike, which showed itself unabashedly by disagreeable remarks to me and about me in my presence. She was also an obsessive borrower, almost a spontaneous borrower, of everything from my shoes to the baby's clothing coupons, which scarcely covered more than the infant's nappies, anyway. Nothing borrowed was ever returned, and in most cases I could not afford to give away the requested article, in which case I was abused for weeks. She seemed to have no orthodox feelings about this genteel annexation of another person's belongings, and laughed heartily as she told Mrs Cardy about going to the parish priest, that old Irishman built of granite and rustic shrewdness, and asking him for ten shillings.

'Get out of here, you're worse than a field of tinkers!' he said. She found this not at all mortifying.

'Oh, that Father Denehy, he's made of iron, God bless him!'

I could not attribute her attitude towards me to jealousy, resentment or revenge. Thus her animosity differed greatly from my own Irish grandmother's persecution of the unfortunate Philomena, a good girl who became engaged to Grandma's sole and idolised son, Poor Jack. That persecution, it was plain even to us grandchildren, was grounded in murderous jealousy. Yet, like Philomena, I had no answers. There are no real answers to irrationality.

Before we married D'Arcy had told me of her obstinacy, her fixed ideas, and asked me to be patient.

'She's had a hard life,' he said. 'Two children dead, nothing but poverty always. I owe her. Think of the ninepenny dictionary.'

As a little boy, mad with desire, he had led her to the shop window of the Chinese storekeeper, Kwong Sing, and shown her a little dictionary. 'Is that really what you want?' she asked. And he answered, 'It's words.'

She didn't know where the next meal was coming from, but somehow she found ninepence and bought it for him.

'I think I learned every word in it. I used to recite them for her, like a litany of the saints, she with this look of wonder on her face.'

How could I not promise to be patient? It did not enter my head that the time would come when I broke into a cold sweat every time I heard her voice.

I plotted simple stratagems. I tried to talk to her, to draw her out about her mother, a wonderful woman, but her answers were vague and disjunct. All I learned about her family, the Egans, came from her older sister Bid, a darling old woman with what Beres called chaotic feet. He was indignant on her behalf, for she had spent her life as a presbytery housekeeper, running here and there and everywhere on her broken tortured feet after her thoughtless and often lazy masters.

'If I get to heaven first,' proclaimed Beres, flushed and passionate, 'won't I tell God about Auntie Bid's poor feet, and that pig of a Father X calling her in from the kitchen to hand him the tomato sauce, when all he had to do was stretch out his holy paw and get it from the sideboard.'

Auntie Bid did not complain. All I ever heard her say with a sigh was, 'All them black socks!'

As with Barbara, her religion was without spot or stain of doubt. It was a mythic world, but a true world for them both.

Barbara knew nothing about me and didn't want to know. She had no interest in my background, family, achievements, aims or opinions. I had sprung fully-fledged into her life, a kind of freakish manifestation more than anything else—educated, peculiar, speaking like a Pom. She spoke always as if D'Arcy did all my writing.

'I liked that story of his in the *ABC Weekly*.'

'But that was one of mine.'

'Yes, he's very good, always was.'

I understood D'Arcy's feelings for his mother; I truly did. I loved my own family and thought all children felt the same way. There was a tender, non-tensile bond between Barbara and her son, perhaps with all her children. I never saw D'Arcy kiss her or even hug her; I think she herself was an affectionate woman but her wretched life had taught her to fear rebuff. D'Arcy knew so many things for which he pitied her. He remembered her as a soft-faced, fuzzy-haired young woman who didn't deserve the life she got as unwanted wife. When he was fifteen he tried to run away with her and the young children. They were like a tribe of penniless tinkers, with bundles and baskets and one boy half-dead with the whooping cough. Yet he got them all to Sydney, settled them in a little house, found the children a school and himself a job of sorts. 'I was like a dog let off the chain. I thought we'd left it all behind, all the fights and humiliations, the miserable, hopeless life any family leads with a drunk. Because you know, I knew we had potential, I knew *I* had potential.'

As soon as the family was settled, up turned Frank, full of penitence and promises, and his wife gladly took him in, giving thanks to God that he had changed.

'But he still hasn't changed, and that's eight years ago!'

'Well, that's my Mumma. She has faith that if she waits long enough her marriage will be what she wants it to be.'

'That doesn't explain why she's so unfriendly to me. Or excuse it either. It's not fair.'

'I'm not asking for fairness, girl, I'm asking for kindness.'

'She's not kind to me, not one little bit.'

'I'm not asking for a trade-off either.'

'But it's upsetting me dreadfully, can't you see?'

'She is who she is, and you are who you are. You're strong.'

'Bloodyminded blarneying Irishman!'

'How about a bit of a cuddle then?'

So, for love or what I thought was love, I kept my tongue between my teeth, was civil and pleasant, behaved like a girl of whom my loved teacher Sister Laurencia would approve. Still, D'Arcy's request should never had been made. No one should be asked, for love or anything else, to permit a third person persistently to erode one's self-esteem, not even for malice, merely for sluggish mischief.

Mrs Cardy took another and cynical view.

'Don't forget I've known Barbara since she was a youngster. She'll never let up on you until you put a flea in her ear.'

'I just couldn't.'

'Then I'll put one in D'Arcy's ear.'

I asked her not to, hypocritically, hoping she'd do so, anyway. Yet that very night he took the wind out of my sails once more. As I lay in his arms, our little baby asleep in the canvas bassinet squashed in beside the table with the typewriter, he told me of the time she'd saved him from getting his head cut off. A magician had visited Glen Innes, where the family lived, and somehow Frank had scraped up enough money to let Barbara and the children have this rare treat.

'The showman asked for volunteers to come up on the stage, and naturally I shot up there like a rocket. I had to kneel down and put my head on a block, while he brandished a huge axe. Even at the age of eight I knew my head would remain connected. But suddenly there was a fearful commotion in the audience and up rushed Mum. First she kicked away the block and then she kicked the magician, and I was dragged down the centre aisle and out of the tent, all our little kids shrieking. I was so mortified I can feel the pain yet.'

'Very funny,' I said coldly, though secretly I thought it was comical. I could feel him thinking, 'What else can I tell her? I have to make her understand somehow.'

So he came out with another story, of a time when he worked at William Brooks's printery, proofreading directories and telephone books. One afternoon when it was pouring rain his mother waited outside with his coat wrapped in newspaper.

'It must have been an hour until I clocked out, and she didn't have a coat herself. Wasn't that just like Mum!'

The vision of Barbara, standing outside the printery, soaked with rain, but with her son's coat wrapped in sodden newspaper struck me as both sad and hilarious, as we both began to laugh. But I could have kicked him. It was just like Barbara, a woman who had nothing in her life but her kids, a woman with nothing to look forward to but more calamitous quarrels and lovelessness. She had but one hope, that her children would turn out to be decent people, with better lives than hers. And in this she succeeded almost perfectly.

I don't know whether there was any coherence to her perception of the exterior world. I don't think there was. But I have noticed that inaccessibility to the external world is a frequent characteristic of very ill, or very distraught people. The noises from within are deafening.

In the end I could bear her harassment no more and gave her a dressing-down. I had rarely been rude to a person older than myself; it was not the way of the young in those days. I felt bad about it for years, but as things turned out, Mrs Cardy had been right. Barbara flung out of the house, but that was the end of it. After that she treated me as a human being. In later years I became very fond of her.

I thought often of what her youth must have been, isolated on a starveling farm. Her father was a brutal man from Offaly, then called King's County. He was a travelling blacksmith and wheelwright, and had a wagon fitted up as a forge. When he was away for months at a time, his wife, her four daughters and one retarded son lived as best they might. The mother became a bush nurse, and on her small earnings they lived.

Mrs Cardy said, 'No one ever called in vain for Nurse Egan. I can see her yet, going off on her horse, with a storm lantern and a little oilcloth bundle on the saddle in front of her, with clean starched white aprons, and scissors and string for the cord, and sometimes baby clothes she had made herself for the poor mother.'

As a midwife, Margaret Egan became famous in New England. This did not stop her husband beating her and the girls whenever he returned from his travels. It must have been a relief when he fell off his wagon when drunk, and the startled horses trampled him. He was buried far from home, and no one in his family cared a jot.

But first he forced Frank Niland to marry his daughter, and such was his reputation for ferocity that one fancies the handsome young man jumped to it. Frank was engaged to another girl, whom he loved dearly and, it appears, all his life, but he had done the common thing and got another young woman pregnant. Lonely Barbara had fallen for his carnation cheeks, his summer blue eyes, his slender wiry frame. Perhaps he had a sluthering voice, though God knows when I knew him it rasped like a file, ruined by coarse wine, griding on and on saying nothing. But when young he must have known how to get his own way and the soft Irish voice is often the way to do it.

Frank's love was a girl called Alice Gunn. Often when he was drunk he would get out her picture and her letters and weep over them. This small tearstained packet has come to me at last. I look at Alice's direct dark-eyed gaze, her strong face and level eyebrows, and think that if Frank had married her she would have stood no nonsense with the bottle. She would have straightened out that young tearaway and made out of him the man he was capable of being.

For he came of a long-established, well-respected New England family, several generations of prosperous saw-millers and coopers who sprang from the emigration in 1841 of Original Thomas and Original Mary Niland. Thomas had been a cooper with Guinness's Brewery in Dublin; when D'Arcy Niland and I visited that brewery 123 years later there were still Nilands working as coopers there. We met two of them and they were the dead spit of one of D'Arcy's brothers, Joseph, as well as a cousin, Professor John Niland of Sydney, and several remote cousins once and twice removed and living in the Northern Rivers district.

Frank Niland's father was the fifth living child of Original Thomas, one of the first Nilands to be Australian-born. When this grandfather died in 1924, he was described as being of a refined and pious nature, esteemed and loved by all. Something of this disposition remained in D'Arcy's father, in spite of alcoholism.

Queer little fragments of good manners used to pop out in him. When sober he was quiet and well-behaved, reading the newspaper through glasses he had picked up at the flea market, one earpiece being made of ginger-beer wire, and lopsided. On one occasion, which touched me greatly, he looked up from his paper, and said in a melancholy voice, 'This would have been our boy Jack's birthday.'

Jack was the lost son John, whom D'Arcy remembered vaguely as a beautiful jolly little fellow, who died in terrible pain from an intussusception of the bowel when he was two or three.

I saw then that Frank, scallywag as he was, mourned the death of his two children, and my hard judgment of him was gentled a little.

But how much he didn't want to marry the daughter of furious William Egan the blacksmith! She was older than he, almost thirty, and he longed for Alice, it seems, with all his soul.

On Barbara's wedding day he thrust a dagger through her heart, though probably he didn't think of it that way. A train passed through Tenterfield, carrying Alice Gunn to a destiny we do not know, and he went to the station to say goodbye.

'When he came back his eyes were red,' Barbara told me in later years, and at the thought of that cruel humiliation tears filled her own eyes.

There ensued for her the ignominy of the unwanted woman. Every degradation, some unspeakable, was inflicted upon her. She was arrested for begging when Frank had left her and the children penniless for weeks. She had sold the children's beds. They slept on heaps of newspapers and old clothes. The parish priest paid her fine, and St Vincent de Paul's Society found her some shelter when she was evicted from her house and was discovered sitting in the park with her little children. Someone had given her some money, but had she bought milk or bread? No, the children were eating saveloys and drinking lemonade.

'I wanted them to remember it as a picnic,' she said, 'not as something frightening.'

She had the variety of wisdom that in a mother is passed on to good and mostly happy children.

Nevertheless her life was one of unremitting deprivation and adversity. She was a person capable of loving greatly, I think, but Frank did not want her love. He wanted Alice's.

She said to me once, 'It makes you wonder what a body's born for.' Was there ever such a summing up of her life and those of countless other women? Ah, not just women. Men, also.

Barbara outlived both her husband and her eldest son. In later years we were able to get them a little house, and

Frank became interested in making a vegetable garden. But he still got drunk whenever his pension arrived, raging around, 'arging' about everything, driving his wife mad with his torrents of meaningless talk. She faded away into arteriosclerosis.

For years she was lovingly cared for by her youngest daughter, that rosy little one who had offered things up when they became too hard for her.

I often ponder Barbara's life. It was a historic quality, as though it belongs to times long gone, when entrapment in intractable hardship, especially for an ill-educated woman, was probable. Yet today people endure in the same way, for the same reasons. They are simply not as noticeable, even in the mass, until they begin trashing great cities.

Yet one cannot deny that the character of such a woman contributes to the sadness of her life. Thinking of her long struggle, I hear music, faint and unrealised. She and those like her seem born to find solace in religion and nothing much else. The music I hear is Irish traditional music, which always sounds to me as if it is saying goodbye—not sorrowfully, but submissively.

This woman is not, of course, Mumma of *The Harp in the South*. That fictional character is a younger, livelier, quicker-witted creature. But she and Barbara shared some of the same experiences. It was the common way of Irish Catholic women of their generation.

All this time we worked steadily. Long before, we had learned not to allow emotion to interfere with the pursuit of writing. We had chosen to earn our family living that

93

way, and though our existence was close to the bone, we were surviving. I have been looking again at our first, faintly pencilled 'account book', and I see that between us we earned the basic wage for six months of that year, not consistently or consecutively, but on an average. The Australian Broadcasting Commission was still the backbone of life to us; through writing steadily for the *Children's Session* I had learned a great deal about radio, which I still think the most challenging of media, because the listener, that blind third, must be your colleague and collaborator.

It teaches you, too, as with a bang on the head with a brick, that dialogue is not talk. This great truth has been entirely lost in television, except by certain European filmmakers.

Through Elizabeth I met Frank Clewlow, a large enthusiastic flossy-haired Englishman who was Director of Drama. What bliss one morning when we received from Mr Clewlow a letter saying that there had been a splendid response to our first adult dramatic effort, *Night Tales of a Bagman*, that the ABC was going to repeat them, and would like some more ghost tales in the same format! He also enclosed a clipping from *The Listener-In*, the most influential radio journal of the day, stating that we were the most promising young radio writers yet seen in Australia.

Now we were two dogs with two tails, or four tails as the case might be.

'Tiger, do you realise we may make it after all?'

'We might even be able to buy a radio!' I said.

It was true. We promising young radio writers had no radio. When we listened-in to the first broadcast of the

Bagman tales, we had, with trepidation, gone next door to the Hing family, and asked if we could listen to theirs. It was a vast skyscraper of a thing, its front decorated with frayed golden silk around a kind of gob of black celluloid, which was spouting static and Chinese as we were invited into the living room.

'Oh, blast, it's a Chinese radio!' I said absurdly. Tyrone Power Hing, an astute Australian-born boy of twelve, said curtly, 'Shortwave. Pop likes to get Hong Kong if he can.'

He flicked a few buttons and in came the ABC. The entire family bowed, and ascended with the greatest dignity to an upstairs bedroom. There behind the grocery shop we first heard the plays we had written in a lamplit bunkhouse on the north-west plains, with the heavy dew dripping off the trees outside with the sound of blood-drops plopping.

We saw the errors we had made, too, and retired to Mrs Cardy's not knowing to be thrilled or ashamed. So much we had learned about radio in the interim between writing the script and hearing it broadcast.

Getting our ideas for ghost stories was no problem for us. Our jubilation at being offered a chance of further work acted like a drug. Our imaginations went off like fireworks. I recalled old bush stories my father had told me; D'Arcy suddenly remembered goose-pimpled evenings when he and the other tikes listened to the Irish stories of Grandma Niland, who had lived with them for a while. We took these stories by the scruff, dragged them out of their original settings, banged them around a bit, and gave them voices. We almost frightened ourselves to death, sitting there late at night in the kitchen, the candle flickering, the baby getting her 2 a.m. feed and looking around with drowsy blue eyes.

We received £14.14s for our first set of *Bagman* plays, and for the sixth, £31.10s. The ABC was still devoted to guineas. In time the repeats paid more than the original. Years later, the plays were also broadcast on the BBC, and some of the fifteen-minute scripts were converted into television programmes in other languages. The format was simple: a bagman or wanderer sitting beside a camp fire with his friends, telling ghost stories of the countryside. We sometimes moved locations from the true Outback into homesteads and country towns, all of which were familiar to D'Arcy, and some now familiar to me.

All human beings like uncanny stories. By accident we had happened on a most successful idea. We were led through this apprenticeship in radio writing by the ABC's senior Play Editor, Leslie Rees, a much experienced and highly skilled man in the dramatic field, as well as a successful writer of children's books in his own right. I admired his expertise no end, as well as his tact.

When I first met Mr Rees he smiled and said, 'But I know you already. Didn't you submit a verse play for one of our competitions?'

'Well, yes,' I admitted. The poet Douglas Stewart had won that competition with his classic *Fire on the Snow*, a play about the Scott expedition to the South Pole in 1912. Very rightly, my play had come nowhere.

'I remember your play well,' said Leslie Rees gravely. (For a split second I thought he might be going to say it was good.) 'Who could forget that escaped convict swimming fifty miles in flawless iambic pentameter?'

If you look at photographs of the war years, you will see that almost everyone carries a newspaper tucked under the arm. Every 'extra' edition was eagerly bought. What was happening over there, so far away? Had Darwin been bombed by the Japanese yet again? Whose familiar name would be on the latest casualty list? Yet, by 1943, the population was largely submerged in drear acceptance of life as it was. We fell over and cursed the piles of sandbags outside every important building. We looked cynically at the many slit trenches dug to save us from air-raid death, and observed that when they were not filled with rainwater, they were choked with junked tyres and old prams. We knew in our hearts that if the Japanese Army invaded, we were probably done for.

Yet by the beginning of 1944, we began to dream a timorous dream. Politicians were heard to speak, though vaguely, of peacetime plans. For by the end of 1943 the long battle of Berlin had begun. The Russians were holding their own against the vast German forces deployed in that country and as the Japanese were hammered more and more in the Pacific, American servicemen began to disappear from Australian cities. We began, in spite of severer food rationing, to feel confident that sometime the war would end. Characteristically for Australia, Saturday race meetings, banned in 1942, recommenced before Christmas 1943.

Beres came back from cooking and deckhanding on one of the River Murray paddlewheel boats and said the countryside was full of Italian prisoners-of-war working on farms, singing, and teaching people like himself every form of Italian from Romano to Calabrese. Australia held something like 18,000 Italian prisoners during the war; they were not kept under restraint, but in open camps, and greatly alleviated the country's manpower problems, especially in rural areas. They were not the first Italian 'migration' by any means, but many settled amiably, brought out their families, and became part of what is probably Australia's most adaptable and highly valued migrant race.

Beres was overjoyed to be back in Sydney. He had missed everyone.

'Yes, I'm glad to see you, and you, too, but where's my Tanglefoot?'

He hugged Anne, but looked astonished.

'Hey, what's this? It's a rib! I didn't know little bubbas had ribs.'

It was true that Anne was underweight. Any mention of ribs made me feel a failure. Though she had a merry spirit and was as lively as a grasshopper, she had chronic bronchitis and the pallid, peaky look of slum babies—at least those who were not fed on watered-down condensed milk. This concoction, syrupy with sugar, was a favourite Surry Hills replacement for breast milk.

As they grew older, slum children often became plump and well-fed in appearance; this is observable even in old Victorian photographs. This 'bonniness' was because of the children's high carbohydrate diet, a common thing still in many districts where the housewife has little money and no nutritional training. In Surry Hills bread was the most important food, white, doughy, generously daubed with tinned raspberry jam. Yet at the time minced steak was threepence a pound, and a large bag of yesterday's vegetables was obtainable at the greengrocer's for sixpence. But the bread and jam were easier to prepare than a stew or casserole.

While we were with Mrs Cardy we constantly looked for other accommodation, but when Anne's bronchitis was no better even in spring, we became desperate.

'We'll just have to get out of the city, into a country town even,' I implored. While this promised us good air and perhaps healthier accommodation, the idea also brought many problems—a higher rent, distance from editors and markets generally, fares.

At last we managed to rent a room in a crochety superannuated beach house at Collaroy, some distance up the northern coast. It had a gas stove on a roofed verandah; water had to be carried from a tap outside; we shared a bathroom with the human flotsam and jetsam who rented the other rooms. The bathroom had no hot water, the bath had no drainpipe. Pull the plug and the water shot straight through a hole in the floor. Things came up that drainpipe—spiders, large red slugs like leeches, once a lost gecko that lived on our ceiling for weeks, tick-tocking forlornly and looking more and more translucent as time passed. Anne treasured its mummified body for days.

There was no sewerage, only a desolate corrugated-iron dunny standing in the middle of the sand and blowing grass, or grass and blowing sand, depending on the wind. As it was extraordinarily noticeable, we called it the Sore

Thumb and cringed every time it had to be attended. To make matters worse, the old bachelor in the front room used to lean against it and sunbathe, exposing his unpleasing blue-white chest and singing 'Ramona'. Delicate hints, outright requests were ineffective. That was his sunbathing place and he was sticking to it. Finally a new lady, a robust pensioner with eight cats, all with worms, went out and told him she'd kill him with an axe if he didn't move quick smart. So he did, and I was most impressed at what a little terrorism can achieve.

The owner of Wits' End, as we came to call it, was a kindly elderly woman, and though the rooms were comfortless to an almost melodramatic degree, they were let at a cheap rent—and no key money.

'At least we'll be by ourselves,' said D'Arcy.

So we said goodbye to good Mrs Cardy. She was Anne's godmother; I have always thought of her with gratitude. We all hugged her and promised we would never forget her little house, or the tomato-sauce bottle, or the Biblical tiles around the fireplace in our garret.

But I never saw her house again. When I next visited Devonshire Street all was gone—the Ming house, the little shops, the brick backyards, the long covered or half filled-in cesspits. Only Mrs Cardy's chimney stood, resisting destruction, still bearing the stout hook where she had hung a candle, in a cocoa tin, to light the stove whilst she cooked. All around was what appeared to be an archeological dig—smashed sandstock bricks, slivers of green glass, twisted gaspipes, fragments of broken cups and plates from the Victorian age. One of the demolitionists told me that the uncovered cesspit of the Hing dwelling was chockful of bones. At first I thought shudderingly of Mrs Cardy's previous comments on cesspit murders. But eventually it was proved that the Chinese grocery shop had, a century before, been a butchery, and the butcher had the habit of disposing of animals' bones in the cesspit.

'All kinds of things down there,' said the demolitionist cheerfully. 'Goat's skulls with the horns still on, horses' hooves. Et everything, I suppose they did, in them bad old days.'

It was incredible to me that because I had lived with Mrs Cardy, she had to leave her home. I would not have made her unhappy for the world, but so it happened.

Who in that bitter wartime could have guessed that within four years I would write a book which would be seized upon by the State Minister for Housing? He was already interested in the prospect of slum clearance, and like many such Ministers had become enamoured of the highrise building, the tower block, which seemed to solve so brilliantly the postwar problems of expanding population and shrinking land availability. Clive Evatt was a handsome vital man, a King's Counsel, imaginative and energetic. He set out to change Surry Hills housing, but in fact began the process which altered not only the face of this inner-city enclave but its character. People who lived in the demolition area were moved to distant, newly created settlements such as Green Valley and Mt Druitt. So isolated, so devoid of the cosy contiguity of crowded Surry Hills and its adjacent suburbs were these model settlements that the unfortunate emigrés felt they had been dumped willynilly in the scrub.

Many years after that time, these districts and others are still 'problem areas', occupied mostly by social-welfare families, single mothers and other people having a hard time.

Yet I was the person who officially declared open the first new blocks of Devonshire Street flats. Neat little apartments they were, and are, with all the light, ventilation, and modern conveniences the aged cottages and terraces lacked. At the time I thought it was wonderfully progressive, but since then I've often pondered over the entire high-density, highrise phenomenon, and all the personal and civic problems it creates. There seems something profoundly psychologically wrong in forcing people to live in beehives or wasps' nests. We are, it seems, rather like the koala—each to his own tree.

So we moved to Collaroy. We had no furniture, only the typewriter, the baby's things, her bath and bassinet and a little suitcase of the clothes my mother had made and sent to her. Most of our baggage belonged to D'Arcy, suitcases and grocer's boxes and kitbags filled with paper, mostly written upon. For although he was a packrat, he was a paper packrat only. He had hardly any personal possessions otherwise.

Perhaps owning nothing in youth causes some people to hoard. Others grow up believing that the fewer objects which clutter up one's life the better. I am that kind. My ideal architecture is Japanese traditional. When in my middle years I first entered a Japanese room, with no furniture beyond one sprig of bush clover in a bamboo container, I felt I had never seen a place that suited me more.

*

D'Arcy's father and Uncle Charlie had promised to help us move.

'Carry a few things, no worry. Help you get shipshape. Do anything for a mate.'

When we were packed I went over to fetch them. It was early afternoon. Sometime in the interim they had found some money, bought some grog, and were dancing together in the dim kitchen, reeling around skittishly, finickily avoiding the hole in the floor.

Charlie was making noises like a Jews' harp; the father, half-delirious it seemed, had draped an old dress of his wife's over his shoulders, its sleeves hanging down over the black singlet he invariably wore about the house.

'We're dancing the varsuvienne,' he explained thickly.

'Twing twang twong,' added Charlie, unhanding his nose for a moment.

The two brothers had once had the beautiful silky wavy Irish hair, black as crows. For years now they had been shaving up the sides of their heads to hide the grey. Now they were two old Mohawks. The kids used to salute their father Frank with 'How!' which made him mad, flailing about but taking care not to touch them. Under all the nonsense and drunken flim-flam I believe he was gentle in character.

It is a picture that has never left me—the unventilated, dusky kitchen which was lit only by a skylight so filthy it was merely a blackish square in the skillion roof—shadows listlessly lolling on the damp-stained walls, and the two men, two lost men, one sadder than the other, lurching together in some memory of their agile, light and outflowing youth, dancing the *Valse de Vienne*.

'I missed me step somewhere,' Frank used to say of his life, sitting by himself, crying over tattered letters, writing a good deal in his handsome old-fashioned handwriting—anecdotes of his young days, hoping his son would use them in a story and all would not be completely lost. He reminded me of the workman in Lord Dunsany's story, who, falling from a high building, tried to scratch his name on the scaffolding as he fell. Frank Niland, intelligent as he was, knew that he had thrown away his life; his only hope that he might be remembered lay in his son.

'I had a huckaback weskit, cream it was, with little cornelian buttons cut on the cross so they shone. And a tan billycock hat, seven inches high. Wasn't I the darling of the girls, Charlie, me in me billycock hat?'

'Twing twang twong,' uttered Charlie dreamily.

Returning to Mrs Cardy's house, I told my husband that we'd have no help from his father and his uncle that day.

'Ah, they're a pair of poor bedevilled bastards,' was all he said.

The Hing family farewelled us with a fusillade of fire-crackers, and the old grandmother pressed into my hand a little pot of green ointment. From her gestures I gathered that it was to increase my breast milk. She had often ruefully shaken her head over Anne's fragility. Certainly, my baby wasn't a patch on Winston Churchill Hing.

6

Up and down the eastern coast the ocean hurtled towards the land as though the fetch of each swell originated in South America. Far out at sea the surf began to furl, perhaps at the edge of the continental shelf, and by the time it smashed on the beaches it had grown into green mountains, blue mountains, marbled with froth and streaks of sand. The water was so clean, so clear, it was fluid glass; the little sprats flipped through it like tossed coins. Often we saw dolphins playing in the surf, and once, at an inconsiderable distance, two humpback whales bottling—rising vertically out of the water in a fountain of foam.

The coast was scattered with tiny, far-apart settlements established in the fishing and timber-getting days of a century and a half before. Beyond them rose abrupt cliffs, bristly with scrub, infested with ticks. They were prehistoric shorelines. In the rock, if you scratched aside the flowering vines, showed bands of fossils, scallops and limpets and what I thought were australwinks, their unearthly blue bleached to white. If you succeeded in scrambling to the top, and we often did, Anne riding on her father's back, you came to Collaroy Plateau, scrubby, windswept, scarcely built on at all.

As far as the eye could see was bush and scrub, sometimes gauzed with smoke from a bushfire struck from a broken bottle or leaf litter too heavy and humid to resist the summer. One could easily understand why the early settlers were so disturbed by the Australian landscape. After Europe they saw it as endless disorder, an anarchic and deathly place.

The writer Xavier Herbert lived on the lip of the plateau, we were told. D'Arcy much admired *Capricornia*, published just before the war.

'You can smell the dry saltpans and the hot rock in that book.'

At night we looked up the cliff, saw a dim light solitary in the engulfing darkness, and told each other, 'I bet he's working on something great!' He was, of course—the monstrously long, sad, and now neglected book, *Poor Feller, My Country*, published years later.

The light may not have belonged to Herbert's house, but we believed it did, and the sight of it strengthened our resolution. We too were writers, little unrecognised ones; we were part of a movement towards indigenous Australian writing, and we were proud of that.

Often in our explorations we came across broad sandstone outcrops, dimpled by puddles of rainwater or dew, and inscribed with archaic drawings of wallabies, sharks, and women with swinging breasts. There were also ruins of the 'stone arrangements' that had puzzled Captain Phillip when he first traversed the almost impassable upland country. Gibbiegunyahs, the aborigines called them, not houses but shelters from rain or wintry winds.

Of those dark people, who seemed like an emanation of the land itself, there was no other sign and had not been for a century.

The coast settlements sheltered, in the lee of headlands tall and blunt as the brow of a sperm whale. Each had a scalloped beach of purest sand. Industriously the Defence authorities had lined these beaches with small pyramids of concrete; there were thousands of them. Mysterious creations, they were called tank traps. When the Japanese landed their tanks anywhere from South Steyne to Palm Beach, they were in for a horrid surprise.

Why any person in his right mind believed that the enemy would land tanks on these particular beaches continues to be an enigma. Still, we were reassured that New South Wales was alert, prepared, sharp as a tack.

In summer, living at Wits' End was not so bad. Certainly Anne's bronchitis improved because the only place she could play was on the beach. She chased the gulls and gulls chased her.

Around the house the grass was befouled in new and livelier ways with the worms the eight cats ejected from one end or the other. One could scarcely walk unsmirched to the Sore Thumb. Everyone protested, threatened the police, the RSPCA; the cats' mother wept, shouted and begged that her darlings be left alone. At last the poor beasts began to vanish, two in this bag, three in that. God knows what happened to them. Their mother retreated into a clinical depression. All night she wept and honked, until at last her daughter arrived and hauled her away, hurling choked curses at us all.

The houses looked out to the sea. In the twilight we watched Peeping Toms prowling around in search of young lovers entwined amongst the dunes, or, more interesting still, fishermen hauling out of the sand the grotesque beach worms that come by the metre and have heads like bunches of chewed string. At first we thought the hunters ate them, then discovered that the worms are the best bait of all.

'What else leads hidden lives down there under the sand?' I mused, but really didn't care to know.

A disconcerting discovery was that Wits' End was unlined. That house gulped up every wind that blew; a mere skiffle of spray and sand, and through someone's wall it went. We plugged the worst cracks with thick wads of newspaper, or nailed over them scraps of linoleum and fibreboard found at the tip. The floor was equally airy; I used to lie in bed writing scripts and watch the line undulating across the boards like a caterpillar.

My husband and I were unable to sleep together; we used to call across the intervening space like lovesick geese in separate pens. D'Arcy slept, if that is the word, on a chaise longue of inordinate length, made for crinolines, he said. The curved headrest was as rigid as a spinal brace. If he tried to sleep sitting up, his chin squeezed his Adam's apple.

'I can feel the pips, I tell you.'

The chaise longue was stuffed so rigorously it was convex. The aspiring writer in repose was a sight to marvel at. If he was not stretched precariously on the ridge, he was rolling off on to the floor. Once he fell off on the wall side and vanished altogether. Between the four little bandy legs he lay and snored. Mad with sleeplessness, I accused him of doing it on purpose to annoy me, and we had a fight.

My own procrustean couch was a stretcher which had stretched. In the middle, the frail wire mattress had sagged almost to the floor. We propped it up with suitcases, butter-boxes, piles of driftwood planks, so that both my head and feet were at a lower level than my navel.

The mattress also rolled under at the sides. Pain was my nightly lot, as there was always some portion of me caught between the mattress and the iron frame. My back felt broken in three places.

At Wits' End, in fact, we reached our lowest ebb. All we had feared, the remoteness from the city and our markets, the cost of fares, the impossibility of getting a telephone, even if we could have afforded it, lost us much work. Our métier had been immediate writing; we had made our reliability valuable. If some other writer had let an editor down, that editor knew he could ring or telegraph us and get the vacant space filled without question.

This was the major reason why D'Arcy often worked all night. If he had promised a short story or so many thousand words by ten the next morning, that editor had it delivered. Often I stayed up, too, and typed the pages as he finished writing them. He had an extraordinary capacity for thinking out, plotting, and then writing short stories; the short-story form must have been native to him, for later when he began to write novels, he had great trouble with structure.

'It's too dispersed,' he groaned. 'Too many side tracks, subplots, minor characters. There's too much obscuration of *the story.*'

Even more than I, he was wedded to the story, the first of childish and the oldest of human pleasures. He liked the particular, the strong backbone of the short story, the premise posed and answered, under the guise of entertainment and human satisfaction.

Financially we lurched along, always with a week's rent in reserve. Often despondent, we drew close to despair. Once we heard an established novelist, Eleanor Dark, speaking on the radio about Australian writing and its terrors.

'No one in Australia can make a living from writing,' she stated with such curt authoritativeness that I began to cry.

'Now, look here, what's that for?' D'Arcy demanded.

'She's so famous. She must *know.*'

I had forgotten entirely (as I still do sometimes) all the bloodstained lessons I had learned about other people's opinions—that they are very often self-excusatory or self-serving, and more importantly, that you can be influenced by them only if you concur.

He was thoughtful. He had nothing whatsoever against Mrs Dark; he respected her writing. But he disagreed with her ideas.

'What she knows, is that *she* can't make a living. That's because she sticks to novel writing. Haven't we agreed that diversification is the answer to making a living by writing?'

'Yes,' I sobbed. 'But . . .'

'Always remember that wonderful saying of Uncle Charlie's—there is a tide in the affairs of men which, taken at the flood, leads on to fortune.'

Uncle Charlie had his own endearing characteristics; one of them was the way he attached his own authorship to anything that struck his fancy. He had written all of Stephen Foster's songs.

'To hell with Uncle Charlie,' I said brokenly. 'Leads on to fortune, or maybe drowns you. And I feel we're slowly drowning.'

He tried to rally me by stirring references to my propensities as a risk-taker; no use at all. The truth was I suspected I was pregnant again, and had no idea how we would deal with this further complication. I didn't want to tell D'Arcy and have to keep my equanimity throughout all that husbandly blather about 'How the devil did that happen?' as though he'd never been within a mile of the place where babies are made.

He put his head down on the typewriter and was silent. A few minutes later he raised it, the letters q, 1 and o plainly imprinted on his brow, and said, 'Tell you what. You keep on writing. I'll turn it up temporarily and get a job somewhere.'

We talked it over. It seemed the most sensible thing to do. But at last I said, 'Let's give it another week or two. We've been in awful spots before.'

111

'Are you sure you're not just being pigheaded?'

'I've always liked pigs.'

Aside from the many problems of our day to day life, I was consumed with anxiety for Mera, my father, whose chronic heart condition had worsened. He often endured fibrillation of a severe kind. Careful not to waken my mother, always anxious to the bone, he would creep from the bedroom, and for the rest of the night sit huddled close to the kerosene heater in the living room. Such a heater was the only kind procurable, for during the war New Zealand had intermittent but drastic power cuts. I imagined him falling asleep, his dressing robe catching fire. There was no calamity I did not imagine. Mail was so uncertain, airmail often delayed for a fortnight, and even when I received it, I suspected my mother was making the best of things and not telling me how very ill he was. It was torture, of a kind hard to describe, but of the same kind he endured on my behalf.

'Not an hour went past but I wondered how you were,' he told me later.

Unexpectedly D'Arcy had come to understand the spiritual rapport between me and my father. He had never felt homesick, and his only bond with his own father was one of pity. But there it was.

'Of course I understand homesickness,' he said. 'I'm Irish, aren't I?'

'Does that help?'

'Weren't the Irish always being forced to leave home and their families, and longing to go back ever after? Understanding homesickness is in my genes.'

112

One evening he came back from the city and plunked £75 on the table. I was dumbfounded. For us that was a vast sum.

'I cashed in my investment.'

Now this investment had always been a Niland myth to me; God knows how many others floated about in the family, half-forgotten detritus from a hundred memories. But this one was factual. When D'Arcy was sixteen, beginning his career as copyboy at the *Sun* office, Auntie Bid, that good old presbytery housekeeper, had been left a little legacy of £50 by some priest for whom she had cared like a mother.

She had invested it for her nephew because he had, she said, more brains than the rest. This caused some ill feeling and many attempts to 'borrow' it. But Auntie Bid had tied it up until he was twenty-one.

'But we aren't that hard up, yet. Maybe you shouldn't have.'

'Yes, I should. You're going home to see your Dad. I mean it, so shut up. What's more, I have a passage booked for you and Anne, and you leave in a fortnight. I said, shut up.'

He admitted he had been going around shipping offices for months. The end of the war was not in sight, but it was on the horizon, as it were. Thus restrictions had been relaxed a little, and civilian travelling for emergency reasons became a possibility.

'So you did know how I've felt about Dad being ill,' I said, ashamed. I had always had my doubts of that mystic stuff about being Irish.

113

'I know a lot of things. Now, how about a bit of a cuddle?'

With what excited joy I carried Anne aboard the decrepit P & O steamer for the three-and-a-half-day journey to Auckland, and with what thankfulness I introduced her to my family fifteen days later.

Preposterous mystery surrounded that old ship. Why was she carrying passengers at all?

At the time I did not think the voyage a nightmare. In wartime you expect anything, and endure as best you can. Even when the vessel left port, and instead of heading east, turned due north and engaged in gunnery practice off Broken Bay, nearly shaking her aged frame to flinders, I merely thought that the captain knew best and hoped that my fourteen-month child's hysteria would not leave permanent trauma.

Either that ship was carrying distinguished personages whom we never saw, or a cargo of bullion like the torpe-doed *Niagara*, because she was elaborately armed. On the foredeck, where we were allowed to walk for an hour or two each day, almost all space was occupied by huge sinister humps covered in oily tarpaulins.

We carried life jackets at all times and were sharply reprimanded if we forgot. For several days we were escorted by a destroyer which scooted round and round the ship like a sheepdog, darting suddenly over the horizon and reappearing from another direction.

We poor unwelcome supercargo clustered together and created rumours. Only eighty in number, we were mostly refugees fleeing back to New Zealand, or whatever the ship's undisclosed final destination was. Mostly these people had been marooned in Australia in mid-escape from Indonesia, Singapore or Sumatra. Several were Dutch women who were the sole survivors of colonial families, either murdered or taken prisoner by the Japanese.

'They did not want me, I am too fat. Oh, my daughters, my daughters! Why am I alive, gross old woman, what is there in life for me?'

The crew was English, and so were the rations. To our spiritual benefit we realised at last that Australian rations were the fat of the land compared with what the beleaguered British had survived on—and indeed were to survive on—for years. Occasionally we were served coarse red meat.

'What's this, steward?'

'Whale.'

'Damned if I'll eat that! Outrageous!'

'Very good, sir.'

Children had not been provided for at all. There was no milk except 'ship's milk' whatever that might be, and how infants younger than my own survived I have no idea. Anne struggled with tinned salmon (urk!) and reconstituted egg (yuk!) and usually brought it up again. She grew thinner and thinner, though her spirits remained blithe.

We rechristened the ship the *S.S. Perisher*.

On the fifth day I noticed a misty sun shining through the wrong porthole. We were not travelling the common route around the top of the North Island and down the east coast of New Zealand to Waitemata Harbour and Auckland. We were going south.

Several of us simultaneously announced this over our reconstituted breakfast. Rumours sprang into life. A sub had been sighted, the *Queen Mary* had been sunk (heavily laden with troops, too); there was a Jap merchantman in the vicinity. Where *are* we headed, steward? Surely we have the right to know.

'Loose tongues sink ships,' announced the steward, a cheeky cheerikins from London, and like magic silence fell. He was a good little man, but not averse to exercising power when he had it.

The days went past, the wind grew glacial; land was not in sight. One early morning, taking Anne for an airing on the drenched deck, I saw that the sea had turned black, and slushy stuff like half-melted ice heaved and disintegrated all along the sides of the ship.

'Oh, Lord, that *is* ice!'

'Very good, madam.'

Why did the *Perisher* sail so far south, down the west coast of the South Island, past Stewart Island, the cold becoming more and more intense so that one could scarcely venture on the deck? She bore resolutely into rougher and rougher seas, sudden squalls of snow, the numbing wind straight from the Pole. Then one day I saw through a rift in the clouds a dreamlike glimpse of land—islands very high, fissured, half dissolved in mist, that shifted along the horizon for a moment and were gone. Far away were those islands, so dolorous and hallucinatory in their effect that I shuddered. I recalled that when Captain Cook had taken his ship down towards the Antarctic Circle, a small wooden vessel amongst floes and bergs of an enormity never seen before, that 'a strange silence fell over all the people and one man began to pray aloud'.

Looking at the map now, recalling how the *Perisher* had dodged back and forth in the Tasman and then set so inexplicable a course for the Antarctic, I believe that what I saw were the uninhabited Auckland Islands, halfway between the southern toe of New Zealand and the iceberg line, old sealing islands hazardous to shipping, forever lost in snow and fog.

Almost immediately, our ship turned north, steamed briskly up the east coast of the South Island, now in sight of mountainous, sunny land, and within two and a half days berthed safely at Wellington.

Anne and I were taken in charge by old friends, Barbara Silver and her brother John. So exhausted I barely knew what was happening, we were cared for by this generously kind pair, telegrams were sent to my unfortunate family, in the dark about our non-arrival, but knowing that if the *S.S. Perisher* had been torpedoed mid-Tasman, weeks would have passed before the fact was made public.

In a day or two we were on a train for Auckland, eight hundred kilometres to the north. It was basically a troop train; civilians found themselves space where they could. The luggage racks were full of soldiers, not luggage; even the toilets had sleeping occupants. I sat on my suitcase, on the platform outside the carriage, Anne asleep on my knee. Someone had given me a large bag of spagnum moss in case I ran out of nappies; there were, of course, no disposable nappies at that time. Out of a nightmarish drowse I saw that Anne had disappeared from my knee and was sprawled

117

asleep across the legs of a young soldier, her spagnum-stuffed pants sticking up like a hummock. So, through the night, through part of a day, with many stops and jerks, carriages shunted off and others shunted on, we travelled, and at last arrived in Auckland. My child, whom I had so yearned to show off to my parents, was thin, pale, soggy wet, and coughing like a chain smoker. Wisps of dripping moss stuck out of her pants, her nose ran.

I looked at this bedraggled elf somewhat rancorously and thought, 'That can't be mine.'

'She looks just like you,' said my mother bravely.

After the ship cast off and I could see you no more, I raced up on the Bridge and saw her clear the Heads, lurching like a drunk. God, she looked frail; I had a new worry to take home with me. Anne's little shoe was on the floor; she must have taken it off the way she does. I remembered times before we were married, out on the Plains, Nyngan, Moree, looking at the stars, hearing silence, and thinking I was the loneliest bloke in the world. Didn't know what I was talking about. Better work, I thought, take my mind off things. I picked up the typewriter; it wasn't properly locked into the case and the whole guts fell out. The carriage is off its feet, the reels won't turn. Hell, I thought, how am I going to get that fixed?

Sitting there looking at it, glad to have an excuse for the tears running down my face. In came Mrs Hislop from next door with a hot casserole (good woman, that), and I said: 'I've ruined the bloody typewriter, that's why I . . .'

'No, you're not,' she said.

She was right. I didn't know you were the sunshine. I suspected, but I didn't know. You and Anne being the meaning of everything. I didn't know. A man's so dumb I could cry. I am crying.

What a queer thing it is that the exiled always expect everything at home to be exactly the same when they return. And those at home expect you to be the same excited, reckless little girl in a green suit made by her mother.

'You've changed,' said my mother, and I could not disguise from myself that she said it accusingly.

'You've changed,' said my sister wistfully. She too had unfolded from a little teenager into a beautiful young woman, but she hadn't noticed.

During that visit I pondered on the mystery of 'change' which is, of course, really growth or evolvement. The familial attitude towards it is both troubling and mysterious. People take change in others as an undeserved personal affront. They never say, 'You've changed. Isn't that wonderful?' No, they sigh.

Probably change in a person who has been absent for some years is an uneasy demonstration of the instability of things, the invalidity of the baseless concept of permanence.

I, too, noticed differences. The city was not as I remembered it. True, it was as rundown and dilapidated as Sydney, but now I noticed things I had never seen before. The light was astonishing. In Australia it was an assault from the zenith, imperious, demiurgic; there was nowhere to run from it. Eventually I was to see the aubergine sky of Egypt, the plumbago blue of Ireland and England, and northern skies as blanched as bone, but nothing was like the Australian sky. Sumptuous I had called it when I first saw it, but the light it poured forth was more than that. The light was the shaper and definer of the land.

In New Zealand the light was lovely, gentle, sifting through gauzes of moisture, miles high. I looked at it by the hour, that island light, committing it to memory, to words if I could, for perhaps we were being too hopeful about the war, and I might not return to New Zealand for years. For now I realised that my homesickness had altered its character; even as I had longed for my country and my family, so now did I long for my man and my other country. This realisation did not give me peace, I knew that ever after I would be like a migrating bird, home in two places, always going from one to the other, loving each equally.

In truth, I had become just like a million other Australians—those who are called New.

The aunties, rushing over to see me *en masse*, gaily lied. I had not changed. How comforting they were! They exclaimed with delight; everything about me pleased them.

'Isn't her hair long, she's as slim as ever, is that how girls are wearing scarves in Sydney? Oh, you do smell good, what perfume is that? And look at that baby, auntie's teeny weeny girlikins, she has blue eyes just like auntie, clever kid.'

'Oh, do simmer down, Rose, why must you fizz?'

The aunts seemed just the same, loving and frivolous and pretty as ever, even Rose, who had lost both son and husband since I left New Zealand. Now that I was older, I could see that their gaiety and nonsense was how they coped with life, a peculiarly feminine defence mechanism against a creative scheme that appears indifferent to humanity and its woes and foibles.

'When you get to the nub of things, what else is there to do but laugh,' said Aunt Wendela to me in later years, reminding me that my unlucky friend the writer, Eve Langley, had said the same. It came to me then that if it were not for women's irrepressible sense of the ludicrous, the human race would have worn out long ago, for I learned that Aunt Rosina, so skittish and amusing by day, spent her lonely nights grieving inconsolahly.

'How did it help the war to have my only child killed at twenty-one?'

All the sisters were very good to Rose, especially my mother, who had a special gift of solace for those in trouble.

Once my aunt showed me Stuart's photograph, the big blond fresh-faced kid of whom I had been very fond. When he was little and Auntie was between marriages he had lived with us for long periods.

'It's terrible. It's not fair,' I cried, 'all these beautiful young men just thrown away as if they were dirt.'

Auntie Rosina was alarmed. 'Oh, darling, don't get yourself upset. Cissy would kill me. You being pregnant and everything.'

'How on earth does she know I'm pregnant?' I was furious.

'Oh, we all know, sweetie. You have that look.'

I was aggrieved. I had not even informed the new child's father, because I thought he might have voted against my going home to New Zealand if he knew. I was not at all unwell as I had been with my daughter; *that look* was not visible to me.

My mother was not pleased about my pregnancy. 'You're having these children too close together; how will you have time or energy to be a writer? A woman deserves time and freedom to fulfil her own aims in life.'

Remembering very well her own frustration when young, when my father would not allow her to work at her profession of dressmaking, for no rational reason except his fear of an occasional jeer from a workmate that his wife was 'keeping him', I gave her a hug.

'I expect this will be the last one.'

Once I would have told her we wanted a largish family, but now I had become discreet. She was older, there was grey in her pretty hair; she was anxious day and night about my father's cardiac condition. For my Mera was different too—his broad shoulders bent, his eyes which had been like two bits of sky, the keen sharp blue of the Scot, a little faded. But we were still very close and spent every spare moment talking together. How I loved him! There was not a thing about his character that I would have altered. In some curious way we shared a soul, and so it was to be that when he died I died too, a little. I know—life for me was never the same.

His frailty was obvious. He hated being a burden on my mother, so much younger than he and 'the kindest, grandest girl that ever lived'. He accepted humbly her many scoldings, for that was her way, about his refusal to stop smoking. Undoubtedly she was right; smoking did contribute to or even cause his illness.

'Don't be too hard on me, old hen,' he would say in his gentle voice, and she would sigh and go away.

'Look after your health, Din [for such he called me]. Once it goes there's so much to put up with.'

'Oh, me, I'm indestructible,' I answered gaily, and I truly believed it. But the gods were listening, and they hate a big head.

Mera told me once again that I was not to fret if I received bad news from New Zealand. He would let me know first, in some way I'd understand.

'Don't talk about it.' I could hardly speak. 'I can't bear it.'

'It has to be borne,' he said. 'You be my good girl and fight through it by yourself, no matter how hard it is.'

Ah, that was bad advice to give me, for when he died I kept my grief to myself and almost succumbed to it. It was the wisdom of his generation and his stock, proud, independent, stoic, the wisdom of the pioneers from the British Isles who built the South Pacific countries. It was the way they survived Fate's hardest blows.

There is a story told about Mera's ancestor, Mungo Park, the African explorer. It is recorded by Sir Walter Scott, a friend of Dr Park's and an intimate of his family.

Mungo's parents were farmers. One late summer night his mother awakened, thinking she had heard a sound in the skillion room where oats and wood were stored and where her son, as a boy, had slept.

Taking a candle the worthy woman rose from bed and went to see, thinking a wildcat had broken in. For the space of three breaths she saw her son Mungo, pale as death and dripping wet.

Returning to her good man she said, 'Our son is dead.'

He was silent a long space and then replied, 'Wife, we shall thole it until the hay's in.'

On his last exploratory voyage, Mungo Park was drowned in the Niger, the source of which he had discovered years before. The word *thole* means to endure, to suffer unshrinkingly. All his life my father had done that; he relied on me to do the same.

But mine was a different generation, and ours was a diluted blood.

How fortunate it was that I was in New Zealand when my Irish Grandma began running away. My relationship with her had always been so close, full of delight and learning, that my being with her as she was dying completed the circle.

She had always had remarkable health; she had no doctor for her many deliveries. In her mid-eighties she entered into that state of extreme old age which is not dementia or Alzheimer's Disease, but leads to wandering. Though all day she was as sprightly as ever, about four in the afternoon her cheeks flared crimson and she'd leave the world she was in for another—sometimes her turbulent life with Karl Johann, her husband, sometimes with reference to the daughters' childhood which made them uneasy and angry, their cheeks as flushed as hers.

At night, several times she crept out of the house in her nightgown, in bitter weather, to be found hours later, bewildered and lost, once with her head deeply cut where she had fallen in her travels.

Theresa was looking after her at that time, and at last it became too much for her. Grandma was put in hospital. She did not object, she merely relinquished her hold on life. She had dwindled into a small, light bundle. What had become of the tall strong girl with the thick red hair, the green mischievous eyes, who had sailed all alone to Auckland to make a home for her father, the poor tenant farmer of Ballindrum? The splinter of a body had borne all those children, most surely unwillingly, into a desperate world of hard work, and (perhaps, for we never knew) a drunken husband who knocked them around. But what was in her head, behind the closed-up face, that like all aged Irish faces had become heraldic in character, the flesh hardened into stone or wood by hunger, sorrow and rage?

I had not visited Ireland then, but when I did, finding the house where she had been born, brought up motherless— where her father John McBride had died, having a stroke and falling from his chair to strike his head on the hearth— ah, then I spoke to Grandma, and D'Arcy listened.

'Grandma,' I said, 'here I am in your home, standing beside the white-washed hearth where your grandmother taught you to cook. Your father's rocking chair is still there, and the stone bench where he slept when the weather was cold. The roof was pulled off long ago, when Great

125

Grandfather went to heaven, but the rain hasn't spoiled things—there's still a homely feeling here. There are only three rooms, the largest being the kitchen, with one wall nearly all chimney. The walls are so thick that sills have been built into the thickness, handy places for the tea caddy, the candlestick and maybe a little statue of Our Lady. Are you glad to hear these things, Grandma?'

'Why for should I care about them poor old things when here I am with the blessed saints, me ma and me da, and little Johnny? Get away with you! Weren't you always an irksome thing to me?'

So we drove away from that little cottage which had not been occupied since 1912 when John McBride died. It was a 'soft' day, lakelets by the score, some with water lilies folded, their hands over their eyes; water belting down the hillsides like streaks of polished steel. Turf cuttings everywhere, and occasionally a soaked workman with his slane and wheelbarrow, and wet, gloomy dog.

'I wish she'd said something to you before she died,' said D'Arcy. 'Something to remember, seeing you loved her so much.'

'Oh, but she did. She opened her eyes one day and said, "Duddy the Draper".'

'Who the devil is he?'

'Not a clue. "Duddy the Draper," she said. "He's gone and tangled the ribbons again." So I said, "Were they ribbons for your hair, Grandma?"'

'And were they?'

'No, she gave me such a glare and said, "Devil take ye, aren't ribbons the reins for the pony in the cart. You idjut."'

D'Arcy said nothing but I could see he liked my Grandma all the more.

In February 1945 I flew back to my other home. The trip took almost seven hours, with Anne airsick the entire time. It had not been hard to get a trans-Tasman passage. Civilians were now allowed to fly to and from New Zealand five times a week. This near-freedom of movement gave me an uneasy feeling; it had been so long since we were allowed to do anything without the permission or interference of Authority.

'I thought you might stay over there. Crikey, I got the wind up.'

'I can't be where you aren't.'

'The more I thought about it, the more I came to the conclusion I wasn't much for you to come back to.'

'True. It's Australia I'm coming back for, you know.'

I was teasing, but he smiled and said, 'All the same difference.'

He must have felt a very strong identification with the country his forebears had chosen more than a century before; he did not speak much of this profound love, but he wrote constantly of it, especially in short stories and in the novel, *Call Me When the Cross Turns Over*.

The housing situation was as desperate as ever; D'Arcy had not succeeded in getting more than a few nibbles to his advertisements.

'And you have no idea what these people were letting—you wouldn't put a chook into them. *And* £300 key money!'

In spite of the excitement of going home, and all the joy of seeing my husband again, I felt queerer and queerer, and soon it became plain that I was ill.

'She has a severe kidney infection,' said the doctor. 'Get her out of this damned draughty hellhole!'

Like many people in comfortable homes he had little idea of the extent of the housing crisis, which was, indeed, to continue in a lesser degree for years. I suppose that, against the massive tragedies and upheavals of the war, it had small significance except to people like us.

'I'm afraid to give you a sulphanilamide because of the baby. We don't know everything about possible side effects on the unborn.'

It is strange to think that because one is ill at the wrong time one could die; true antibiotics were not yet in use, or perhaps even formulated. It is painful to think that men in the second World War suffered frightful wounds, and the only manner they could be treated was with mercurochrome, iodine and similar disinfectants. The sulpha drugs appeared in time for the Korean War, and thus the casualties were not as great.

Day by day I staggered onwards, dictating ABC scripts to D'Arcy, some days feeling well enough to get up and wash Anne's hair or even my own, but mostly consumed with lassitude and fever. At night I had such chills that the stretcher clicked and squeaked with my shaking; D'Arcy used to get into bed with me to warm me, his extra weight pushing the wire mattress fair to the floor. Sometimes I had waking dreams, very sharp and positive, confusing my early days in journalism with events that had happened while

Beres and D'Arcy and I were in the country, at the opal fields at Lightning Ridge, or in that homestead kitchen in the north-west, listening to the *Children's Session* for the first time.

'There's so much static,' I complained. 'I want to hear Elizabeth. Why don't you tune the wireless?'

But we had no radio by then. D'Arcy had sold it. Often I was delirious for brief periods. Where is it you travel in your head when you are delirious? Sometimes I believed I had crossed over into a conterminous universe, where things were just the same as in my own, but ran smoothly and joyfully. I knew I had already what I truly wanted in life, a faithful and funny man for a lover, a darling child and hopes for another, a little talent with which to please myself and other people. My hard life was simply because the environment was wrong. But I didn't know what to do to make it better.

'I'm a hapless creature,' I said once.

'Just hang on, don't give in, and God will send us a hap.'

'All you Irish are wrong in the head.'

It was a bad worrisome time for D'Arcy. Most of the Wits' End refugees had moved, even kind Mrs Hislop. All we had for neighbours were shiftless strangers and the old man in the front room, still trying to blow up the house with his primus and not speaking to us at all. There were no effective locks on the doors, and my nervousness was abject. The scrub around Collaroy was full of eccentric people mooching about—probably they were simply home-less, poor creatures. When D'Arcy was away in the city, sometimes all night, when the Manly ferry wasn't running because of bad weather, I spent the night in terror.

Once a strange man did creep along the verandah and into the bathroom. He seemed just to stand there, listening at our kitchen door. I stood listening at the door, too, the frying pan in my trembling hand, resolved to emulate my bold cousin Helga who had fractured a man's skull with a similar weapon.

But he made no attempt to open the door. He simply piddled in the bath like a dog leaving a sign on a post or bush. The sound of this waterfall was the last straw. My throat was too constricted to scream, so I gave the door an almighty whack with the pan, and was answered by the sound of scuttering feet. From the front room came a detonation from the primus stove. It was 3 a.m. but the tea was in the pot and all was normal.

Yet on the literary front things were improving rapidly. D'Arcy had an informal agreement with Murray Publications, a company which had prospered producing magazines with particular interest for the Forces—action stories, informative articles, cartoons and pin-up girls. From our account book I see that the last week we spent at Wits' End D'Arcy earned nearly £9. Except for my radio scripts, my income was nil. But it was evident that in spite of Eleanor Dark's despondency about the future of Australian writing, we would soon be able to afford a higher rent.

It was a phenomenally cold stormy autumn, with tides so high they flung haystacks of drying seaweed against Wits' End's fallen-down front fence. An easterly rose somewhere in the South Pacific and blew for days, weeks, on end, with all the urgency and muscularity of a river. The air was hazed with spray, salt formed on our lips. At night the sea was black, edged with luminous foam; the clamour of the huge surf on the headlands was deafening.

'Oh, shut up!' yelled D'Arcy, trying to plug with damp newspaper a crack through which the wind squeezed with the squeal of a stepped-on cat.

Some of the occupants of nearby houses and beach shacks became alarmed.

'The ruddy nails are falling out of my walls,' said one man. 'If you could wring out the front door you'd get gallons. I'm moving to the daughter's place.'

'Look here, you young 'uns,' said another, 'you ought to move out if you can. Storms can be tricky. My granddad saw one that washed ten feet of water right over Pittwater Road.'

But we had nowhere to go.

'Oh, it will calm down when the wind swings around,' I shouted.

'I'm tellin yer, girlie, clear out while yer luck holds.'

Two nights later an appalling crash shook the house, followed by explosions, fizzes and spitting sparks as the electric power died. But before darkness covered us D'Arcy saw one of the most fearsome sights of his life—the light shining through the window into the depths of a huge green wave. The next moment the room was dark, the window blew in, and in poured a cascade of seawater. The waves broke on the roof, two, three, four, then with a hideous sucking sound withdrew.

I seized the yelling Anne and some blankets. D'Arcy the typewriter and an armful of the current work spread out over the table, and we ran. The roadway was full of refugees, some with torches, most with children. Pittwater Road, even as our kindly neighbour had warned, was rushing like a shallow river. Seaweed, beach chairs, clothing, swimming dogs, spun past. We reached a derelict shop high on the west side of the road, kicked in the door and sheltered for the rest of the night.

The storm seemed over; the wind swung due north, the moon shone out, far up the coast we could hear the wolfish yell of the sea as it besieged the more distant headlands.

'If I hadn't been wearing Sister Roche's scapular we would have been a goner,' said my husband smugly.

The next day sparkled; the sea purring in over kilo-metres of splintered wreckage, piles of bricks, uprooted outhouses, a garage on its side. The water had swept away the sand from under fifty houses, which now stood on one corner or fell on their chins. Most astonishing of all, the storm had been so powerful it had lifted the Defence Department's concrete tank traps as if they had been made of plastic and deposited them by the dozen along the grassy verges of the road, inside houses, upside down, heavy, immovable, doomed in some cases to be there for years.

D'Arcy went off to see how Wits' End had fared. He came back long-faced. Our room was a total wreck, a metre deep in seaweed, even the ceiling sodden and dripping. It stank horribly.

All the crockery was broken, shoes and what few clothes we had totally spoiled. Even the baby clothes my mother had so lovingly made for the newcomer were stained and thick with sand. I looked at this ruination with despair.

'Do you think it's possible that someone up there hates us?'

'We could have had a tank trap in the kitchen . . .'

'Thank God we stored our books with Auntie Bid, at least we'll have them when we get a flat.'

'People who live in flood areas sometimes do this three or four times a year, more fool them,' said Beres, magically appearing. We were much solaced by his arrival. Anne and I were sent off to a boatshed that had somehow escaped damage. She spent her time fishing through the cracks in the floor; she was always an adaptable child. The boatshed owner, a cheerful woman who sold fresh bait for a living, took the new baby's clothes, washed them and returned them almost as good as new.

'You look a bit brighter to me,' she said. 'Thought you were going to be a real cot case when you came in here yesterday. You get up and sit outside and get a bit of sun. Do the nipper good, too.'

She was our first bit of luck. Only a few days later D'Arcy had a telegram asking him to phone one of his editors, who had found a flat due to be vacated. It was the converted residence above an old empty shop, and the rent was triple what we had been paying. But there was no key money.

'Sister Laurencia has come through,' we told each other. I had been praying to my old English teacher, who had gone to heaven just before Anne was born. Having no patience with the Church and its formalised union tickets—*you're* a saint, *you* aren't, *you* may be in five hundred years—it has always been my habit to keep in close communication with those I love, and Sister Laurencia is one of these. She it was who put me in touch with D'Arcy Niland in the first place and had a terrible fright when we decided to get married. I had placed our housing problem in her compassionate hands.

Both D'Arcy and Beres understood. They said they prayed to their Granny Egan all the time.

'Oh, crikey, I can't believe it, we can't believe it, can we?' they said as we walked around the clean, newly painted flat in Petersham, marvelling at the huge airy bedroom, a living room, a kitchen, a bathroom of our own with real hot water. There was even excellent furniture and a queen-sized bed.

Probably it was an ordinary little apartment, but to us it was a miracle. I felt as though my life had been saved for I was able to rest comfortably until my baby arrived, knowing I would carry him back to a safe and healthy house, the kind Anne had never had.

It was a major battle to bring that baby alive into the world, for it was a breech birth and seemed to go on for days. I pleaded with the elderly Jewish doctor not to let the baby be hurt, no matter what, and he said what I have always remembered as a wonderful thing.

'I promise you, my dear. To me, any newborn child may well be the Messiah.'

Our son Rory was born alive and well on May 5, three days before war ended in Europe. I remember lying in bed feeding this battered little fellow, so bruised and scraped, and listening to Ben Chifley, the treasurer, announce that war was over. Our Prime Minister, John Curtin, who had effectively killed himself by his labours during the war, was too ill to make the announcement, and indeed died a month later.

It was magnificent news, but not so magnificent for us nations of the Pacific, still with the formidable Japanese to defeat. Nevertheless, two of the baby boys born in the hospital that week were christened Victor.

We southern people had to wait until August 15, the Feast of the Assumption. I was at Mass, and halfway through a little boy ran on the altar and whispered something to the priest. The latter turned to face us and said, 'Thanks be to God, the war is finished.'

Almost at once the entire air was filled with the braying and bellowing of sirens, air-raid warnings, ships in the harbour, factory whistles, strange sounds like those of dinosaurs or other uncouth beasts. People in the congregation turned to each other with tears and laughter. It's over, it's over! And one or two undoubtedly said: Ah, but it's too late for Kenny, too late for Bob.

We ordinary people did not lack comprehension of the terrible potential of what was then called the atom bomb. Younger generations seem to believe that we did not understand what we were watching. Hiroshima, Nagasaki, boom boom, and that's the end of *them*! The Establishment might not have told us everything, but were not stupid. We knew from the moment Hiroshima died that the world would change; we had entered a new mode of existence.

Weeks went by while I convalesced, never to be again the robust country girl of earlier years, for the long kidney infection left a condition that flared up often, and was indeed to be a kind of brake on the leading of a full life.

Nevertheless our luck had turned, and did not cease in its onward flow until my husband died.

As he would say, 'Good luck doesn't wear a label; bad luck doesn't either. Maybe that was my time, my good time, to leave you and the children. Who knows things like that?'

Ruth Park, aged twenty-six

Anne Niland, eighteen months, on Collaroy Beach at Wits' End

Rory Niland, B.Sc. a week after his father's sudden death

Deborah and Kilmeny Niland, fifteen months old

D'Arcy Niland and
second son, Patrick,
thirteen months old

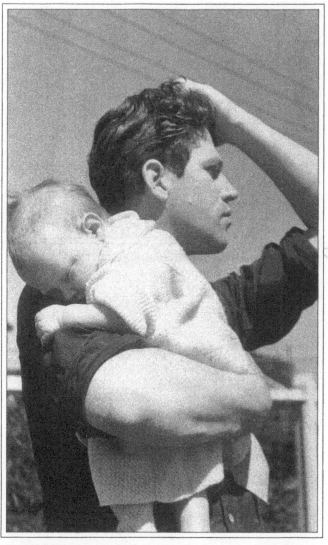
'How did a man get into this?'
D'Arcy Niland, aged twenty-four. Anne Niland aged two months

Anne and Rory Niland, at Petersham, where we lived next door to Gilles de Rais

D'Arcy Niland, at the time of writing *Call Me When the Cross Turns Over*

Barbara Lucy Egan, aged seventeen. D'Arcy Niland's mother

Barbara in her thirties, with her sister Bid, the presbytery housekeeper with the tired feet

D'Arcy Niland and actor Peter Finch, discussing their copyboy days on *The Sun*, 1956

Beresford Niland, aged
nineteen. Our constant
companion

Elizabeth (Ida Osbourne), 'The
fair and lightly sparkling girl' of
the ABC's *Children's Session*

Interviewing Surry Hills residents about the new housing scheme, 1951

PART TWO

1

'You sound like a dog with two dinners,' said my father, Mera, of the letters I wrote after we moved into the Petersham flat.

Indeed I lived in a daze of bliss. The war had ended, our son was born safely, and we had our first real home. Nevertheless, the housing famine continued for years for thousands of other young families, and was exacerbated by the country's immigration policy.

Such were the consequences of my confinement I could do little more than creep around for months, so D'Arcy's younger sister came and lived with us for a while. Anne loved her. She was Anne's dear Dordie.

Rory had a much better start in life than Anne had had. He was not only healthy and sociable, but so well-dressed that his father addressed him as Bub Brummell. My mother sent us parcels of charming garments, for in New Zealand as well as Australia rationing had been stealthily relaxed. No longer were we tied to the scanty clothing coupon allowance which had scarcely bought Anne napkins let alone the horrid 'austerity layette', a collection of baby garments made of a greying fabric so thin you could spit through it. Even so, while we lived at Collaroy, Anne had been the victim of a mugging. A passing mother, seeing the child asleep in her pram outside the butcher's shop, removed all her clothing and fled with it. Wartime brings out the closet anarchists.

'Still, we've been lucky,' I thought. 'At least we've survived by writing, when everyone predicted we couldn't.'

Unceasing practice as freelances had taught us some valuable lessons, some of which I have detailed elsewhere. The growth of market sense was one; another was the ability to gauge, as distinct from his magazine's require-ments, an editor's likes and dislikes. Some editors always gave careful reading to a story about an animal; others would not consider any piece about a child in jeopardy, even though the ending was both safe and happy. Another, for reasons of his own, detested stories which showed a woman doing anything but wash up the tea things.

'Preposterous!' he would cry. We nicknamed him Old Preposterous and wondered a good deal about his wife.

Though many magazines which had been published primarily for the troops sank like stones as soon as demo-bilisation began, D'Arcy was able to find other short-story markets and sold his work with increasing steadiness. One reason for this was that he suddenly ceased being confron-tative with editors. This lamentable propensity had done much to hold him back.

Either some particularly burly editor had hurled him into the street or at long last good sense had prevailed. He wouldn't tell me which. He merely grunted.

This does not mean that he ceased being confrontative with me, nor I with him. If either one of us disliked a piece written by the other, the reasons why had to be stated and argued out. In this way we learned from each other, usually with the accompaniment of flashing eyes and snaps and growls, backs turned to each other in bed, and finally tickling matches and a bit of a cuddle.

Gradually I acquired knowledge about the writing of short stories. D'Arcy made me read the best, which in his opinion were largely the European classics. His perfectionist taste centred around Tchekov, Isak Dinesen, just beginning to be translated, and Thomas Mann. Amongst those who wrote in English he admired James Joyce, particularly for *The Dubliners*, Somerset Maugham ('cunning as a rat') and Mary Lavin, a new Irish writer.

And he, so adamant that he would never get the hang of writing factual material, profited by my years in journalism. Within a year of our marriage he was writing fact prolifically—articles, personality profiles, radio documentaries.

'How, when, where, why, and who, who, WHO?' I yelled at him until he told me I sounded like a bloody morepork. He was hopeless at research, which enraged me, perceptive and intelligent as he was. Somehow, when reading books or other sources on his subjects, he could not pick out the salient points required for his own piece. He brought home notebooks filled with laborious trash.

'Who cares whether he had a boil in the armpit?' I raged at his notes on some explorer's hazardous adventures. 'What supplies did he take? Who were his companions? Why was that particular route chosen? Why did you waste energy recording that he had an innoculation scar on his right arm?'

'Oh, shut up!'

We had more fights over this than most things. At last, as I regained health, it was agreed that I do all the library research, mostly in the Mitchell Library and the reference section of the Public Library, now the New South Wales State Library. These marvellous repositories of knowledge were then far more open and freely designed so that a bloodhound researcher such as myself could browse at will, following tiny clues, lateral speculation, or my own allusive thoughts.

It became my great joy to spend two evenings a week at the library, rushing home at last to give the baby his ten o'clock feed, sort out my notes, maybe type them.

Out of his own knowledge, D'Arcy commented on my short stories, much as my old mentor, Sister Serenus, had done. He suggested the replacement of inexact words with hard-hitting ones, or that I should shorten sentences, sharpen themes.

Often I argued fiercely, preferring my own choice. He accepted this placidly. I have never known anyone so impartial, so able to give another person his own space, even if that space were filled with stuff one wouldn't like to get on one's shoes.

*

The modest comfort of the Petersham flat made me realise, almost with disbelief, what hard times we had had until then. Our life had been so full of work, children arriving, difficult relatives, and the thousand frustrations and deprivations of the war, that we'd scarcely had time—except for thirty minutes of despair or fury here and there—to think about it.

It had been rather like D'Arcy's own battling childhood, of which he said, 'We kids would never have known that we were poor except that people kept telling us about it.'

When I reflected upon our apprenticeship—usually as I lay in one of those endless hot baths which were beatitude after nearly three years of none—I saw clearly that we possessed an abiding joy. Each of us had been lonely before we married, not only in body and mind but in that mysterious place where literary creativity resides.

But now we were dual; we set off sparks in each other. Providence had also spared us jealousy, that frequent devil that haunts creative partnerships and which destroys so many writers, even writers we knew well, such as Charmian Clift and George Johnston.

D'Arcy's failures made me weep; my successes made him burst into song. I suppose our mutual aims were the same in both the literary and the natural worlds. From his letters I pluck two sentences which reflect upon his philosophy of life and work:

The greatest thing in life is to produce children who'll he pleased that you did.

And also:

The real test of a writer is whether people are grateful that once he was around.

While he was alive I did not see that somewhere in his mind he had made some curious identification between the fathering of children and the production of literary works. So I did not ask him for his thoughts on this subject. But I recall his saying that posterity would judge which were the more valuable, the kids or the books.

So many writers are inimical to children, or cope destructively or not at all with family life. They feel they are, because of talent large or small, external to common humanity.

Such a thought would not have entered D'Arcy Niland's mind.

Nevertheless, in most ways, he was what I can only surmise an ordinary young man. Not selfish—indeed generous and kindly—but self-absorbed to a degree that frequently made me think he was wrong in the head. His own purposes and requirements dazzled on his horizon like an all-consuming sun. If his attention were drawn to the ineluctable fact that other human beings, such as myself, had needs and desires different from his own he blinked as if I had suddenly stuck out a foot and tripped him.

When we entered the Petersham flat on that first happy day he made a beeline for the dining-room table, excitedly opened the typewriter and spread out his dictionaries, papers, and reference books.

'Look!' he cried. 'I've a proper place to work at last.'

And he immediately sat down and whacked out qwert, asdfg and poiuy£? with as much enthusiasm as if he were playing the first bars of something nervewracking by Wagner.

'It's like a miracle!' he said, looking at me with such innocent rapture that I couldn't find it in my heart to kill him. All his life he had yearned for a desk or something that would serve as a desk, and now he had it. All my life I had done the same thing, and I didn't have it.

'And where shall I work?' I asked.

'Oh, yeah,' he said thoughtfully. 'We'll think of something. No need to worry about it just yet.'

The question then passed from his mind. Thenceforth I worked with the typewriter on the kitchen table, the ironing board, our bed, my knees. Everything I ever wrote in D'Arcy Niland's lifetime proceeded from one of these situations. At one stage, I did have one end of the table, but gradually his papers encroached; files ostentatiously fell to the floor; the carriage of my typewriter constantly hit things—books, old jam jars filled with dead pens, half-eaten apples, ash trays.

At last I went back to the ironing board. It may be asked why, as I was doing equal, or even more work, I did not stand my ground. Why didn't I call him a selfish son of a sea cook and demand the table for myself? I have no answer, but I suspect that, in my estimation, the ironing board was a miniscule price to pay for all the good things in his character and in our relationship—the lack of jealousy, meanness or vulgarity, his alacrity in accepting the care of the children for the day, or cooking a meal if I hadn't finished a script; the way he would walk into town to the G.P.O. at 1 a.m. to post a script that had to get to the ABC in the first delivery that morning.

Besides, I understood very well how that fierce, underfed kid he had once been had longed for a desk, a proper desk where he could write and not have to shift his work all the time. Why shouldn't he have it?

By that time I had heard many explosive outbursts from other wives of my age. The self-centredness of young men seemed to be a major cause of discontent in marriage.

'I thought only Dad was like that,' said one girl.

There was a prevailing female belief, as there is at the present, that such peculiarities in the male psyche arise from a radical misunderstanding of a woman's identity. Whatever it is, women of my mother's generation mostly accepted it, working their lives around it as water works around boulders in a stream. They had not much choice.

In the early postwar years there were observable stirrings of revolt.

Two women of a much older generation had interesting things to say. Mary Gilmore said it was little to do with misunderstanding of a woman's identity.

'Do men think you have one? No, it's radical misunderstanding of *human* identity. We have to confront the fact that, always speaking generally, few men are good with people of any gender. Read history and see for yourself. Objects, events, movements—those are the male forte, never the welfare of human beings, *en masse* or individually.'

On the other hand Bertha Lawson, with whom I became friends in later years, had another theory. Bertha was a sagacious, passionate little dot of a woman, very different from the way she is depicted in the many books about her famous husband, Henry.

She thought the problem was, in a word, hormonal. I disagreed, because as far as self-centred women were concerned I had met some corkers.

'Not as many as men, perhaps?' she suggested. 'But maybe for the same reason?'

'In some persons adolescence goes on for a very long time,' she continued. 'Few adolescents know there are other people in the world. Perhaps your man is a late bloomer. By the time he's thirty he'll have become a man in every way, a complete human being. Some never do, of course,' she added, and I thought I detected a sigh.

She was right, anyway, as Mary Gilmore was right. Gradually the infuriating singlemindedness of my partner concerning his own imperatives diminished. Sometimes when I yipped about his thoughtlessness or lack of consideration or even good sense, he reminded me mildly that he had to put up with me.

'And what's the matter with me?'

'You're weird.'

'Well, if you try to be less heedless I'll try to be less ...'

'Gee, no. I like you weird.'

The Prime Minister, Ben Chifley, exhorted us brusquely to win the Peace. The prime folly of politicians is that they do not study historical cause and effect; neither do they heed folk memory, which is directly related. History does not repeat itself. Repetitive patterning rises from the same old mistakes committed by governments.

People of my father's generation wrote letters to the editors of this newspaper and that, speaking of the chaos of disorganisation that follows long wars, the protracted difficulty of repair to community services neglected while priorities were urgent and elsewhere. Where were the jobs for the half million young Australian men still in the services on VP Day?

The official solution was to tip out the women who had held down those jobs for five years. But then *they* were unemployed. Not a large percentage were content or even economically able to return to the prewar tradition of domesticity.

We young ones were just as obtuse as the politicians. We read the letters of often constructive suggestion with a disinterest that leaned towards the kindly rather than not. We dismissed as outmoded the older people and the wisdom originating in hard experience.

When the Budget was brought down in September, a month after ceasefire, we learned of a new tax on income, to be known as the Social Services Contribution Tax. Here was the original brick, so to speak, upon which the vast structure, superstructure, annexes and outbuildings of modern social welfare was to stand. As I recall, this initial tax was 7½ per cent. Gradually it was subsumed into ordinary income tax and forgotten, so that other social services loadings could be imperceptibly added. It had been in place only a fortnight or so when militant labour unions associated with protected industries such as coalmining and steelworking, organised a series of strikes. Power shortages, and then total blackouts, lasted until after Christmas. The first Christmas dinner for returned soldiers was a cold one, or, like ours, charred intermittently over an open fire in the backyard.

'We can heat the baby's bottle in the living-room fireplace. Why didn't we think of that before?'

The midget Victorian grate, a cast-iron basket, had not given out its meagre warmth for at least two British reigns. The chimney caught fire with a whoomp! like a volcano. What drama! The fire brigade, children squalling, neighbours blaming, the landlady's lounge suite freckled with greasy smuts, some iniquitous person taking advantage of the commotion to steal all our towels from the backyard clothes-line.

One of the firemen, seeing me snivelling, said paternally, 'Cheer up, missus, this is the first Christmas for years that no one's killing anyone else. Youghta think of that.'

'Oh, shut up, you brass helmeted smug-O,' I thought, but didn't say. He didn't have to clean all that moquette. Besides, he was right.

In those days I was so happy with life that when I look back it seems to have been a shimmering time.

Historically, it was not.

The war was over, but the peace was restless, often irascible and disillusioned. Incalculable social changes had occurred; as far as many returned men were concerned, the old Australian ethos had disintegrated. They could not

149

cope with children they did not know, wives who weren't the girls they had married in some heavenly hasty romance. The housing shortage had reached catastrophic levels; many of these men, sick or exhausted, traumatised by years of dreadful experience, found they had to share houses with relatives whom they didn't know either, and whom they couldn't bear a bar of.

One of D'Arcy's old mates confided that he did not even recognise his wife.

'She was this little blonde dolly, and now all I've got is a big old walloper with dark hair. I think she's a ring-in, that's what.'

Judging from the letters to the advice columns in the women's magazines, women also had discovered, either with resignation or shrieking fits, that their returned heroes were not the lovely boys they had married. Estrangements and divorces were rife, the consequences of which lasted for at least one generation and probably two.

If one could temporarily set aside all the monstrous tragedies of war, one might significantly call those five shattered years the Time without Fathers. Certainly many, many families reconstituted themselves and submerged contentedly into history. With others it was as though a *tsunami* had swept across society, leaving inextricably tangled debris when it receded.

We lived next door to Gille de Rais, aged four.

He was really Ray, handsome, sturdy little Ray. It was Beres who rechristened him. Beres was camping with us for a while, while he looked for a room of his own, and delighted we were to see his feet sticking out over the end of our sofa. I didn't still like him more than my husband, but I liked him just as much. We spent a good deal of time hearing of his adventures as a circus rouseabout, pulling down the Little Top.

'Isn't it the Big Top?'

'This was a very small circus.'

He had also shoved elephants around, filled in for the Charlie when he was drunk, and acted as bouncer.

'You a bouncer? Don't believe it.'

'Well, I sort of coaxed.'

The only thing he really hadn't enjoyed was sharing a bunk with a midget, a delicate baby-faced man who had trained as a schoolteacher but had, perforce, to take a job as a clown. The midget slept at the bottom of the bunk and Beres at the top. He said it was like having a pillow at both ends.

Like our residence, next door was an ex-shop, once a greengrocery. A phantom smell of bananas still hung about it, as there was sometimes an elusive whiff of cheese in our flat, as though the walls had soaked up the odours of long vanished goods. Once Sydney had thousands of these small islanded shops, decades since starved out by supermarkets. The old grandfather next door, crippled by arthritis, had been the greengrocer, but had found he could not manage once his son was called up.

'We was Buckle & Son, you know. First of all the Buckle was my father, and I was the son. And then I became the Buckle, and Jim was the son. And I thought that one day—but then the Big Stoush came along. Changes things.'

151

His eyes filled with tears at the knowledge that his family's humble dynasty had come to an end. The son Jim, who had left Australia before the child Ray was born, had been a Japanese prisoner-of-war for several years.

'How'll he come back, that's what I'm asking,' lamented the father. 'Treated like an animal. My Jim. Thank God the wife died long ago, it'd kill her. And what will he think of that young Ray?' he added dubiously. 'I dunno, really I don't. And as for that tyke there . . .'

The tyke was a three-months-old baby, a tightly wrapped bundle in a pram. The old man, sitting in the sun, mechanically rocked the pram whenever the bundle miaowed.

'She ain't a bad girl, you know, just careless and wants a bit of fun. Very good to me, she is, and only daughter-in-law, you know, not daughter. Yes, very good and patient.'

The son had survived Changi and the Burma Railway; he was in a hospital in Singapore and soon would come home. His wife was carefree about her new baby, tossing her head flirtatiously, laughing, 'Oh, he'll make a fuss, go to market a bit, but I'll get round him, always could. Got round the old Dad, didn't I, and he's a Methodist.'

Our kitchen window overlooked the next-door back-yard, but I rarely looked out of it; it was not a view that said much to me except neglect and the sadness of the old man struggling to walk a few steps to the outside lavatory.

But Beres, who had resumed work at the Tivoli, the last desperate stand of vaudeville in Sydney, had mornings at home, and usually occupied himself doing the cooking for the day. He liked cooking. He looked out the window while

152

he was beating or stirring things, for everything interested him. One day I came into the kitchen to find him holding Anne up to the window, pointing out this and that.

'See that little shed at the bottom of the yard? That's what you call a loo. Yes, I know our loo is inside but some loos are outside and Mr Buckle's loo is right there. And Mr Buckle is inside. I know because I saw him go in. You know perfectly well what he's doing, don't be rude. And there's Ray. No, he's older than you and he's years and years older than Rory. Look at him piling all that paper and rubbish and stuff outside the loo door. It's a game, I think. Yes, it is a funny game. And now he's setting fire to it . . .'

In a split second Anne was on the floor, a rapid drumbeat of feet sounded on the stairs, and Beres appeared in our backyard, scrambling over the fence. It was a high fence, but he had long legs. He fell over the other side, kicked away the flaming rubbish before the lavatory door, and Mr Buckle staggered out, half suffocated by smoke, tripping over his trousers, his gammy leg giving way and throwing him on the ground.

'That bastard will be the death of me,' he stammered.

It was an alarming situation. The child, though obviously intelligent, was homicidal. All his games were directed towards the death or injury of someone else.

I have often wondered what happened when he grew older and his imagination developed. While we lived in Petersham, his instincts were mostly towards pyromania. Of course, he had tried to put his baby sister in the incinerator, squashed the cat under a rock, and jabbed a wire through a crack in the fence, through which Rory, aged two,

153

was looking at the time. Fortunately it missed the blue eye and only left a scar near the corner.

He made several attempts on his grandfather's life; the old man, growing steadily more helpless, must have been in terror. I went over the fence myself to rescue him when I saw the child pouring kerosene on his legs while he was dozing.

The mother ran around like a hen with its head off, whine, whine all day, aiming vague slaps at the child, saying she hadn't an idea in the world what to do.

'Don't you hide the matches?' I asked. I was afraid that Ray would not only set fire to his own house and everyone in it, but ours, too. 'And how did he get hold of the kerosene?'

'I don't know,' she replied distractedly. 'No matter what I do, he always finds things. It's awful, really it is.'

I even asked advice at the fire station, but they said that fires were their business, not arson. See the cops. The police said the boy would grow out of it; the mother was obviously incompetent, try a social worker, the church, a doctor.

The social worker said Ray would change his ways when his Daddy came home; little boys were often disturbed, wet the bed, had bad dreams, when there was no father figure in the house.

'I don't know that Ray does those things. All I know is that he tries to murder people.'

'Come now, dear, surely that's rather extravagant.'

'What makes a kid like that hate everyone?' asked Mr Buckle despairingly. 'Just a little thing he is, not much more than a baby. What's happened to him, missus, do you know?'

It seemed to me that Ray was a casualty of war, but I did not say so.

Into this dangerous household returned the young father, Jim Buckle, a skeleton yellow of skin, with a face like a Gothic effigy, so attenuated, long-nosed and speechless it was. What had been his dreams while slaving on the Burma Railway, of which he was one of the infrequent survivors? But what he had was an infant daughter not fathered by himself, an old helpless man, half crazy with harassment, and this murderous son. I never heard him speak, even when the child, now bigger and stronger, tipped him out of the long chair in which he used to lie in the backyard. He just tottered to his feet, righted the chair, and lay down once more. He was, I think, a dead man, aged twenty-eight. Before very long he disappeared from our view, perhaps to hospital or the grave.

D'Arcy wrote a short story about a wicked child harassing a blind old grandfather with the threat of non-existent spiders. It appeared in several international anthologies. The ABC Talks Department turned it down because they felt no listener would find it credible that a child could act like that.

While we lived at Petersham we saved enough money to take the family to New Zealand for three or four months. My parents had not seen Anne since she was an infant, and Rory not at all. They had never met my husband, and I longed for them to do so.

'It's going to be tight financially, but we can work from there. The airmails are so good now there'll be no trouble sending your scripts. And I'll get ahead with a few stories before we leave.'

We travelled in a converted hospital ship, the *Katoomba*, through one of the Tasman Sea's spectacular storms. Early morning, hastening on deck, we found the sea placid, the skies bluebell-soft, and my native land's green velvet hills dozing in the sunlight.

'Why did you ever leave?' said D'Arcy.

As I had done with Australia five years before, my husband had fallen in love with a strange land. This love expanded as time passed, for he made frequent journeys to New Zealand in his lifetime, and explored it more closely than many New Zealanders. He spoke of the little country with such possessiveness that one day I became impatient and said, 'Why don't you rechristen it Niland's Islands and be done with it?'

'I will, I will, and I'll write a book about it, too,' he said.

'Get away with you. We don't write books. It's all short stuff for us—stories, radio plays, articles, scripts for children.'

But in fact I was the one who wrote a book while we were in New Zealand, a novel called *The Harp in the South*.

2

The first thing my father and D'Arcy did when they met was to shoulder each other around, grinning. Then they retired to the garden and could be seen hunkered down, rolling cigarettes and frequently uttering the traditional peaceable laugh—the soft uh-uh-uh used by men meeting as strangers, each wanting the other to know he is non-confrontative, open to possible friendship.

'*Now* what are they doing?' asked my mother, who wanted them inside to have their tea while it was hot.

'Being men,' I thought, having seen these rituals many times when I was in the outback, men sussing each other out by means of familiar moves and old, worn sentences.

'He's all right,' said Mera briefly, when we were able to talk privately.

Being with my father once more was a wonderful thing for me, although I could see his health was precarious. With a pain at my heart I observed his big bony old frame, clothes hanging on it, hair scant and silver, eyes like bits of summer sky now turned to winter. Even his hands were different, still warm and strong, but now smooth skinned.

'Not a man's hands now, Din. A man's hands should always have a bit of bark knocked off them.'

But he is active in the garden, spending hours grafting fruit trees. Grafting is his great interest and hobby. Trees are the first love of the old bushman, even niminy-piminy trees like apple and plum.

'I feel like a boat with the bottom out, tossed up on the sand.'

'He's got too many women around him,' says D'Arcy. 'A man needs men. But he'll latch on to Rory. Teach him how to bang a nail in straight, tie a knot, never cry, handle things in a fight.'

'But Rory's only two!'

'Can't start too early.'

My father has changed a little in that he speaks more often of his family's history, his mother Mary Ann Dunne, born in the married quarters of the barracks at Hobart Town, in Tasmania when it was Van Diemen's Land.

'Her father was from County Clare in Ireland. He was a regular British Army man, a sergeant. He died before I was born, but Mother had a photo. One of those stone-grey Irishmen, face like a roughcast wall. Trousers tied around his shanks with leather bowyangs, a pot hat. Knock you down as soon as look at you. He ended up buried under Grafton Bridge in Auckland with other old soldiers.'

Mera's mother, Mary Ann Dunne, was a small dark-eyed woman who had three sons before she was twenty-one.

'She was only sixteen when my father courted her. He used to swim across the Waikato with his clothes in a bundle on top of his head. Her family were glad to get her off their hands. They were like that with girls in the old days, with those huge families.'

This story and that. He has a certain urgency. He doesn't want his memories, his life, to be lost. 'You'll remember, Din, won't you? Write it down somewhere. Tell Anne and Rory.'

'Yes, I shall.'

I watch him often. He seems a little lost, a little unfamiliar in this world of women, wife, daughters, sisters-in-law. Very few men come to the house. His surviving brothers live in distant towns. The clan is now so large, his nephews so many he hardly knows them, never sees them. Two of the aunts have already lost their husbands, good men who were his friends. My cousin Stuart, whom he loved as a son, died in the war. It is true my mother's sisters, the aunties, are merry, loving and solicitous, but they are after all chirping, finical little creatures alien to his life as a countryman of the far ferny hills and the dusky intractable forests.

In an effort to bring the light back to his eyes I ask him for the old stories.

Tell me again about the bullocks, Dad. That farmer who had you yoke up his prize bull to take the devil out of him.

Dad, tell me about the time when there was an explosion in the deep mine at Huntly and your father went missing.

Dad, tell me about your mother left alone in a raupo hut with two little children, and being frightened to death of roving warlike Maoris, and how she heard a scratch-scratch at the wall in the dead of night, and . . .

'Your father's tired, lovey. Let him go off and have a rest before tea-time.'

He goes off obediently.

I see with terror that something has knocked on his heart. Get ready, old man, it has conveyed to him. You know not the day nor the hour.

But he doesn't know how to get ready. He isn't religious, and what he knows of Catholicism from my mother's turbulent family hasn't persuaded him to inquire further. The idea of a Divinity or an afterlife embarrasses him. But he doesn't want to blink out, either. He can't speak of his unease to me or my sister, though we are his beloved little daughters. And we can't speak of it, either, or he will jump up and go out and begin pruning the gooseberry bushes. I want very much to tell him his whole life has been a preparation. Courage, stoicism, honour towards his fellow men, all have been his yardsticks of life. I want to remind him that his own father, old Hellfire Jack, would not see a pastor on his deathbed because as he said, he and God had never squabbled. But I don't. I could have tried, I think.

We had scarcely unpacked before Beres airmailed us the announcement of the *Sydney Morning Herald*'s first literary competition, the largest and most impressive ever held south of the equator. And our freelance writers' blood boiled.

'Get off your tails, you two!' wrote Beres, ringing the fantastic £100 prize for a short story. He didn't bother pointing out that a novel might win £2000, because he knew our meagre circumstances dictated that we write only short material which was quickly paid for. Novels were things we never thought of—so much work, dependent on royalties which might or might not come in. How could we waste time on insubstantial enterprises?

But I looked again and again at that announcement. Obviously it didn't apply to me; I was largely a children's writer and preferred, given the choice, to continue as one. But D'Arcy could write a novel. With his gift of vivid characterisation, his ability to tell an unusual and substantial story, he could produce a novel.

'Ah, come on!' I urged. 'Have a go! The Great Australian Novel!'

'Great Australian Horseshit.'

'Semi-great Australian Novel?'

'Now, knock it off. I'm going to enter for the short story and maybe the poem. I have this idea, see . . .'

'What about all three sections, then?' I argued. 'If you don't want to write a rural novel you could write about Surry Hills. Goodness knows there's enough drama there for six novels.'

'That's boring old stuff to me. *You* write about it.'

'I'm not a novelist.'

'Who knows? Anyway, you know I don't like the novel form. I never read a novel if I can help it.'

This was true. He never was to read any of mine.

I pestered and pestered. It seemed to me that these competitions offered a marvellous opportunity. At last he said, 'Shut up now, or I'll put you in the wardrobe.'

Nothing moved him. He was, anyway, going off to spend a month exploring Niland's Islands, mostly on foot, hitching rides, making friends everywhere in his usual style.

My mother was querulous about his leaving me to cope with the little children, but I could see that D'Arcy might never be able to return to New Zealand, whereas in time of family emergency, somehow I would always manage it. She had no idea we were as close to the breadline as we were most of the time. To her, as to other people, I found it impossible to explain the complicated financial side of a freelance writer's life—the long waits for payment, the failed and aborted ideas, the manner in which magazines flourished for seven issues and then dropped dead, owing the writers and artists considerable sums. Our lifestyle was based on total insecurity, and as insecurity was the thing my mother feared above all, I certainly wasn't going to tell her about mine.

'Blow him anyway. I'll have a shot at it. I can work on a novel in the evenings, in the kitchen.'

'I expect you'll be able to get on with it more easily, with him away,' agreed my mother paradoxically. She believed that men always got under your feet one way or another, though this was an inconsiderable fault in a good decent man.

Upon reflection, I felt that I knew very little about anything, especially nothing that would stretch to eighty thousand words. Dismally I asked my mother, 'Could I write about the *Auckland Star*—really dramatic back-biting, backslapping and favouritism went on there?'

'They'd sue you.'

'I don't want to write about the sawmill.'

She shuddered, for her prison term in dark, freezing Tanekaha Valley had been much longer and harder than mine.

'Don't *ever* write about that place. Readers don't deserve it.'

There was nothing left but Surry Hills. My life there had been like a visit to some antique island where the nine-teenth century still prevailed. As I pondered its idiosyncratic nature, I began to remember things—lanes with no gutters, just a line of inclined setts in the middle to carry away the rain. The smoke from kitchen fires, rubbish heaps. Most memorable of all was the pink-lit smoke spilling over the lip of the smallgoods factory chimney, white as milk it was, heavy too, flowing straight down amongst the cottages. How that smoke had smelled, a stench of acrid chemical, strong enough to taste, pervasive enough to taint one's hair and clothes!

'Don't ever touch them frankfurters,' said an old woman with no teeth. 'You can't trust nothing but eggs, honest.'

In my mind I could see that smoke, poisonous and enigmatic, like so many things in Surry Hills. It recalled my loneliness and unhappiness, and I thought suddenly, 'Why, if I write about that place it might exorcise the bad memories.'

So I began writing every night after the children were in bed, for two hours only, for there was a nine o'clock curfew on typing. Some evenings I could achieve only a page. I missed D'Arcy's constant interest and encouragement, though he wrote almost daily letters.

Those letters, often marked KEEP THIS, TIGER, were paradoxical, for he wrote about my country as seen through a fresh and amazed eye, while I was writing about Surry Hills, which he knew so well, and with almost total recall.

Still travelling like a traveller, not a tourist or sightseer, he booked in only occasionally to a hotel for a bath, a good meal and a long night's sleep. Wherever he could he hitched rides, not to save money but for the conversation, and truckies and long-haul delivery drivers on the road were not loath to invite him aboard.

He left me at the Thirty Mile and I took the turnoff, walking. It was a mongrel road, clay covered with metal for a few miles, then clay itself, each side sopping flats reaching away from it, and cascades bolting down the hills to flood them. Watch out for MacPherson's gate, he said. I found it. Far away there was a light like a fuzzy yellow ball.

I splashed up the rutted drive, chained dogs shrieking somewhere behind the invisible house. When I reached the verandah a man was waiting for me with a hurricane lamp, the blue tongue flapping

*and swooping at its moorings. How would a warm bed
and a feed go, he said.*

This letter appeared in extract in his short story 'A Cargo
for Topacki', one of the first he sold in America.

He also reproved me briskly for my grumbles.

'Don't give up. What does it matter if this book gets
nowhere? Later on you'll be able to rewrite it. You've got
the skeleton of something good there, I'm confident. Get
cracking, will you?'

The novel took the natural form of a chronology.
Early on I asked myself: 'What am I writing about?' And
the answer was clear. 'This story is about no particular
protagonist, but about a group of people, a family and their
friends and neighbours. They are all descended from Irish
immigrants except two, Irish born—one from Northern
Ireland and one from the Republic.'

With such a group of characters there certainly could
be a plot, but I did not want a plot, I just wanted to tell
about these people as if they were real human beings. Plots
rarely occur in life, and life, as far as I was capable of
depicting it, was what I wanted.

I was already enough of an experienced writer not to
find writing easy. Those people who find the craft facile and
enjoyable are nearly always beginners, or people who don't
really understand what writing is about. You do not find
Flaubert saying, 'I just pour out the words', as I have heard
innumerable apprentice writers say. This is what he says:
'When I find I haven't written a single sentence of worth
after scribbling dozens of pages I collapse on my couch

and lie there dazed, bogged in a swamp of despair, hating myself. O, if you knew the torture I suffer!'

And Vladimir Nabokov—'I am a snail carrying its house at a rate of two hundred final pages a year.'

When I wrote that first book I was not an experienced novelist, but I was experienced in the creation of character, the enlistment of humour, and the use of dialogue rather than talk. What literary strength the novel had came from these things.

In later years D'Arcy Niland was to say, 'After I finished writing *The Shiralee* I felt as if some kind person had lifted a heavy suitcase off me. No one had told me extended creative action battered the body.'

I felt much the same at the conclusion of my first novel, and determined that I would never write another one. Radio plays, and little tales for kids were my destiny, I told my husband.

'I'm calling it *The Harp in the South*,' I added.

He was by then in Stewart Island, the third large island of New Zealand, which also encompasses more than a thousand small ones.

'Good title, and tells exactly what the book is about. *The harp* representing Ireland and the Irish, and *the south* for Australia. The Irish in Australia. Excellent. You're getting near to closing date. You know I sent my poem and short story months ago now. Don't miss out.'

It seemed to me that typing a clean copy of the book was probably a fruitless exercise. With despair I rifled through the wad of much-corrected manuscript kept for safety in an old *Esquire* magazine. By ripping out a Hemingway story,

The Old Man and the Sea, I had provided room for mine. I felt it wasn't worth the labour. But there, nothing attempted, nothing done, you fool; so I whacked out a presentable copy of the novel, a short story or two, and a long poem which I thought rather good. All were airmailed to the *Herald* with a few days to spare.

Competition entries had to be submitted under *noms de plume*. Mine was Hesperus because I felt a wreck. I cannot remember D'Arcy's, but it was probably something joke Irish like Barney Rafferty.

In early December we returned to Sydney, leaving behind Anne and Rory for three months, at my mother's behest. It was good for them, not only because of a close association with an extended family of grandparents and amusing and doting aunts, at that stage lacking grandchildren, but because at last they could play as freely as little children should. The tiny backyard behind the Petersham flat was not only bare and constricted, but to my mind always menaced by the fertile criminality of Gilles de Rais. Who knew what he would think of next; maybe a fire bomb?

'Look for a house with a garden, a *big* garden,' my mother urged. We promised, knowing that the extent of the housing famine in huge Sydney was still incomprehensible to her.

It was a wrenching parting, especially from the little girl, a pale fragile child, whose fading cry, 'I want to tiss you again, my Mum!' long echoed in my memory.

We resolved grimly that somehow we would find a house with a safe garden.

'And we won't rent. We'll buy it.'

'My family hasn't ever owned anything,' said D'Arcy definitively, as though this fact was inscribed in the book of Fate.

'This is where we begin.'

Beres had looked after the flat in our absence, and he and D'Arcy now made plans for a lightning trip to the opalfields of Andamooka and the grape country of South Australia. D'Arcy had some idea in his head about a woman with hair the colour of poured beer, 'like yours'.

'She hasn't a mother. The country is her mother.'

I was used to his talking to himself, or to me, it didn't seem to matter which.

He was one of those writers able to use selected people as sounding boards. It is not a happy situation for the sounding board, especially when that person is trying to work, and when that person is herself darkly secretive, never speaking of any work until it is completed.

'But what shall I call this girl?'

'Oh, for God's sake, can't you shut up? All right, then. What about Barbie?'

'Barbie what?'

'Get the hell out of here, I have to finish this script by the afternoon's post.'

'You're huffy with me because I'm going walkabout again,' he said, narrowing his eyes at his own perspicacity.

'No, I'm not. At least I'll be able to work without you jabbering.'

He went away, hurt, but walking on the sides of his feet like a parrot. What could I do with such a man? My

168

eye fell upon the *ABC Weekly*, which published the radio programmes for the week. On the cover was the name of a popular actor. I yelled after him, 'Barbie Casabon!'

First he wrote a short story about Barbie. It was called 'Away to Moonlight', Moonlight being the name of one of the abandoned gold settlements he had visited during his New Zealand walkabout. The woman, strong and solitary, appealed to him. She was in many ways, I think, a feminine projection of his own character. At last, in 1959, she lived again as the protagonist of the glorious novel of the opal-fields, *Call Me When the Cross Turns Over*.

In bed that night he asked, 'Do I really jabber?'

'Often. Get on with what you're doing.'

The boys decided to leave in March, when the inland weather was less than furnace hot. I noticed that Beres, though he was delighted to be going on an expedition with his brother, spoke no more about getting grist for his acting career. Slowly he had realised that the road was too hard, too precarious.

All this time we had almost forgotten about the *Sydney Morning Herald* competition. There was too much other work to do. When, just before Christmas that year, I had a telegram from the newspaper I had my characteristic fit of panic—anyone who had lived through the war ever after identified telegrams and cables with bad news—and then ran to show D'Arcy.

'They want me to ring for an appointment!'

'Your poem, betcha!'

The boys were more excited than I was.

169

'My elbow itches,' said Beres, flushed with exhilaration. 'And that's an infallible Kilkenny sign that something wonderful is going to happen to us.'

I was touched that he included himself in this possibly upbeat event, as he had always done in our hard times.

'Would you like my scapular, chickie?' he asked tenderly as I prepared to set off for my *Herald* appointment. 'Just for good luck? I'm told it was blessed by a one-eyed bishop, and you know what *that* means.'

Off we went to the city, by now a little nervous. Somewhere in the hallowed upper halls of the old *Herald* building in Hunter Street, I bumped into Old Preposterous, who gave me a sour, crumpled stare. He probably thought I was leaving rather than arriving to hear whatever news there was.

'There'll be trouble,' he said out of the blue. 'Terrible trouble. Oh, I told them, you may be sure.'

With that he doddered off, leaving me feeling rather as I had as a child, when eight out of ten adult utterances seemed to me to be raving potty. Shaken, I went on my way, finding at last a palatial office and an agreeable elderly gentleman called Mr Threlfall, who informed me that I was one of twenty-eight finalists.

'In which section, please?'

'Good God, did you enter more than one?'

'Everything except the war novel,' I confessed.

It was revealed that I was, incredibly, a finalist in the novel competition. I tottered out to rejoin the boys, twitching restlessly from spot to spot in the *Herald*'s classic portico.

'Oh, crikey, I can't believe it.'

'Mr Threlfall couldn't believe it either. I could tell by the way his nose swivelled around. He thought I am too young, too goofy . . . something or other.'

I could not bring myself to tell them of my enigmatic encounter with Old Preposterous. I had no clue at all about the meaning of his words, but I suspected they indicated I was a lot closer to the prize money than twenty-eighth.

The *Herald* management kept us waiting for a week before they called me in and told me that *The Harp in the South* had won first prize. Then, with a hushed air I was led into the office of the managing director, Rupert Henderson, a dark and terrifying person who fixed me with a practised glare and with little preamble offered me a job on the *Herald* at £20 a week. As I was a girl who earned more like £20 a month, this sum was the stuff of fantasy.

'But I have two little children,' I said, faintly.

'Good heavens!' he cried, disgusted at the very idea that children could get between me and the *Herald*. 'Get a nanny or something!'

I could see he thought I was soft in the head when I declined. He spun his chair around and presented his back to me. Not knowing what else to do, I tiptoed out. This extraordinary procedure was Mr Henderson's manner of indicating extreme rage. It happened to me several times in succeeding years, but regrettably I saw it not as a majestic gesture of contempt but as a refined form of mooning, or the presenting of the bare butt to the disapproved person, and went away chortling.

'If you really want to take that job, I'll look after the kids,' said my husband. I knew he would have done it, and done it well. He was much better with babies and very young children than I was, for he had been nursemaid and caregiver to all his mother's younger children. He was an old hand at croup and colic, and he had perfected mysterious ways for putting infant howlers to sleep.

'And I'd make a beaut nanny,' added Beres. 'Say the word.'

Though appreciating their offers, I wished to look after Anne and Rory myself. I liked those little creatures, and liked being around them. As a member of a largely female family, I had no damnfool ideas about maternalism, a concept created by men so that they would never have to endure the murderous tyranny of the infant. Though I loved all my children as babies, and was tigerishly defensive of their welfare, they did not become interesting to me until they got up on their pins and began to show personality. My children were now at charming and ever-changing ages. I did not intend to miss any of their company.

Nevertheless, it was fortunate, though by chance, that the children were in New Zealand, for this left me free to cope with a most painful and incomprehensible circumstance.

Probably people who win large lottery prizes felt as we did. Having got by on the barest minimum income for almost five years, £2000 seemed a colossal sum to us. It was certainly enough to put a deposit on a home. How I wanted a little house! The desire burned in me day and night. Small enough to put in a walnut shell—I didn't care. Just as long as it had a safe place for Anne and Rory to play, a little garden where I could grow things, and privacy. I had spent years almost in the pockets of other people, often people alien to me, finding that contiguity is not cosy, but the root cause of much human dissension.

Already D'Arcy and I could see that house in our imaginations. We dreamed and built on those dreams like any young couple.

'In my mind's eye I can see a whole wall of filing cabinets for our writing stuff.'

'Oh, yes! I'm just so tired of keeping my papers in a suitcase under the bed.'

'And a desk.'

'Two desks.'

'Eh? Oh, yeah, two desks.'

We did not guess that the prizemoney would not only be taxed, but that provisional tax would also be charged as though I were bound to win the same prize the following year. I was to appeal to the Tax Department without success.

What I eventually received was less than £800, but nevertheless that was a windfall which proved a turning point in our life together.

On December 28, the *Herald* announced the results of the novel section, giving also synopses of the three winning novels. This first literary competition had drawn a magnificent response; many of the runners-up, which were also serialised, seemed to me stronger than the prizewinners. But judges are judges. Messrs A, B, and Madame C will not choose the same books as Messrs

D, E, and F. It was my luck, and Jon Cleary's luck, to have our work judged first and second, and thus be given strong impetus in careers already precariously established. All three prizewinners were guaranteed publication by Angus & Robertson Ltd, then the country's oldest and most prestigious publishing house.

Almost at once a hideous clamour burst out, not only in the literary world, but in Australia at large, and this on the basis of the synopsis only of *The Harp in the South*.

Normally I would not enlarge on this extraordinary row, for after all it happened long ago and far away, and very nearly in another galaxy. But it is, in its way, a unique psychological study of the popular mores of the late 1940s and early 1950s of this century. Old Preposterous, hard-nosed journalist attuned to that peculiar thing, the reading public's common denominator, was right. There was trouble.

The first nick of the knife at my throat came in a church, where D'Arcy and I attended Mass. It was a thanksgiving Mass for us. D'Arcy, as I have said, was extremely devout.

We were stricken when the celebrant devoted his sermon to the *Herald*; its scandalous judgements; wicked books; immorality in print and to what it would lead; young women and their conscienceless slandering of that great race, the Irish. Nay, it was his sincere belief that I had taken the axe to the foundations of Ireland itself, island of saints and scholars.

'Can you believe this?' hissed my husband.

The priest was now well away on Our Lady and her chaste example to all. He implied strongly that in her lifetime she would never have stooped to writing a book of any kind, let alone that to be published in the *Herald*.

'Ah, that a great newspaper should . . .'

'It's not fair!' I muttered. 'He hasn't even read it!'

'Bugger needs a poke in his godly snoot.'

Ten years later I would have risen and marched out down the centre aisle, but then I was so shocked, so humiliated I felt faint. My husband was all for going around to the vestry and pulling the priest's biretta down over his lugs, but I needed him to lean on on the homeward journey, for my knees intermittently gave way.

'Why? Why?'

'Don't ask me. Gone mad with all that celibacy.'

The next day Mr Threlfall rang, gentlemanly creature, who confessed that he'd had the legs knocked from under him by the torrent of phone calls, telegrams and mail the *Herald* had received since the announcement.

'Do you want me to send some of it on to you?'

'My goodness, no! Please read it yourself, Mr Threlfall.'

'Well, as a matter of fact, we *have* . . . and well . . . it's quite, quite baffling . . .'

Serialisation commenced to the accompaniment of appalling hullabaloo. True, of the letters to the newspaper the majority were in favour of the book; it was just that the letters against were far more forceful, angry and abusive. My distress was aggravated by the fact that I had no idea of what people were objecting to. The gravamen of their complaints varied perplexingly. Conclusive statements were made that Sydney had no slums, therefore the novel

175

was a cruel fantasy. Other correspondents maintained that yes, there were slums, but they were populated exclusively by criminals and deadbeats. The novel, which dealt with decent people, was therefore a sentimental fantasy.

Some took a stern, political view of me rather than the book.

Because I wrote about poor people I was a Communist. On the other hand because I wrote about poor people I was a capitalist—I wrote about them only to jeer, or, alternatively, to make money.

The book was immoral, filthy in fact, though no specific filth was ever mentioned.

Some letters were well-intentioned and written by people who gave their names and addresses. The filth-protestors mostly signed their letters *Yours Prayerfully*, *A Christian*. Or, *Catholic Mother*, and gave no addresses.

I have often wondered how these timorous souls would react to the prospect of martyrdom.

To those correspondents who were patently well meaning, I wrote to suggest we form an organisation liaised with the City Council and various social services departments, which could work to improve the lot of the underprivileged whose daily lot was so bad it should not be written about. But I never had a taker.

Similarly, when I offered a personally conducted tour of Surry Hills and adjacent slums to those who maintained there were no such places, I had only one answer. This was from the beautiful little Welshwoman, Pixie O'Harris, who devoted most of her life to producing comforting artwork for children, especially sick children. Pixie did not simply inspect Surry Hills. She organised a vociferous group that over weeks and months harassed the City Council and the Housing Department into accelerating their sluggish slum-clearance programmes. Much of the public housing in the Surry Hills–Redfern area owes its genesis to Pixie O'Harris and her energetic friends.

It was a bad, agitating time, full of conflicting currents. More than anything else I was perturbed by the writer Miles Franklin's mysterious enmity. I can see her yet— slight little lady, spine ruler-straight, rimless glasses, an ornamental hat set straight across a fine forehead and still dark hair, a seventyish woman, to whom I was introduced at some literary bunfight. I was delighted to meet her, for although she had published so little, she was (and is) one of the legendary figures of Australian literature. She responded to the introduction mutely. With a brisk nod of acknowledgement she moved away.

At that time I did not know she was an unsuccessful entrant in the *Sydney Morning Herald*'s novel competition. Still, not for a moment can I believe that disappointment could have been the only cause of her untiring hatred. There was something obsessional about it, for although she was openly and venomously defamatory about everything I wrote, my personal life, and even my appearance, it seems she continued to read my books, view or listen to my plays, even attend any function where I was speaking. Thus she fed her inexplicable ire for years.

What was the reason for such an intelligent woman's capitulation to malice? Was I a symbol of something she detested? Or something she had missed and lost? I sometimes think it might have been the latter, for although she was cruelly disparaging of most women writers, the only other person of whom I know, and whom she actively traduced for a long period, was the clever and charming sixteen-year-old, Catherine Gaskin, whose first book was a bestseller, and who went on to write many others.

This darkness in Miss Franklin has not been adequately addressed by her biographers. The question remains why a person who was, in several ways, an exemplar of the old-fashioned virtues, would indulge herself in so base a manner.

We looked forward with nervous excitement to the publication of *The Harp in the South* by a real publisher.

'Our first book!' exulted Beres.

But even that was a disturbing matter. Beatrice Davis, senior editor of Angus & Robertson Ltd, sent galleys by the *Herald*, told me, 'It's not the kind of book A & R cares to publish but we have a gentleman's agreement with the *Herald*.'

Even then I suspected that a reluctant publisher is no better than no publisher at all, and left Angus & Robertson in deep dismay.

A week later I had a cable from London. As soon as galley proofs were obtainable we had airmailed a set to Michael Joseph Ltd, whose booklist I had always admired. Michael Joseph had H.E. Bates, hadn't he?

The cable shook me.

HARP IN THE SOUTH SUPERB MAGNIFICENT STOP
EXCEPTING HOW GREEN WAS MY VALLEY BEST NOVEL
MICHAEL JOSEPH HAS HAD PRINTING DOUBLED
ROBERT LUSTY.

After Angus & Robertson's blunt expression of indifference this was too much. Weeping, I babbled, 'I don't understand publishers. I'm going back to newspaper work.'

D'Arcy was decoding the cable. 'This means they've accepted the book. We know that much, anyway.'

Tremulously we celebrated. Would this be the big break for which we longed? But how could two publishers have such different opinions?

A week later a delayed letter from Michael Joseph himself arrived, enthusiastically accepting the book and enclosing a contract—as fair as all subsequent contracts from this publishing house were to be.

Later Sir Robert told me how, home in bed with the flu, he had read the *Herald* galleys, reached for the phone and increased that print order. A reserved, stately man, Lusty was the active spirit of Michael Joseph Ltd, and later of Hutchinson's huge operation.

On the same day as the cable I received an English letter addressed to The Harpy in the South, which was bad enough. But worse was the fact that it came straight to me without any readdressing or Please Forwards.

In a high state of confusion, I no longer knew which way to turn. I was, I think, nervously overwrought almost to extremis. Yet at this time I met many wonderful people, and made four or five friends whose loyalty lasted a lifetime.

The trouble was that without warning my trust in people had been publicly and severely damaged. Not until more than twenty years later did I trust them again, but then I approached humankind along a different road.

D'Arcy could not understand the extent of my agitation. He burned obscene letters, wrote fiery answers to the sanctimonious, cursed Earnest Christian and Catholic Grandmother.

'Oh, let the silly bastards go hang!' he fumed. 'What's the matter with you? Michael Joseph loves the book, and you've just heard that the New York agent has sold the novel to Houghton Mifflin in Boston. Are you jumping out of your skin? No, you're having fits about something said by some unknown knucklehead who not only has never gone without a meal but won't admit there are thousands of people who have and do. I thought you had more *nous*.'

'You don't understand.'

'I do. Maybe more than you.'

'Then why don't you postpone your trip?'

Day by day, as I watched him prepare to go off with Beres, leaving me to the wolf pack, my resentment had grown. I believed it his husbandly duty to remain and support me in my tribulation, and the longer he did not offer to do so, the madder I became.

'You'd only have to put it off for six weeks.'

'But I can't. You know very well Beres is going off in a month.'

Beres had agreed to help out with the circus while it was in winter quarters. He had a rare touch with elephants.

Did I say that I needed D'Arcy's presence, that though I conceded he might understand my agitation, he didn't understand it enough? No, I snapped, 'There is plenty in life external to Beres!'

'Yes, but he makes it all such fun,' he explained, putting his arms around me. He was perfectly correct about Beres; I was the last person to deny it, so, having no answer, I made myself into a plank and stayed that way until his arms dropped down disconsolately.

'Go then!' I said coldly.

'Sod it, I will.'

Long afterwards he told me that if I'd said I needed him, he would have stayed home.

'Anyone in his right mind would have known I needed him!'

'But I thought you a warrior woman. Aren't you?'

Four hours after he left, I had a wire from a railway station *Missing you like BillyO* already. The next morning there was another: *Don't be crook on me, I'm not such a bad bloke.* In a week yet another arrived: *Ag Pigen.* After a while I worked out that this translated *At Pigen* and meant I could write to the post office there. I looked up Pigen on the map and in the gazetteer; I searched over the border in South Australia and the Northern Territory. Certainly, it was an extraordinary name, but a country that can produce place names like Pantapin, Galiwinku, Gnarpurt and Liapootah can come up with anything.

In fact, the message that D'Arcy had entrusted to the untender keeping of the telegraph service was *Aw, Tiger.*

'I thought it simple and moving,' he explained.

But soon he wrote from Port Augusta and I was so pleased to hear from him that thereafter we fired back and forth our usual fusillade of letters.

'I've a new assignment from the ABC,' I wrote. 'An adult radio serial. Half an hour. It's called *Stumpy*, and the ABC is paying £4 an episode!'

This serial ran to 140 episodes, and provided the first starring role for the much-loved actor, John Meillon, who was eight or nine years old at the time. After I accidentally heard him auditioning at Station 2UE for a radio version of *Tom and the Water Babies*, I pressed the ABC to try him out. A consummate actor, John Meillon had a half wry, half sad personality. He was a witty man, with an expressive, crumpled face, and a beautiful comedic talent. His life however was somewhat unhappy and he died unexpectedly in middle age.

That walkabout of D'Arcy Niland's, undertaken in the face of my wrath, was one of the most valuable he ever had. He had chosen for his travels just the kind of country he needed for stimulation at that point in his literary growth. Though he loved the succulent scenery of the green east coast, thereafter what drew him most was the pitiless wilderness, the yellow light over the shelterless plains, the sun veiled with whirling silt.

Remembering, Beres often lifted his voice querulously. 'If there are two ways of doing a thing, he'll always choose the hardest. I don't *want* to sleep rolled up in a blanket on the bare ground. One night we camped on the fringe of an aboriginal settlement; they came shyly into the firelight with a plateful of pink iced vovo biscuits. Real nice people with eyes like possums. In the night frost settled on my blanket, and I had to get up and throw on another dog.'

The brothers struck west into the drought country, boarding a train illegally to do so.

'We were the greenest pair of rattler jumpers in the business,' wrote D'Arcy. 'We travelled down to Port Pirie in a truck of lead-ore concentrate. We were so frozen we couldn't get out of the truck when the guard saw us. But he was a lovely fella. First he kicked our backsides and then he brought along a billy of hot tea. We looked like redheaded Fijians with the rust and the dust.'

They zigzagged across the southern end of the continent, ending at Andamooka, an opalfield now fully developed but then only a desolate corner of a vast cattle station. The heat was so great that most of the miners lived underground.

The sky was bluemetal, sandpapered smooth.
The land is up and down country, brooded over by
space and silence. Sand, stone—it lives on the lip of the
sun. We were stony broke and hungry as hell. That
night we camped in an abandoned dugout, wrapped
up in sheets of the Port Augusta Examiner *against*
the killing desert cold. We spent some time discussing
whether we'd eat meat if we had it (it was Friday),
and we ended up agreeing we'd eat the priest. The
dugout was dry and full of spiders. Every time we lit
the candle you'd see every cranny sparkling with a

faceful of eyes. Crikey, it was woeful. Then there
was the crack of stoping giving way and the whole
thing caved in with the sound of thunder. We got
out by the skin of our teeth, and there was a man
with a hurricane (lantern). He'd walked half a mile
over the field to ask us over for a feed and a
shakedown. His name was Wally. Mrs Wally said
they'd gone to the pitchers for their honeymoon.
Reminded me of us and the Chinese opera.

The man called Wally gave D'Arcy half a threepence and
kept the other half. D'Arcy's half was in his wallet when he
died. Like Sister Roche's scapular, the half-threepence was
a testament of friendship and so he treasured it.

D'Arcy always kept a store of tiny cheap notebooks in
his shirt pocket. Mostly his notes are about people—'near
the dugout door he has a barrel, a water barrel. Harsh
artesian water. It's lidded with a blue circle of sky and this
is his mirror when shaving or combing his hair.' 'The storekeeper threw away a couple of dockets when we paid our
bill. It is his way. His name is Absalom.' 'I saw the Southern
Cross turn over, Wally said it's the old drover's signal for
changing the watch. Call me when the Cross turns over,
they used to say.'

Many of these scenes and people turned up later in
the novel *Call Me When the Cross Turns Over*, and several
short stories, notably the fine 'Without You in Heaven',
which won so many prizes that the writer had a mind-
boggling discussion with the Taxation Department which
was inclined to categorise him as a professional prizewinner.

To reinforce his rebuttal of this accusation, he took our account book to the Taxation Department, and showed the officials one page, dated from June 11 to June 28, fifteen submissions and three acceptances.

'How do you write so much in seventeen days?'

'It's necessity. When we have fifteen submissions and say, ten acceptances, we'll take it easier.'

But although our percentage of acceptances did naturally become higher in time, he never did take it easier.

On this expedition, Beres confided, D'Arcy had occasional chest pains—perhaps indigestion because of long periods without food, and then, probably a hearty meal at 'the Greek's' in some small handful of a town, steak, eggs, chips. Or the boys had been forced to drink at some dying waterhole, blowing aside the scum to get at the water.

That was, I think, the first intimation that his cardiac condition was worsening, though I had no thought of that at that time.

By the time he had settled in again, most of the uproar about *The Harp in the South* had died down, but I was still at a loss to explain it.

The literary people who had written to me—Kylie Tennant, Jean Devanney, Christina Stead, Vance Palmer—gave literary reasons for the extraordinary outburst against the book. The public had a pinched, hysterical cultural imagination, they wrote. These self-righteous ravers either were not readers, or were burdened with a modified illiteracy. Though illiteracy was common in Surry Hills, I had no idea of the percentage of illiteracy in the general population. Dame Mary Gilmore said it was 10 per cent amongst army inductees at the beginning of the war. This may have been one reason. These people had read scarcely anything else, and the realism of the story and the locations shocked them.

The *Herald*, overjoyed at the publicity for their competition, had orchestrated the protest by printing daily the number of letters for and against. The righteous love jumping on the wagon no matter what the wagon carries, so long as it's in the news. If on television, a hundred times better. The themes of today are different, but the type of person is the same.

All through this time of trial D'Arcy put aside reviews, letters and clippings, growling as he did so. He was the packrat, not I. For over forty years I did not glance at them. Things happen, they hurt, they change your life, but it's not good to keep picking at the scab. But for this current book, this autobiography, I had to go through them carefully, and I saw at last the reason for the inexplicable public reaction of 1947 to a modest book which, after all, has never gone out of print; has been translated into thirty-seven languages; was never badly criticised internationally; became a Book Society and Book Club choice not only in English, but three or four other tongues; was shortlisted for several literary prizes including the Vie Femina, and was destined to end not as a controversial novel at all, but as a book on secondary schools' reading lists for the Higher School Certificate.

'When did all the hue and cry begin?' I asked myself, as I read through the detritus of a bygone time.

The answer was, with the synopsis. Yet the synopses of the other two novels appeared at the same time. The third prizewinner was a traditional, unexceptionable country tale. Jon Cleary's was different, far tougher than mine, set amongst petty criminals in Paddington which was then an old, rundown slum. Did Jon Cleary's book, let alone the synopsis, attract any flack at all? The answer was no. No public harassment. No letters to newspapers. No private abuse either. Here was a carbon of my 1947 letter to him, inquiring; here was his answer.

In 1992 I contacted Jon, now living in Sydney, to check again.

'All I got was the usual single ratbag letter when the book was serialised,' he replied.

Aside from a basic similarity in the backgrounds of our books, Jon Cleary's age and literary apprenticeship fairly well paralleled my own. How did I differ from Jon? In two ways only. I was a woman and I was not an Australian. In an age when the words *should not* and *ought not*, with or without justification, were profusely applied to women, I had stepped over the invisible boundary line. Similarly, though Jon Cleary with photographic realism depicted an underclass of Sydney society, he was an Australian, an insider, and thus allowed to do so. I was a New Zealander, a foreigner, and could not be permitted to do the same. My novel had to be either misrepresentation or derogatory criticism. In other words, the mob was not objecting to the story at all, it was objecting to the writer. But excuses had to be produced, as the true objections were too prejudiced, too embarrassing to be stated.

Jon Cleary went forward to become the most consistently successful Australian writer. A master technician, he is the author of forty odd novels, several of which have been filmed. By turning his face away from the freelance world, he and his family probably had a calmer and more prosperous life than D'Arcy and I had. But for us novels were only one variety of writing. We were to continue with our richly varied literary endeavours all our lives.

Just before I left Sydney to bring my children home from New Zealand, the little Gilles de Rais, now six and ever more inventive, stretched a trip wire across the stairs and caught his grandfather, the old greengrocer, Mr Buckle. He was taken to hospital with several broken bones and I never saw him again.

With foreboding I brought Anne and Rory back to this dangerous place, only to find that the remnants of the de Rais family had gone. A large group of music-loving, goat-rearing Turks took their place. Very kind and sweet they were to our two little infidels.

In Petersham our second son Patrick was born, I wrote *Poor Man's Orange*, and D'Arcy, temporarily putting aside his hatred of novels, wrote *Gold in the Streets* which won a prize of £500 in another literary competition.

'I don't know,' he said. 'Maybe there's something in this novel writing after all. But it's the short stories that really come out of whatever I am.'

Still, the financial returns were, after tax, small or very moderate. Our own home was as far off as ever, and sometimes we despaired of ever having one. We missed Beres's cheerful presence as well. Tiring at last of his peripatetic life in Australia he went to New Zealand, whence his younger brother Joe was soon to follow him.

Both boys were to marry in New Zealand, Beres to my sister Jocelyn.

3

At the close of 1949, in a fury of ambition contaminated beyond all reason by optimism, we gave up our Petersham flat, put into storage our few pieces of furniture, plus the four herring-gutted folders that contained what I cared to preserve of my literary lifework and D'Arcy's eleven tea chests packed with books, manuscripts, notebooks, letters from forgotten people and certificates from children's pages in newspapers. I protested, pointing out that this packrat treasury added to our storage charges. All I got was a wounded look and an indignant, 'But they're all my Things.'

I have read that literary men almost invariably gather and protect such a store of Things—no collective word correctly covers these items—all of which are based on paper. Often very small pieces of paper, with one word written on each.

'There is no doubt in my mind that you are the Great White Father of all the packrats,' I informed him, an insult which brought forth nothing but a modest smile.

We were about to set off for England via New Zealand, where we planned to stay briefly with my family. After seven years of financial pillar to post we had decided to chance the old country with its broader and better-paying markets. But I had grave doubts.

'Jon Cleary did it,' I encouraged myself. 'Morris West, too.'

'And look at Katherine Mansfield,' urged my partner.

'Katherine Mansfield didn't earn a living, she had a rich Dad.'

'You've got that awful don't-want-to-go look on your face again,' he accused.

'I can't help it. I've a bad feeling.'

'What kind of bad feeling?'

'Like the feeling you have when you swallow too hot coffee.'

This was a lie. My bad feeling resided in that small awkward corner of my psyche where I kept my handful of second sight. I could not share D'Arcy's excitement, this conviction that as freelances we could manage to make our way in England. Our savings were modest, my health unreliable, and we now had a third child prone to chest ailments. It was true that by nature I was a risk taker but now I was also a mother, and as Sean O'Casey justly remarks in one of his plays: 'A mother with a child at foot is a desperate coward.'

'Michael Joseph promised to introduce us to all the editors!' my husband reminded me.

My London publisher, youngish, handsome, charming beyond all anticipation, had visited Sydney recently, and had assured me of all kinds of good prospects. But I feared that maybe he was a promiser, expansive as so many people are when far from home.

'Come and stay with us for as long as you like!' they press. 'Don't worry about work, I have contacts everywhere!'

And then when you turn up they don't remember your face. Or so I've been told.

'And then there's Ireland!' added D'Arcy. The Republic was already murmuring about bestowing tax-free status on visiting artists and writers.

'It hasn't happened yet and it mightn't.'

'There you go, wet blanketing again. I've had enough of it. You've got cold feet, that's the beginning and end of it. And it casts a man down, I can tell you. It discourages a man, takes the wind out of his sails.'

Like other Australian men my husband always dropped into the third person when any emotion or even sensibility made its appearance. A declaration of love from him was, 'A man can't help being fond of you,' as though a man had battled bravely against it.

Off he went to have a farewell beer with a few more old mates. But the feeling of impending failure, disaster, something adverse, remained with me. Every Celtic ancestor I had rose up and growled.

'Oh, for one year without tax,' I thought. 'What a difference it would make! Then we wouldn't have to go.'

For in Australia, payment for literary work was still pitfully low. When the *Sydney Morning Herald* serialised my second novel, *Poor Man's Orange*, they paid £121.5.0, take it or leave it. When I objected to such low rates the editor concerned said they could buy Daphne du Maurier for £19, an unfair comparison as the du Maurier book was syndicated, and the *Herald*'s publication the forty-fifth instead of the first. Even the Australian Broadcasting Commission paid only £25 for an hour-length play and five guineas for a read short story.

Royalties did not provide a fortune either. I had one royalty statement from the US that was $6000 at the top, and $87.25 at the bottom. Withholding tax of 30 per cent was still imposed, and inexplicable fees, State taxes and agents' cuts occurred all the way down the list. I felt I was working for a great many people other than my own family.

In my heart I acknowledged that I often despaired of ever raising our standard of living above that very moderate one we had struggled to reach in our years together. When I thought of my children I was fiercely determined that they should not have the austere childhood I had had. I wanted them to have books, good education, music, a comfortable home. But perhaps D'Arcy was right, I had cold feet. Had I become too timid to leap out into the unknown once more? What was I afraid of? I could not tell my insistent husband of the shadows in my mind, for they were nothing but shadows.

I wanted to be large-souled, confident, even audacious, as surely I once had been, in vain I repeated to myself Carlyle's infuriating words: 'Miserable biped, wherefore dost thou pip and whimper?'

In the end I muttered, 'All right, we'll go.'

*

After D'Arcy's death, during the many cold months and years, I stood back and looked at my marriage. It was a monumental thing, at the same time mysterious and declarative. Here I am, it said, to begin with unwished for, often unwanted, unalterable now. By that time it had ruled more than half my life, neither full of light nor full of darkness. That year in New Zealand, (for we never got to England) was the darkest yet. Betraying my instinctive foreboding, I had gone against that and my own good sense, believing that because I was married, I owed my marriage partner some acquiescence in his resolution, though I knew it unwise.

'You should have told me to jump in the lake,' said D'Arcy later, with a certain cheerfulness. 'A man expects that from his missus.'

'I did what I could,' I retorted, in the churlish tone of all women invited to be the prime cause of their men's bad judgement.

It was a very unsettling year for everyone. Shortly after I arrived in Auckland I discovered I was pregnant. My mother, dismayed, went into her usual chambermaid seduced by Lord Byron lament, giving the author of my misfortune reproachful looks and little beyond chill courtesy. Even he understood that her attitude was based on solicitude and anxiety for me, but life became painful. Poor dear, it was an afflicting time for her. My sister and Beres married that year, again to my mother's great uneasiness. She was overworked and overtired, worried about Mera's health, not young herself.

Nevertheless, many of her forebodings originated in her own highly imaginative nature. In her mind, I think, girls never grew up, remaining tender creatures blown about by cruel chance, bullied by menfolk into doing things they shouldn't, such as having too many children. Men, on the other hand, had heavy moral responsibilities, possibly beginning at the age of twelve, which they tended to dodge if they could. In the face of her exquisitely kind care of my father, she was very tough on men in general.

The touchy situation was exacerbated by the fact that we and our three children were castaways. Unable to go forward to England, or to return to Sydney because of lack of accommodation, we were marooned.

'Surely you could get something!'

'We're trying very hard, honestly. All our friends are looking out for us.'

'D'Arcy's mother could put you up for a while, of course she could.'

Glumly I thought of the poor Nilands squashed into their two damp, dark, crowded rooms, victims of the housing shortage as much as we. To make matters worse, the old house of which they rented a small part had recently been sold, the new landlord entering upon a campaign of terrorising the tenants, so that they would leave him in vacant possession. We were homeless now, and soon they would be homeless and helpless as well.

The atmosphere was tense; we all suffered the nervous strain caused by too many people in one small house. I often felt depressed to the point of desperation, and if it had not been for my father's unchanging congeniality I could not have survived it.

All this time both of us wrote doggedly, I my ABC scripts, D'Arcy short stories for the publications to which he regularly contributed. And constantly our friends in Sydney sought accommodation for us.

'Anything, anything!' we implored. In retrospect the Petersham flat seemed paradise. Even Wits' End at Collaroy took on a delusive desirability.

'After all, we were happy there,' we reminded each other. 'It was just that bed—hard on the backbone.'

'And those creepy things that came up the bath plughole.'

'And the primus stove going bang at three in the morning.'

'Never mind. We're together, Anne and Rory and Patrick and you and me. And the new bub will be a beauty, if he's not a calf.'

D'Arcy looked somewhat thoughtfully at my middle. Certainly there was a lot of it. Still, it was no more than a week before delivery date that the doctor discovered we were to have twins. The news was not received well. My mother wept.

'You'll have three babies under a year old!'

Even my dear Mera said it was a catastrophe. But suddenly my world had righted. The confusion I had endured about the meaning of our aborted voyage disappeared; I began to see the road ahead, and it was a good, if difficult road.

'Don't worry,' I said to my mother. 'This is the most wonderful thing that ever happened to me.'

'You are *crazy*,' she replied with doleful conviction.

'Everything will be fine now,' I assured D'Arcy. 'Maybe tough for a while, but fine in the end.'

'Do you feel it wherever it is that you live?' he asked.

'Yes, no need to worry any more.'

Our twin daughters were strong, blonde and identical. Later in life they decided not to be twins, achieving this by means of the many arts known to women, but that is no business of mine.

After the numbing months I was aware once more of the immediacy of life and the hope of future contentment. I felt like a mother cat with kittens, very delighted indeed that my room in the nursing home had originally been the bedroom and study of Michael Joseph Savage, New Zealand's first Labour Prime Minister, who had always been my hero. I felt this a splendid omen.

No more was their arrival considered a catastrophe. The twins were no more trouble than a pair of puppies, and just as playful and good tempered. Nuki and Nui my father called them—Big and Little, one being minimally smaller than the other.

Meanwhile our friend, Cyril Hume, the ship modeller, had tracked down an old house at Neutral Bay. So eagerly were houses sought after we had to pay three years' rent in advance, this taking most of our savings. This was not exploitation of a malicious kind, as I think the owners of the ancient house in Ben Boyd Road were not aware, as we were not, that such an arrangement was illegal.

Poor Cyril was dismayed when we cabled our decision to take the Old Manse, as it was called. He said he'd only told us about it because it was his duty, that his wife Leonora had looked it over and nearly had a fit, that it was in fearsome condition. Please don't do it, he begged. Why didn't I keep quiet? he berated himself.

But D'Arcy and I didn't think twice. He had been quieter than usual after the twins' birth, though courteous and pleasant in his usual way. When I asked him if anything were the matter, he merely replied, 'Just thinking about this and that. No worry.'

He left New Zealand first, taking Anne and Rory by sea. Cyril had had the electric power reconnected to the Old Manse, and ransomed our furniture, such as it was.

D'Arcy wrote: 'Well, you wanted an old house and by crikey you have one. After I put the kids to bed I wandered through with tears in my eyes and my heart in my boots. The architecture is by Bram Stoker. It has a high peaked roof and false gables through which possums bound and fruit bats fly. Vampires too, no doubt. And under the master bedroom floor there is a cave. A *cave*!'

His tone was lighthearted; I thought he was exaggerating for the sake of fun. And anyway, I knew how Anne and Rory would love that cave and even the elderliness of the house. What if it were rundown? We would soon renovate it, mend it, paint it; we were young and energetic. What made me happier still is that when I flew back to Sydney with Patrick and the twins, my old St Benedict's friend, Ina Ratliff, was coming too. An ardent amateur actor, she was going to try her luck in Sydney.

'If it comes to nothing I can always go back to teaching,' she said. As she was a merry warm-hearted girl of many talents, domestic and otherwise, I was delighted at her decision.

The week before we left, I had another letter from D'Arcy.

I'm going straight out to post this letter, for fear that I might change my mind. I want to let you know what happened to me last night. Like I do most nights I prowled through this calamitous house, the cold loneliness, the dirt, the doors that lead nowhere and the windows that haven't been opened for half a century, knowing that we've done more than half our savings on this bloody incurable ruin. I sat down on a box in a dark room that smelt of mice and listened to the possums widdling through the ceiling. Something happened—a revelation, a kind of clearsighted knowledge, what you'd call a flash, I suppose. I realised that it is absolutely my own selfish fault that we're stuck here, and I feel a bastard. You said we weren't ready for England, but I wouldn't listen.

Do I ever listen to other people? That's what bothers me. If I always follow my own ideas regardless, believing I'm right, walking over other people's needs, do I understand anyone at all, even from a literary point of view? How's a man to tell?

I can fancy you smiling at my bringing writing into this letter when it's really about being a husband and father. But all three seem involved to me.

*Well, when you land here with Ina and the little
kids, you'll notice I'm different, that I've sorted myself
out quite a lot. I wish I'd done it before but I didn't
seem to know.*

*Don't mention this letter to me when we meet again.
I've said all I want to, or indeed that I'm able to.*

So I never did mention it. I saw that he was gentler, more
considerate, had thrown away some of his old prejudices,
both male and family-based. And it was indeed, as Bertha
Lawson was to predict—we did not yet know that fascinating old woman—as if he had become a mature man at
last. Hers, as we know, never did.

So the five of us arrived from Auckland and took
possession of the Old Manse.

'We'll feel better when we've had a good hot meal,'
said Ina, whisking on an apron and approaching the gas
range.

'I don't think much of the cooktop,' she said, looking
dubiously at the four extraordinary, spiky burners, which
D'Arcy had scrubbed within an inch of their lives but which
still looked like charred relics of a bush fire. She opened
the oven door. Two time-pocked batwings of iron formed
this door, and one could hear the oven trays shifting about
menacingly even before she opened it.

There was an instant's dismayed silence and then the
oven spat a fossilised sausage roll at her. For a moment even
Ina looked as though she wanted to go home.

'Renovation of the kitchen is on top of the priority list,'
said D'Arcy firmly. 'Even before the twinnery.'

'We love this house, Mum,' said Anne. 'It's not like any other house in the whole world. It's full of really great horrible things.'

The Old Manse was indeed a fantasy house. In spite of the manner in which it swallowed up most of our earnings even as we earned, its unspeakable discomfort, its haunted room, I was never able to hate it. I wrote comic articles about our efforts to make it liveable, I put it into children's books, including the two *Callie's Castle* books.

We had scarcely taken possession of the Old Manse before the crisis affecting my husband's family became an emergency indeed. For six months now Barbara Niland had endured the kind of wicked persecution which, sadly, is known best to the old, helpless or indigent. The new landlord changed the locks on the doors of their apartment; entered at will and carted away the furniture; constantly harassed this ageing woman who was incapable of dealing even with ordinary crises.

Frank, following his lifelong habit, had cleared out, gone on the shearing circuit, and was now safe in northern New South Wales, firing off a letter of sage advice every two days, and castigating his distraught wife for not having done what he had advised two letters before. He was righteous, sincere and even pious, and his eldest son, accustomed as he was to pusillanimous behaviour from his father, hit the roof.

'Drop off your twig, you hypocrite,' he wrote. 'Running away is about all you can do. I'm ashamed of you. You're no father of mine, you no-hoper.'

To my knowledge he had abandoned his father to the four winds at least twenty times before, so I took no notice.

I was disturbed, however, at his distraught and fatigued appearance. He could not settle to work but prowled about, smoking his head off. Half the night he walked around the house, kicking aside children's forgotten toys, often rubbing his chest absent mindedly.

'Do you have a pain?'

'Indigestion.'

He seemed unable to think of anything but the older family's predicament. Constantly I found myself finishing an article for him, typing out this or that story, writing alone some play contracted to be written by the two of us for the ABC. When Ina went off to find a good life of her own, mine became very difficult. Not only her hard work as cook and deckhand, but her cheerful, laughing presence had made easier our struggles with five young children and the intractable Old Manse. At last I objected; 'Look, this can't go on. I can't carry the whole burden by myself. You have to do some rethinking.'

'I know,' he said sadly. 'But I can't help myself. I feel responsible for them and I don't know how to stop.'

Cynically, I remembered that his brothers had known how to stop. They left Australia and found safe haven in another country.

However well I understood the peremptory nature of the calls upon his lifelong loyalty, it was still an imposition that severely strained our personal relationship. For in this present emergency as in innumerable others throughout the years, I could plainly see it would always be myself and our children who would be forced to take up the slack. Also I didn't like the way my husband looked or behaved;

he seemed like a man on the verge of breakdown. So the problem had to be faced head on.

'There's only one answer,' I said. 'Only one solution for your mother. She has to be settled in some place where she can't be evicted, no matter how much your father tries to bitch up the situation. We have to buy something.'

At the time, after years of hard saving, even after wasting thousands of pounds on our unwise lease of the Old Manse, we had at last enough to pay a deposit on a home for ourselves. We had even begun to look at modest houses for sale.

'Oh, crikey, do you think we could?'

No generosity was in my heart; bitterly I resented our capital, mostly my own earnings, vanishing this way. But if my own family had been in a similarly critical position, there was no doubt of what D'Arcy would have suggested. He would not have thought twice.

'I'll build up our funds again some way,' he promised. 'I'll even write a novel.'

From his expression I knew that this was the sorest trial possible. What could I do but laugh?

At last we found a tumbledown old cottage in Leichhardt, not wonderful at all, but all we could afford.

'It's not all for us, is it?' asked Barbara timidly, so pleased, so disbelieving that my heart misgave me that our funds could not stretch to something better for this unlucky woman who had always lived in places largely occupied by hostile strangers.

She was much taken by the extensive backyard. 'Frank always liked gardening; this will be the making of him. It's like a miracle.'

'You see what I mean?' asked D'Arcy that night. 'She never loses hope that her prayers will be answered.'

'Well, maybe they will be.'

D'Arcy insisted that the family not know we had purchased the cottage. It belonged, he told them, to the friend of a friend.

'If they know it's me, they'll lean all the more. And I want them to have self-respect, responsibility, pay rent, feel that they're making their own way.'

Undoubtedly they paid the small rent from the allowance he made them thenceforth, but pay it they did. When D'Arcy had settled his mother in the house, back romped Frank and moved in, celebrating a place all to himself by a mighty spree. That evening we had calls from the police and three irate neighbours.

'Well, bang goes our money once again,' said my husband sadly. 'Yet how can anyone get a drunk to play a man's part, tell me that? The gutless way he made for the country! You couldn't see him for dust. Well, I give in; I'll never be the bunny again. We can't hope for any improvement as long as he's alive and kicking.'

'Forget it. There was a priority. We did what we could.'

'Of course, there's always a chance he *might* get interested in growing vegetables.'

In fact, Frank did. His garden may have given some satisfaction to that always unsatisfied man. But until his father died, D'Arcy was never free of phone calls from the police, indignant neighbours, his beleaguered sister. Always drunkenness, fights, arrests, bailings out, troubles, tears, misery. Not until the youngest sister, that Dordie whom Anne had loved, was able to take charge of the household, though she too had been left unsupported, with two young children, one very ill, was there any peace from this ancient situation, where the parent had become an uncontrollable child, and the son assumed the duties of a father.

Yet when the father died, D'Arcy had tears in his eyes. He said, 'Don't be too hard on him, Tiger. We don't know what it's all about, do we? And besides, he was a bloody good woolclasser.'

In the meantime we stopped fretting over the parlous state of our finances and set to work at the typewriter and with the paintbrush. If we were stuck with a ruin, at least we could try to make it livable. Even picturesque. People in magazine articles were doing it all the time. We had every do-it-yourself book available, and we learned as we went along. But alas, too many decades had gone by; the Old Manse presented a chain reaction of deterioration. If we removed a window to reputty the glass and paint the frame, we discovered that the windowsill had terminal dry rot. Taking out the sill in order to replace it, we found that the bricks underneath were crumbling, the mortar turned into fine powder.

Once, tackling the kitchen wall—the kitchen was the only room we managed to make bright, pleasant and functional—we actually removed those dead old bricks of 1860, only to discover that the house had no damp course at all. So we had the wall jacked up and a damp course put in, a process I shudder to remember.

Few had loved or cared for the Old Manse since the minister left. It was anchored on the crest of a monstrous breaking wave of sandstone, literally anchored in some places by rusted stanchions of iron clawed into that Jurassic rock. In spite of the gables it had a crouched, cranky look; its knocked-in tin roof leaked everywhere; the gutters were bewhiskered with starling nests; the downpipes gaped with ragged holes that sheltered lizards, stray shivery grass and cockroaches.

Oh, that house! Somewhere in its innards was the core of its being—a small dwelling, built of sandstone, a hall straight through its middle like a tree trunk, large square rooms branching off on both sides, rooms with magnificent red cedar ceilings, and fireplaces and mantels of carved stone or timber stretching up fronded arms that once enclosed family paintings or looking glasses half a century gone.

In the time of the minister's family the garden stretched halfway down Ben Boyd Road. There was an orange orchard below the house, and two Jersey cows in the home paddock.

But through the years, during the Old Manse's journey down the *via crucis* that is the destiny of most ancient houses, people had boarded-in its verandahs, added nasty bits to outside walls, divided rooms. Anne and Rory ran around claiming these almost secret rooms, some now boarded up even from the inside, perhaps to keep out the sweeping draughts, and converted them into castles and cubbies, forbidden to everyone else.

'It was a cheap boarding house,' said Dame Mary Gilmore, 'and I had a room there when I taught at the Neutral Bay Public School at the top of the hill. Let me see, that would have been about 1890.'

Strangely, Beatrice Davis, senior editor of Angus & Robertson, had also lived there as a small girl during the first World War. The school where Dame Mary had taught was her first school. It seems that the Old Manse then belonged to Beatrice's maternal grandparents, and although the dwelling must surely have been in better condition, she clearly remembered the multitude of mysterious little tacked-on rooms.

'I like the outside toilet,' confided my elder son. 'You can read the door.'

The outside toilet, stuck on an exterior wall like a bug, was of later date, and afforded an interesting glimpse into Victorian Australian, for its door was plastered with catalogue pages from Lasseter & Co, a huge firm which vanished about the time of Gallipoli. Lightning Streak rabbit poison drops 'em dead on the spot, boasted the advertisements. Other goods were Safety Rocking Horses and Tin-lined Wedding-cake Boxes, and, amazingly for that time, equipment for muzzle-loading guns such as Wad Punches, Brass Worms and Nipple Keys.

The tail of a sacred snake vanished under the toilet and beneath the house itself, for the golden rock was richly engraved with pictures of whales, hammerhead sharks, wallabies and lizards. In the concavities under the house, sculpted by wind and rain, were dim paintings of human beings, one the faded figure of a man with no mouth and a hat shaped like an ice-cream cone. Traces of black and yellow ochre were still discernible.

Under the clothes-line were strange round deposits of concrete, very old and crumbly, so we chiselled them out, revealing shallow holes where aboriginal women had ground grass seed, wild grains and nuts. And later, in the tumbling masses of unpruned azaleas at the foot of the rock, I found prehistoric pestles of a harder stone, possibly granite, and found that the carefully chipped and ground finger-grooves and thumb-holes fitted my own fingers as they had fitted those of the dark-eyed women of ten thousand years before.

The haunted room was the original drawing room, commanding a southern view of Sydney. A splendid hexagonal room it was, its noble bay looking out over trees, roofs and harbour, even down upon the deck of the Bridge. For the Old Manse was as high as a watchtower, and must have been even more so when there was still dense bush down to the shores of Neutral Bay, where foreign ships were once anchored until their papers were examined.

Surveying the night city from the bay window was like staring into the middle of the galaxy, planetary systems and nebulae, comets and stardust that flowed in uneven spangled streams along the major streets.

Whenever she saw it open, Anne stealthily closed the door of that room.

'Are you shutting something in?' I inquired.

'I don't want it to look out at me.'

She would not enter that room, and neither would the other children, though it was empty of all but an old sofa and a few boxes, and thus good to play in.

D'Arcy did not notice anything odd at all, so we didn't tell him. In the bay he set up a makeshift desk, an old door resting on two boxes, and at night, and in half-hour periods sandwiched amongst our renovating jobs, he wrote *The Big Smoke*, a story set back a little in time.

> I want to do right by Sydney. They're dismantling the old girl already, just look at all the scaffolding everywhere. Of course, that's the way of things, towns grow, like everything else. But I want to do a true picture of Sydney as she was when I first saw her, a leaky old ship, half-foundering, heading out of the colonial era, and not sure of where she was going. Rags and tatters of Empire still fluttering from her masts . . .

This scribbled note I found amongst his papers years later: *The Big Smoke* meant more to him than just a novel, I think. He attacked it furiously; the manuscript shows little sign of revision. He was able to work fairly consistently because of the advent of Tice, houseman and handyperson. Tice took on most of the jobs around the house that D'Arcy had been accustomed to doing. Though with us only six or seven months, this farouche character, who came into our life in response to an advertisement for a cleaner, was one destined for a certain immortality in Australian literature.

Tice was thirtyish, lean as a rail, with a nutmeg face and a sideways, flaring glance. I did not like meeting it head on, as when I did I felt I had collided with something.

'Gee, I don't know about *him*!' I muttered to my husband.

'He's all right. He's a returned soldier. Give him a go.'

Tice's first remark was, 'Christ, what a dump!'

Nevertheless he made it a clean dump, working with speechless intensity. He refused tea or coffee or any lunch, often departing suddenly, returning next day as silent as ever but with a thunderous hangover, to resume window-washing or paint-scrubbing where he had left off.

'You want I should clear up the garden a bit, missus?'

'Yes, please, Mr Tice.'

'I ain't no mister.'

The only time he showed humour was when he called out to me as I typed in our bedroom: 'You there, missus? There's a robin redbreast at the kitchen door.'

Obeying this irresistible summons, I found at our back door the eminent Dr Eris O'Brien, the scholar and historian, who was then stationed at the Neutral Bay church. He was, I think, in spite of his fame in intellectual circles, a somewhat shy and modest man, perhaps lonely, as many of the priestly intellectual are.

'I believe we are both bookish people,' he said, 'so I thought I should make myself known to you. And offer you the run of my library if that would interest you at all.'

So began a formal but rewarding friendship, which ended only when he was appointed Archbishop of Canberra and Goulburn. As a parting gift he gave me a little old book, printed with archaic long S's, Comte de la Perouse's account of his Pacific voyages.

'An indelicate fellow, I fear. I hope it will not offend you.'

In the far future when I was forced to sell it, I discovered that his gift was very valuable indeed. He was a noted book collector.

So *The Big Smoke* was finished, and submitted for the Commonwealth Jubilee literary competition. And Tice went on turning up intermittently, silently. One boiling hot day as he cut overgrowth in the bottom garden, he took off his shirt, revealing a back so monstrously scarred I could scarcely bear to tell D'Arcy of my horror.

'Oh, yes,' he said, 'Japanese prison camp. He was whipped with barbed wire.'

'He told you?'

'I asked. Not a man who confides much. Drinks away his bad memories. Probably sensible thing to do.'

We did not learn if Tice's nightmarish memories ever left him. One day he did not return to the Old Manse. I thought he might have ended his life somewhere, but D'Arcy scoffed.

'Not him. Tough as stringybark. He'll survive. I'm going to use him. I have this idea for another novel, no title as yet, about a wandering man, a seasonal worker, who takes over the care of his kid, not for love but for revenge. A tough unforgiving man with a hard leather face, like Tice. Yeah, he'll do.'

The Big Smoke behind him, his worries about his family temporarily relieved, D'Arcy began to look like his old self. No longer did he rub his chest, or find himself unable to sleep. In those times we did not know about the relationship of stress to heart and other ailments; we did not know that coffee or indeed any caffeine-laden beverage should be avoided, nor that smoking is positively jeopardous. We had scarcely heard of cholesterol.

We would not, anyway, have associated stress with overwork. In our view we led the freelance writer's common life, compelled to grab what jobs we could, to deliver the finished work no matter what it cost us in sleep or energy.

In the month in which D'Arcy was notified that *The Big Smoke* had won second prize in the Commonwealth Jubilee Competition—he also won the short-story section with 'Dadda Jumped Over Two Elephants', and was awarded a special prize for 'A Girl I Knew Once'—I see we had an average output. I wrote eight episodes of a children's serial for the ABC. For this I had apparently already written forty-six episodes, but my memory is silent on this point. I had submitted the novel *The Witch's Thorn* to all three of my publishers and been overjoyed that it was accepted. So somewhere amidst the care of children, the writing of scripts, and floor and wall repairing I had written that difficult story. D'Arcy had submitted the weekly material for a newsletter he did for a New Zealand magazine, and had had accepted four short stories. The account book does not record work written, but accepted or rejected, with comments and payment. I had also written and had accepted two funny articles for a women's magazine's Christmas issue.

Delighted by the Jubilee prize and the comments of the judges, D'Arcy hastened to submit *The Big Smoke* to Angus & Robertson. It was rejected.

'Damn it, why? What does "not really the sort of book we care to publish" mean? Isn't that what they said to you about *The Harp in the South*, and then it sold like salted peanuts and earned them big profits? What's the matter with those people? I'll show them.'

'How?'

'I'll write another novel, that's what. No, hang about. I don't suppose we could afford it. I could write a dozen short stories in the time I'd spend labouring over another clunker.'

This was true. Immediate or near immediate payment was still vital to us. Though my books were selling well, advances were small, and tax and the debilitating provisional tax reduced my income grievously. In the US, *The Witch's Thorn* was a Book Society Choice, mysteriously marketed under the slogan 'a wonderful story about people unlike us'. But although it was thrilling to read that so many copies were sold per day, the royalty statements told the same old story—a large sum at the top, and a smallish one at the bottom.

'You could apply for a grant from the Commonwealth Literary Fund.'

'Hey, hey, my Tiger. We don't believe in grants!'

That was so. We sincerely believed that patriarchal handouts from the State created a dependent, money-grubbing mindset amongst practitioners of the Arts. This puritanical, but bang-on-target attitude rose from our occasional visits to Fellowship of Australian Writers' meetings. There, alas, though the atmosphere was outspokenly Communist or possibly Fabian Socialist, one heard a continuous cranky mutter about the undeserving layabouts

213

who had landed grants, and the sacred old pillars of literary Australiana who had not.

There we also heard a bold man boast about not turning in one line of the mighty work for which he had been given a grant.

'What a parasite!' fumed D'Arcy. 'A no-hoper like that gives writers a bad name.'

'If you did apply for a grant you could specify that it's for travel expenses. For the Tice story.'

'Well—I wonder.'

He applied for the grant, the only one he ever did apply for, and in due course a government cheque for £500 arrived, accompanied by a generous letter from Vance Palmer, a respected elderly writer who headed the awarding committee.

'I wish you had applied for more substantial funding,' ran this letter. 'No young writer is worthier.'

'Crikey, how's that?'

Like most young writers we were either indifferent to or merely tolerant of older writers; nevertheless Vance Palmer's kindly, non-patronising words acted on my husband like a shot of adrenalin. He emitted showers of invisible sparks.

'Do you think you could manage here alone for a fortnight?'

'Why?'

'I ought to run over the route, the shearing circuit that Macauley follows.'

I must have gazed blankly, for he said, 'For *The Shiralee*, the new novel. Macauley's the Tice character. Good name, isn't it?'

'Is this the wanderer story, about the man with the little child?'

'Of course it is. Her name's Buster. She looks the way Anne did when she was three or four. I'm mad to write it. Do you think you could cope without breaking a bone? What's programmed for the next week?'

'That new series for the *Children's Session—The Muddleheaded Wombat*. The ABC wants eight scripts so they can get ahead with their recording.'

'Oh, you'll knock those over with no trouble,' he said sunnily. 'Right then, suppose I go tomorrow?'

Both of us knew how much easier life was with two adults in the house. It was the Old Manse's doubling as a business office that was the problem. Luckily we had been able to site the phone where it could be answered promptly and professionally with no background noise from children scrapping, saucepans boiling over, or the inhuman row of a little boy with a fish hook in his thumb.

It should be said that even without the great array of household appliances common today, housekeeping in the 1950s and 1960s was in the main, easier. *There were deliveries.* If I organised domestic supplies properly, we could easily withstand a fortnight's siege.

It was plain to me that D'Arcy wanted to get away at once to do his research because he could then return and begin that book he was on fire to do. I could not mistake the creative energy that had seized him; he was like a volcano ready to blow its head off. I knew the feeling well. Wanting to write may well be a sensation felt in the ankles; wanting to write some specific thing is peremptory, urgent, almost obsessional. All novels have their optimum time of writing, and any experienced writer (and probably editors) can discern if another man's book was written while his blood fizzed, or whether it was cranked out, sentence by sentence, however skilfully, by means of technique and dogged intent.

Three days later, with all five children sick with chickenpox, I again pondered bitterly the question of which one of us it was who usually carried the shiralee, which I now understood meant burden, though perhaps a necessary burden. This aptly described each one of my itching, blazing-hot, miserable children. By day I anointed them with bicarbonate of soda; by night I shot out of a delirious sleep to answer the dread call, 'Quick, I'm sick in the froat!' In between times I wrote *The Muddleheaded Wombat*, carefully tailored to the talents of three contract actors, on the kitchen table, where I could hear the imperious summons of both phone and sufferers.

My second sight did not let me know that *Wombat*, so precariously begun, would run for many years, proving the foundation of our family finances, particularly after D'Arcy's sudden death, when all funds were frozen for more than a year.

If it had, I might have felt less depressed. For whether it was the chickenpox, the sleepless nights, or the forlorn atmosphere of the Old Manse, I felt very dark and dull of spirit. Perhaps lacking the sound of D'Arcy's busy typewriter, his skylarking and beaming good temper, I had time to think.

As I sat at the kitchen table, half worked-out story-lines of *Wombat* all around me, I experienced a terrible consciousness of futility. For what was it all about? It seemed that from my earliest years I had been running, always catching up on something—often breathless, often with a stitch in my side. It was true I had had, as the world saw it, considerable success. Yet, was the struggle worth it? And I pondered, as I often pondered, Chaucer's words in his 'Parliament of Fowles'. True, he spoke of the nature of love, but his words can be applied to many aspects of human endeavour. I applied them to writing.

The life so short, the craft so long to learn;
The assay so sharp, so hard the conquering:
The dreadful joy . . .

After so many years of hard running, I acknowledged I did not get from my life much that was satisfying. I was the maintenance officer for a reasonably large family, the multiple responsibilities not begrudged but in fact carried out more as a true and caring friend than a motherly person, whatever that may be.

I was also an industrious and dedicated writer, not a novelist, not a playwright, not a journalist, but all three. A writer.

In front of me were probably twenty or thirty years of similar experience. The children's infant problems would evolve into adolescent problems, then into adult problems. Difficulties with editors had already been converted into difficulties with film and television producers.

217

'I need another dimension,' I thought, 'but what is it?'

This disquieting and deeply melancholy feeling may have been what is today termed burn-out, when the validity of what one is doing is in question.

On the other hand it could denote entrapment of my mind in the vast religious and ethical error of constructiveness—that all life is nothing more or less than a storyline, a linear plot moving onwards, onwards, towards The End, which will prove either satisfactory or otherwise. Satisfactory, if they want it to sell. This variety of time-travelling is not programmed by culture into all races, but it is a part of our own, thereby robbing us of awareness of the moment.

But perhaps I was merely worn threadbare with lack of sleep, which affects the mind in many inventive ways.

'Why don't you go and see old Mary?' asked D'Arcy. 'You always come back from a visit sparking on every plug. And I'll cook dinner and see to the kids.'

By this time I knew Dame Mary Gilmore very well, for we had corresponded and occasionally met for eight or nine years. On the other hand, I didn't know her at all; such is the way of things with human beings.

Though she was the first woman in the British Empire to be made a Dame for her literary work, a good portion of the bookish establishment in Australia said it was a crying shame and she should not have had the honour. For what had she done? A couple of books of balladic verse, another two collections of essays, twenty-three years of running the women's section of *The Worker*. A dozen other people had done more.

But Dame Mary was a nonpareil; she could not be compared with other writers. True, she was a commentator rather than a historian, a singer rather than a poet. But she *said things*, she *thought* of her own accord. Almost never did one get from her the echo of some other mind. She wrote many thousands of letters on the small letter paper that was headed: 2 Claremont, 99 Darlinghurst Rd, King's Cross. Thousands and thousands, many to her 'swans', of whom I was one. She never referred to us as geese though most of us were. And every letter contains a referred glitter from an eager, independent, never-darkened mind, always expressed idiosyncratically, often gloriously. The Mitchell Library has, I am told, incredible files of these little letters, and my simple question would be—if she were not a rare person why did we, the recipients, keep them all these years?

The 1950s, with their shameful political battles, the disruption of the Labor Party, the rise of boldly venal, cynical selfseekers in trade unions and the Party itself must have been painful to this woman, then in her late eighties, an old Labor woman, and, more than that, the kind of idealistic Socialist who went off to Paraguay to create a New Australia. But she never mentioned politics to me.

It is true that, in her arresting tales of pioneer Australia, she often placed herself as character when the calendar proves she could not have been so. I don't think this was lying, nor was it fantasising in the usual sense. Perhaps her imagination was so detailed, so vivid, that as she grew older she was not able to ask herself: 'Was I there, or is

219

this something I heard from old men yarning around the campfire?' There is no record of this personal misplacement in earlier years, so far as I have read. I confess that D'Arcy and I often played 'Dame Mary and Captain Cook in Tahiti', or 'Dame Mary and Captain Phillip at the Arrival of the First Fleet'.

'I'm telling you right this minute, Arthur, my boy, that Botany Bay is unsuitable for a settlement.'

'I have my orders from Admiralty, ma'am.'

'Confound them for fools! Can't you see the swamp? Think of the mosquitoes, the fevers, the difficulty of drainage!'

'I should be obliged, ma'am, if you would take yourself off into the next century.'

Oh, she was a wondrous old woman, so full of vitality, fun and originality even in her extreme old age, that I was ashamed to tell her that in the middle of my life I had found myself in a dark wood.

'Who doesn't?' she inquired almost gaily, pouring me a mug full of maté tea, stuff that tasted like cobwebs and a particularly noxious lichen, but which had some kind of stimulating effect on the blood vessels in the brain. So she said.

'It will go, my girl,' she said. 'Hold your horses and don't do anything desperate. Though I did.'

She said no more because of the arrival of a visitor, but I believe she referred to that period of her life between 1903 and 1911, obviously entrapped and frustrated years on and off Will Gilmore's family property in Casterton, Victoria. There she tried to be one of those pioneering housewives she so admired, but though she succeeded, her deprived intellect was tormented beyond bearing. A woman who knew her during those lonely years when Will was away all week shearing or scrub-cutting, wrote: 'She would put her arms around the trunk of a gum tree, still warm from the heat of the day. That warmth was the only response in that desolate place to her loneliness and desolation . . .'

Reading that, I remembered how I had often done the same thing during my first two homesick years in Australia, leaning against the warm and moving tree, the silky, bark-less red gum, full of life and benevolence.

From Casterton, Mary Gilmore left for Sydney, to take up a position on *The Worker*. Will Gilmore and his brother went to Queensland where he lived for the rest of his life. The marriage, it seems, was effectively ended. But that was the kind of desperate action I did not want for myself.

Dame Mary's visitor in that sunset hour was not as old as she but appeared venerable. Soon they were lost in conversation, the old weather-wizard Inigo Jones and she, while I called forth all my cryptic abilities and melted into the stacks of books and papers in the corner. What did they speak about? I cannot recall. All that afternoon and gathering dusk left with me was the awareness that I was a silent onlooker of history, perhaps not significant history, but still part of the continental story. Here were two ancient people, Dame Mary's voice still deep and melodious, Inigo Jones's a little thready. Talking about winds that no longer blew since tall buildings came to Australia, lightning striking down and upwards on the ironstone plains, the sunspots that were the weather wizard's lifework? I do not know. This is speculation.

But I remember night falling, and a neon light somewhere in Darlinghurst Road throwing jellybean colours over that crowded, amazing, spellbound little room, now yellow, now red, a trembling blue.

Having temporarily forgotten the *selva oscura*, the dark wood, I went home bemused, emerging blinking into our bright and noisy house.

'Dinner's ready,' said my husband. 'And I've made a sponge cake for afters. But you'll have to give me a hand lifting it out of the oven.'

4

Some time during D'Arcy's absence on the *Shiralee* field research, a quaint couple came to the kitchen door. Everyone came to the kitchen door, as the front door, encaverned within a porch over four metres deep, was obscured by wisteria and jasmine headstrong with summer and neglect.

'We knew you were here, and we want to know you,' said the tall old gentleman, seventy-seven if he was a day. 'I'm Will Lawson. And this,' pointing to the dimpled butter-ball beside him, 'is Mrs Lawson.'

'But I know your work, of course I do,' I cried. 'Ballads— "round the bend where the pungas grow, I heard an axle groan, The clatter of linch pins knocking slow, in a drowsy monotone". Of *course* I know you, and lots more than "Round the Bend", too.'

'Why, isn't that nice, Will!' said the butterball, delighted.

'I've always loved ballads,' I continued. 'I think I like your sea poems best . . . "When big winds blew like booming guns". Great!'

'Blooming guns. You have to remember the narrator's idiom.'

'I like booming better, though.'

'Don't correct me, missy.'

Will Lawson was carved from cross-grained hardwood, with a face from the British Isles' past centuries. His personality had been shaped by an often tumultuous life as seaman, journalist, wharfinger, battler and drunkard. He was the son of an Anglican bishop, and ne'er-do-well and runaway though he had been, he was nevertheless a well-educated man with old-fashioned courteous ways.

'I'm not Mrs Will Lawson, you know,' said the little lady. 'I'm Mrs Henry Lawson.'

This was our introduction to the historic ménage of Mr and Mrs Lawson who were, I believe, not lovers in the commonplace sense, but affectionate and mutually dependent friends. They were of great interest and pleasure to us for some years. But D'Arcy, whose first serious reading had been the tales of Henry Lawson, was curious about this forgotten female half of Henry's brief, unhappy marriage.

'I wonder would Bertha talk to us,' he said. 'It's time she had her say.'

We obtained Bertha's permission to construct a documentary provisionally called *The Courtship of Henry Lawson* for the Australian Broadcasting Commission.

'You can check every word,' we told her, and so she eventually did. Very soon we were invited to morning tea at her tiny Northbridge home.

'Quong Tart was a Chinese who wanted to be a Scotsman. He recited Robert Burns and wore a kilt on St Andrew's Day.'

Bertha goes back a long way. She married Henry Lawson in 1896, and says she was nineteen. I don't believe it. Her mother would have stopped her, the girl being underage, and Mrs McNamara reading Henry like a book. Only later in the story do I find out that Henry wheedled a written consent from Bertha's mother with his usual convincing lies and false evidence that he'd taken 'the pledge'.

'Mr MacTart, as he called himself, ran a fashionable tearoom in the Sydney Arcade, and that's where Harry told me he had made arrangements for us to be married that very afternoon, at a clergyman's house. Now, what was I wearing?'

'A green dress patterned with red poppies and cream lace-up boots,' Will prompts tolerantly.

Bertha's living room is, without argument, a parlour. Drab Brussels carpet worn to the drabber threads; red rep curtains draped and valanced; glass bookcases that turn the room into a hexagon; dried grasses in urns; a perfect spinney of little tables laden with photographs, porcelain figures, silver boxes, framed letters from Rudyard Kipling, Henry Parkes, S.J. Brady, Billy Hughes.

She administers tea rather than serves it, daintily, ritually. Hot water in the teacups, rinsed out, cups dried with

225

a soft cloth. The china is fine and floral, sugar in lumps, lemon sliced thin, milk called cream in the English manner. The tea is most likely China, but tastes like mud to me, as I prefer coffee. Will has his in a substantial mug. I take it his hand is beginning to shake a little.

'And then we went home, and Mother had a fit. She called me a lunatic and Harry a waster and didn't speak to me for months.'

The belief that Bertha had gone off her head was almost universal amongst those who knew Henry. Kindly, commonsensible George Robertson, founder of the publishing firm, Angus & Robertson, had done his best to dissuade her, even asking her to spend the weekend at his home in the mountains so that his wife could talk her out of it. He also adds, 'She had great big hazel eyes, shining with excitement. They were undoubtedly very much in love with each other.'

For Bertha, girl of a gaslit, hansom-cab Sydney, romantic, impressed by the tall, handsome and already famous writer, love was a natural thing. She knew he was a drunkard, but believed in female folly that with the care, support and adoration only she could give, he would cease being a drunkard. But why did Henry choose young Bertha Bredt, better educated than he, child of a radical, bookish, politically aware family?

Once I interviewed Tom Mills, in his prime days a top New Zealand journalist, who had invited Henry and Bertha to stay at his home when they fled to Wellington in 1897 to help Henry turn over a new leaf.

'Why did Henry fall for Bertha?' I asked.

'Oh,' he said decisively, 'it was the shape that caught Henry.'

D'Arcy, when he heard, laughed. 'Sounds like a music-hall song!' But it was true that even at seventy-five or -six small round Bertha had an hour-glass shape, probably with the aid of corsets.

'They were fighting like wildcats even while they were with us,' added Tom Mills. 'We were glad when they left.'

Bertha's efforts to get Henry away from his boozy friends failed entirely. Henry always preferred his boozy friends to family, even his own children. The former, after all, never asked him to take responsibility for anything. The marriage broke up completely in 1903, his children then being five and three, another dead, and the twenty-six-year-old Bertha without any means of support. Much has been written by Henry's hagiographers of his wife's cruel hounding of him, and his frequent brief sojourns in Darlinghurst Gaol for defaulting on child maintenance. But it is difficult to see what else she could have done. When the children were older George Robertson gave her a job. She was the first woman book sales representative in Australia.

It is impossible to discern what indeed Henry Lawson wanted from women; it does not seem to have occurred to him that they wanted, needed, or indeed deserved anything from him. His remarks to George Robertson about 'the four women I was closely connected with' are revelatory. Firstly his mother, the indomitable Louisa, 'a selfish, indolent, mad-tempered woman insanely jealous of my literary success'. Then came Bertha, 'an insane Prussianised

227

German by birth on both sides, by breeding and by nature'. Of Number Three we know nothing.

She was possibly his dead infant sister about whom he maundered sentimentally, though it appears his daughter was not given the same attention. Finally he scarifies Isobel Byers, who looked after and supported him for years either as mistress or friend. Isobel is a combination of Louisa and Bertha. 'They all develop into the Brute. I . . . was always soft and yielding or good natured and generous.'

'All that was manly in him went into his stories and ballads,' says D'Arcy, who admires him as a writer. So do I.

We wrote *The Courtship of Henry Lawson* with great care, for it was a minor historical document. The ABC had scarcely advertised the broadcast before collectors of Lawsoniana were on our doorstep, and Bertha's doorstep, either to dispute the script or have us sign affidavits that it was entirely authentic. But these things are authentic only as far as the interviewee is truthful, or can remember the truth.

Bertha's voice was on the tape, as well as those of several literary people who were her contemporaries. But somehow it vanished from the ABC's files. Mislaid, they said, but most likely abstracted and sold or given to a collector.

We both found Bertha very likeable. She was durable, humorous and kindly. My impression was that, when young, she had probably been a voluptuous little bundle. Still she gave off that indefinable fragrance that attracts men. But her long life had been entirely without scandal.

Naturally enough, I never mentioned that I knew Mary Gilmore well, for I had heard the long-established rumour that she and Henry Lawson had had an affair, and I did not wish to upset Bertha by mention of Dame Mary's name. But in the interests of history I must record that Bertha Lawson, on the one occasion she mentioned the older woman, did say that some kind of serious love passage between these two unlikely people had occurred. But I found it, and still find it, hard to believe. The dates are difficult to explain or adapt. And *Mary*? Plain, large, strong-minded, bossy, older than Henry? Exactly the kind of woman of whom he was most afraid and most vilified. My personal opinion is that the 'love affair' was one of Henry's little brags with which he successfully wounded his estranged wife. The tale possibly wounded Mary Gilmore also. But the truth will probably never emerge from the shadows of the long gone past.

'Curious the way she found Will Lawson and took him in,' I commented.

In Will Lawson, Bertha had achieved her simple but usually unattainable aim—she had succoured and reformed an alcoholic. Fifteen years or so previously she had found Will Lawson literally in a gutter, 'bust as an old paper bag,' as Will said. 'Sick as a dog.'

He had come to the end of his buccaneering life, his health was ruined, and he had no hope. Bertha gave him a home, fed him properly, and kept him sober. On a closed-in back verandah of Bertha's Northbridge home he had a spartan bed, a table supporting a dinosaur of a standard typewriter, files lining the walls. There he happily wrote his ballads, and books about the old whaling days in which he had a special interest. He was a man completed.

Their contentment with their mutually supportive life was pleasant to see. A memory that always makes me smile is this. One morning I called unexpectedly, and found Bertha sitting on the verandah and Will absorbedly curling her hair with a wooden clothes-peg.

Henry died in 1922, Bertha two years after we met her; Will lingered a little, and died in 1957. To the literary world, which had given Henry a State funeral, Bertha was nothing more than a memorandum, faint and half-erased, of a bygone age.

Will, I fancy, had gladly gone 'where big winds blow like booming guns . . .'

Don't you correct *me*, missy.

Now, all this time we were looking for a house, finding a house and moving in, establishing the older children in new schools, buying uniforms, checking bus routes, writing excited and thankful letters to my family in Auckland about this spacious new home that looked over Manly, picked up the sea winds, and had a large well-fenced back lawn where the little ones could play safely.

All this time too, D'Arcy was writing *The Shiralee*. Half the night the typewriter rattled away, its machine-gun-like bursts interspersed with dead silences. During one of these I crept in with a cup of tea, and saw him staring at the darkened window. I knew what he was doing, in his mind throwing threads up into the air like a spider, hoping to snare a word, a sentence; or dropping them down into the subconscious, trolling for he knew not what.

Over his shoulder I read:

A town that clutched the hem of a mountain, a damp town that smelled of wet sawdust and sopping trees. Wintry lights, blurred by mist into heads of thistledown, marked it like a backcountry airstrip in the darkness of rain and forest.

At the camp men were touchy and spoiling for a fight. Blow your nose and they'd get the notion you were slinging off.

As I read a line was added. 'Get away out of there, you redheaded rat. You hear?'

He finished the book and retyped it.

'Now for Angus & Robertson's.'

It was rejected.

'What reason this time?'

'Wouldn't have sufficient sale to warrant publication. God, Tiger, I really thought I'd hit it this time.'

He was deeply dejected.

'And when I was coming out through the shop I saw a new book of woeful poems by old Jim So and So. If that sells 150 copies it'll be a miracle. What did she mean, wouldn't have sufficient sale?'

'In my opinion it's great. Don't waste time whinging. Airmail it to Michael Joseph.'

But D'Arcy repined. He had his heart set on a success with A & R.

The publishing firm to which I refer was not the present establishment, but the original house, rich in property and bookshops, owning its own printery, and as a publisher by far the most powerful in Australasia, perhaps even south of the equator.

Blooming out of an antiquarian bookshop, it had produced its first book in 1888 to celebrate the centenary of British settlement. By the turn of the century the firm was already honoured not only for its steadfast support of indigenous Australian writing, hitherto lost in a welter of colonialism, but for the remarkable co-founder, plain-spoken, honest, expert businessman George Robertson.

It is difficult to describe with what panting desire we young writers looked upon A & R. There were other publishers in Australia, certainly, but either they were frail and struggling, with no powers of distribution, or the far-flung non-autonomous colonial offices of British publishers who felt it necessary to establish a Raj-like presence in the outposts of Empire. Angus & Robertson were different; self-ruling, independent, wealthy. We approached the old bookshop at 89 Castlereagh Street with awe and pleasure, and if we had already had a book published with the thistle and waratah imprint, a certain proud possessiveness.

The publishing offices were on the floor above, a warren of little cells filled with snowdrifts of paper, clouds of cigarette smoke, and dregs of coffee in styroform cups. But we didn't look for opulence. The fact that the entire building had once been a coach-house, that George Robertson had lived where the editorial offices were now lent a romantic air. A & R had come out of the fresh green colonial days, and the history of those vigorous joyous times was all around us.

But for a long time those of us who had some experience of overseas publishers had felt that there was something the matter with the prestigious firm we so revered. We felt this not only reluctantly but with a sense of betrayal. Yet commonsense can not be denied for ever. Would George Robertson be pleased with his establishment as it was conducted now, I asked myself. And commonsense answered no.

Well I remembered how *The Harp in the South* had been received by Beatrice Davis, the senior editor. If it had not been for the gentleman's agreement with the *Sydney Morning Herald* that novel, for one, would never have been published. Yet it had made a small fortune for Angus & Robertson.

My first meeting with the then managing director, Walter Cousins, widely regarded as a lovable old chap, had left me feeling he inhabited a world not akin to mine. After expressing little faith in the book he stood up and murmured, 'Well, well, we must hope for the best' and was so plainly on the verge of ushering me forth that I gasped nervously, 'When may I expect the contract, Mr Cousins?'

'What contract?'

He then told me that business matters at Angus & Robertson were sealed with a handshake only. Now, this was a lie. When I finally read his predecessor George Robertson's delightful letters, I found they fairly jumped with references to contracts. But perhaps the custom had lapsed under Mr Cousins, for when I finally received the contract I found it was a copy of an English one, word for word—publishing territories wrong, and instead of the

233

agreed royalty scale, a miniscule 'colonial edition' clause. In addition, on the contract I appeared as 'Mrs D'Arcy Niland'. Back I went for revision.

Mr Cousins was patient but puzzled. I wanted a contract, didn't I? Well, I had one.

Clause by clause we rectified it. But he baulked at the Mrs D'Arcy Niland. What was the matter with that?

'That's not my name, Mr Cousins. It's my marital status.'

He was baffled. I explained that if D'Arcy and I divorced and there was a second or even a third Mrs D'Arcy Niland, A & R might be in the soup. Who then would own the copyright?

Oh, I could see he thought I was a troublemaker. But eventually I received another contract, this one made out to Ruth D'Arcy Niland.

Time went by. I had some unsettling chats with older A & R writers.

E.V. Timms wrote high-coloured historical romances. He said, 'He's obsessed with ink, you'll see.'

'Ink?'

'Every time they do a reprint of one of my novels Walter tries to beat down the royalty rate on the grounds that the price of ink has gone up. But they're such good people. They'd never see you stuck if you were in difficulties.'

Leslie Rees, trying to get hold of proofs of a non-fiction book, the accuracy of which was important to him, was promised them immediately by Mr Cousins, left the latter's office and walked out through the shop to discover that the book was already on sale.

'No proofs, no advertisement, not even a notification of publication date.'

'But didn't you get mad?'

'How can one?' He laughed ruefully.

This was the weakening factor. It was what kept us writers, and no doubt artists as well, from screeching blue murder when our work appeared with terrible jackets; blurbs so non-selling that I can recognise them still after thirty or forty years; no publicity whatsoever; few books sent out for review, and almost inevitably the worst publication date possible, such as the first week in January or the week after Mother's Day.

Angus & Robertson, I think, had not put aside the old idea that publishing is a gentleman's profession, though certainly George Robertson had no such high-flown sentiments. Books could no longer be left to find their own way, they sank before the flood of other publishers' books (excellent sellers often already rejected by Angus & Robertson), that enjoyed professional promotion and sales technique.

'Books cannot be treated as if they're tins of beans,' said the chief executive, the gentle, sweet-tempered George Ferguson one day. When I repeated this to Colin Simpson, the travel writer, an intelligent, sophisticated man, he groaned, 'Christ, why not? That doesn't *make* books tins of beans.'

'Aw, cut the pious cackle,' said Frank Clune, one day when I was bemoaning the inefficiency of our publishers. 'Do you return your royalty statements twice a year and have them revised? Yeah? You and a hundred others. The trouble with A & R is that, bloody beaut as all the staff are, they've turned comfortable. They'll lose that firm yet, you'll see.' He snorted.

Frank was an accountant and a smart businessman. He managed to push sales of his rough-written adventure and historical books by sheer cheek and ingenuity. He was an authentic soft touch, but worked hard at being an Ocker, swearing like a trooper and pulling people's legs with dreadful jokes. It was rumoured that he had put the hard word on the regal Miles Franklin as they shared a car on the way to the Henry Lawson Festival at Gulgong—a probable myth that nevertheless seemed to me to sum up agreeably the slightly mad character of Australian literary life.

'You and your bloke get out from under,' he advised.

'And you?'

'Well, writing's not my main source of income. 'Sides, I'm in love with Beatrice. What a little corker she is!'

As was our way, we were so immersed in other jobs we forgot that *The Shiralee* was on offer in London. I was doing an immense book on Australia for a German publisher, who planned to distribute it in half a dozen European languages in the year of Melbourne's Olympic Games, 1956. It was an enormous job, carried out as usual in the night hours and squeezed between the multitude of tasks attendant on the care of a family, but I revelled in it. Always I have most enjoyed writing non-fiction. *The Golden Boomerang* never appeared in English; it is a curiosity in my literary history. Its sale was large, and brought in royalties, possibly from copies sold to European libraries, for many years after-wards. German publishers are, overall, superb—prompt, efficient, and honest, the best of the many I have had to deal with in my literary lifetime. Also they tend to send you spice cakes and little tin boxes of almond paste and cherry confiture for Christmas. The only small problem is getting translations of their royalty statements for the Taxation Department.

Within two months D'Arcy had a cable from Michael Joseph Ltd.

WILDLY EXCITED SHIRALEE. PREDICT SPLENDID SALES.
LETTER FOLLOWS. SINCEREST CONGRATULATIONS.

D'Arcy sat in blinking bewilderment. He couldn't believe it.

'Have I struck it at last? Crikey, I must tell Beatrice!'

'Why?'

'She'll be so pleased for us.'

And indeed she was, and sincerely, for sincerity was the essence of her character. D'Arcy was invited into Castlereagh Street for a celebratory drink with Beatrice and the much younger George Ferguson. He came back triumphantly, an Angus & Robertson author. I was dismayed.

'How did that happen?' I cried.

'Mr Ferguson said that maybe they'd been hasty about their first reading of the book, which you know, Tiger, might well be the truth. And then Beatrice asked me to give them another chance.'

'And you gave in! With Michael Joseph wildly excited?'

'Well you know how it is. I'd walk over burning coals for that woman. And besides, it's what I've always wanted.'

All Angus & Robertson wanted were the Australasian rights. Michael Joseph could have the United Kingdom. But Michael Joseph most wanted Australia, where the sales would be biggest, and being denied them, crossly backed out of the deal.

The novel thus became one of the first Angus & Robertson published from their new London establishment.

'I don't see why you should be so cranky,' complained my partner as I uttered a few dismal predictions. And he put on a mulish look and said I didn't understand the way he felt. He had his own vision of things. This originated in his first days in Sydney, when, a coatless rainsoaked kid on his way home from jobhunting, he had gazed into the windows of the firm's great bookshop, yearning over all those desirable books and swearing that one day his short stories would be between covers in that very window.

'At least get an agent,' I begged. 'You know how effective MCA have been for me in New York. Yes, I know you've given A & R agential rights, but what do they know?'

No use. His publishers showed goodwill, and to him goodwill was all.

I was surprised that he put up a fight when his editor wanted to change the title of his novel to *The Millstone*. Goodwill or not, he could tell that was incontrovertibly a stinker.

Thus *The Shiralee* became a bestseller; a Book Society Choice in the UK; Book Club Choices in the United States, Germany and France. Almost immediately it went into ten translations and several serialisations. Its title word became famous. Little girls were called Shiralee. People named racehorses and beauty salons Shiralee.

But the same waftiness that drifted about the Sydney office operated in London, which was run by a fussy old gentleman who had once, I believe, been a colonial administrator in the remote Pacific, a quasi-writer of sorts. Always with the best intentions, but without the author's knowledge or permission, he gave Ealing Films a free option on *The Shiralee*, meanwhile keeping other film offers to himself. Years later we found out that there had been several excellent ones.

D'Arcy went around as if in a dream. His great success with the novel had not made a dent in his natural modesty, and he agreed to the film deal in the same quiet and almost shy way. But his tense excitement was obvious to me.

'Crikey, Tiger, this is the end of the rainbow. If this film does well, we'll be able to stop freelancing, take it a bit easy, maybe even travel a bit.'

Thus he expressed his most dearly held ambitions. Grand houses, big cars, a highflying lifestyle—for none of these things he cared a jot.

'We'll be able to give the kids the best education on offer; buy Paddy a piano . . .'

Patrick, who was musically gifted, already had a piano, sweet-toned but fourth-hand and subject to asthma. His father longed to buy him a fine instrument. But, as usual, we lacked capital.

Most readers believe that once a writer has a bestseller he is financially secure for years, if not for life. But this is not so. If that writer has another income, or a pleasant nest-egg in the bank from family inheritance or generosity, the case is different. But for the ordinary writer, starting in the basement of the literary world, living from typewriter to mouth, so to speak, he will get mighty little from his first bestseller. If the book has taken him into the top tax bracket he will lose half his income, and provisional tax will take almost all the remaining half. Certainly provisional tax will be adjusted the following year, but in that first year he may find himself poorer than he has ever been.

Some writers, of course, along with other professionals, manage to find one of the now rare tax havens. But even these have their disadvantages.

With what is regrettably called a mega-bestseller, the situation changes. Let it rain, let it hail, let the Tax Department do its direst duty, there will still remain enough money to bank or invest and thus form a nucleus of capital. The same is true of a film sale. If such is your luck, you have a real opportunity to put aside some monetary security for the family.

This is what D'Arcy Niland anticipated.

He was also delighted that Peter Finch had been cast to play the Tice character.

When the film crew arrived in Sydney, accompanied by the usual deafening hullabaloo, he was dumbfounded.

'Those blokes are batty. You've never seen such a carry-on. What's it all about? They talk all day, and eat and drink all night. Yet they get things done. Energy! You'd think they were all on amphetamines. Yet they're cluey, you know. Sort of witty.'

Neil Paterson, the Scots scriptwriter who accompanied the crew and who became a treasured friend until D'Arcy's death, tried to advise him. 'Dear boy, to cope with the film business a man needs stamina, as well as a certain technique to confront what is entirely synthetic. Back out. Leave for Turkey.'

'But they say they need me along.'

'For local press interest. Believe me, dear boy, the writer of the film is on the bottom of the totem pole.'

'But this may be the only film I have, the only chance to make big money, I feel I have to co-operate where I can,' D'Arcy said desperately. Neil shook his head kindly and said no more. Probably he had been in the same position, for he was also a novelist.

Peter Finch was brutal. He had met his old friend exuberantly. Still lean and haggard, older after seven years of phenomenal dramatic success and even more phenomenal hellraising, he was still a fascinating mixture of urbane actor and what D'Arcy called the original tin-roof bloody hooligan. He still fantasised—'When I was two years old my father sold me to a Tibetan lama.' Peter's marriage to the beautiful Russian, Tamara, had gone bust; he had survived and indeed thrived on the international scandal of his affair with Vivien Leigh.

D'Arcy and he spent considerable time together, laughing and drinking beer.

'Don't take all this film business seriously,' he advised, 'It's bullshit.'

'And I think he meant it,' said D'Arcy, wonderingly. 'But he's worked hard. No matter what romances he spins

241

about himself no one can deny he was a battler. Still is, in his way. Yet, in spite of all the fame and adulation he's at a loss for something. What is it?'

I had a good idea. Peter was suffering from the 'Is that all there is?' syndrome as much as I was. The melancholy truth, or shadow of truth, that had revealed itself to me at the Old Manse had not dissipated. D'Arcy's intense involvement with the film and the film crew, while I stayed home, managed a large household, listened to children's woes and joys, wrote scripts for the *Children's Session*, and finished a novel that required much historical research in a poorly documented period, had demonstrated conclusively that things could only get more complex, more burdensome, less rewarding for me.

'You're looking like a wet week. What's the matter?'

However solicitous the question, it was impossible to put into words my unstructured discontent, my feeling that I was not only in a trap with no way out, but that I didn't know why I felt I was in a trap. I did, however, resist the common feminine response of 'Nothing,' uttered in a brave tone, which translates 'Something is very much the matter and it's your job to ask me sympathetic questions to find out what.' But whenever I said 'Nothing' to D'Arcy Niland he believed me, and said happily, 'That's great!'

'I'm fed up,' I said.

'Of course you are. But you've finished your goldfields book, and there'll be nothing more doing on the film while they're editing, so why don't you go over to New Zealand and see your Dad?'

My father was now intermittently bedridden, often very ill. But when I arrived from Sydney he was sitting up in bed, reading *Moby Dick* with a magnifying glass.

'This joker writes like the sea,' he said, and I thought how exactly his words described the long swell and dwindle of Melville's incomparable text. This old man, whose only teachers had been bush and river, and the talk of men old when he was young, had been my support and friend all my life. He had written to me every week during the fifteen years I had been away from New Zealand; he had kept that country ever present in my heart. Now he had written a little book of memoirs, though I don't think he cared any more whether his life experiences were remembered. Long illness dissociates a person from his personal life.

'Are you happy, Din?' he asked. I couldn't bring myself to say I wasn't and lied in my teeth. Afterwards I was sorry. If I had admitted it, he might have been able to tell me what to do about it. He took my hand and kissed it, a strange thing for an old bushman to do.

'I'll let you know,' he said, as he had done twice before.

Probably we both knew that was the last time we would meet, for, although I had said goodbye, I went back quietly to have yet another look at him, and saw that he had put the blanket over his head, as Maoris and many other races have done when they know all is finished.

Here is the way he told me about his death. As I have never told anyone, perhaps the time has come when I can write it. As one inevitably does, I have pondered it for many years; was this experience subjective, was it some commonplace thing misinterpreted by me, was it a waking dream? I would say no to all these questions.

It was months later, the depths of summer. In Sydney, summer heat does not rise to airy heights; it sinks down and down into entranced depths, dark and moist, leaching out energy, so that the land and its people seem to lie in a moveless dream, waiting for sundown.

It was a listless, stifling day, All Saints' Day, and the four younger children who attended Catholic schools consequently on holiday. The house was full of bickering, music, the chirping of the little ones making toffee in the kitchen, and the maddening thud-thud on the exterior wall as the boys played handball.

In the study D'Arcy tried to work out a storyline for a novel set on the opalfields, about his character Barbie Casabon, who had been in his head for years. But the distractions were too many.

'Come on, we're going for a picnic.'

Our house was in easy reach of many beaches, and we all swam well. From North Head to the far point of Barrenjoey, the ocean side of this noble peninsula is scalloped into long shallow curves, swagged between sphinx-like headlands, marvellous beaches of fine bistre sand and never-ending surf.

'Freshwater! Freshwater!'

We liked it best, the odd one out amongst the sweeping bays, much smaller, a half moon clasped between two headlands, more like a submerged volcanic crater than anything else. In those days the beach was not popular; people said there was a villainous rip off the southern rocks, and so

Freshwater had been left to itself. Low velvety dunes ran down to the beach; coarse marram grass blew in the ceaseless wind; the fresh water of its name glistened out of the sand, grew, found deep runnels at low tide mark, and spread out into a web of fissures like the roots of a tree.

We put up the big umbrella amongst the dunes, D'Arcy dozing, I reading. The book, I recall, was about the cultivation of roses. The smaller children slid down the dunes on sacks; the older swam. There was no one else around. The afternoon heat was so great that the further seascape, even the horizon, had been absorbed into the hyacinth haze above the ocean. For the first time in months I felt at peace, doing nothing but watch the breakers scrolling and unscrolling into the glassy shallows, gulls flitting along their crests, dipping their hard red feet.

From the north end of the beach a man came running, a tall man with a lanky stride, too far away for me to see his face, but close enough to see that he wore an old-fashioned bathing costume, dark in colour, all of a piece from thighs to shoulders, with one strap, the left, broken or undone. Aside from the strangeness of the bathing costume, there was nothing strange at all. He was just a tall man running.

Immediately in front of me he dived into the sea, flipping through the base of each wave as a penguin does. Two, three, four, and he was almost out of sight. I caught a glimpse of his dark figure before he, like the sky and the sea, disappeared into the hyacinth haze. I waited for him to come back, watching all along the beach, to the north and the south, but he did not come back.

245

Awakening my husband, I said, 'Dad's dead.'

'We'll go home straight away,' he said, and called the children in from the beach.

As we opened the door at home, we could hear the phone ringing. It was my mother calling from New Zealand.

This happening was one of freedom, delight, boundlessness. I can see that. But it did nothing for me. I suffered a very dark, moveless grief which did not lift for a long time. I thought of that afternoon at Freshwater again after D'Arcy's death, when life seemed to have stopped, but again it did nothing for me. There is a truth in there somewhere, but like all truth no statement of it can be final. I still have no theories about it, except that it says something about everyone's death.

Bringing the twins home from
New Zealand, 1952

Opening of first Housing Commission blocks of flats in Devonshire
Street, Surry Hills, 1951. Residents whose existing terrace homes had
been demolished were dubious

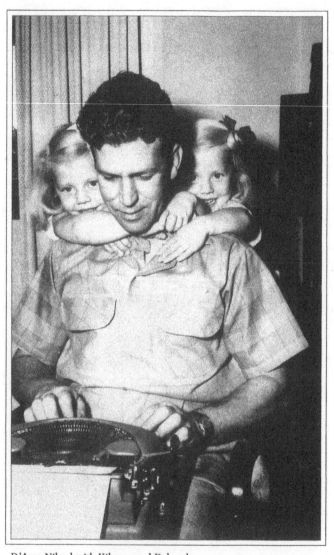

D'Arcy Niland with Kilmeny and Deborah.
'Posterity might judge that being a father was more important than being a novelist.'

Bertha Lawson, wife of
Henry, publisher's sales
representative 1907
(Courtesy of the
Mitchell Library,
State Library of New
South Wales)

Will Lawson, unrelated writer who looked after
Bertha in her last years

Dame Mary Gilmore when she was a journalist on *The Worker* (Courtesy of the Mitchell Library, State Library of New South Wales)

Transcript of the letter reproduced on opposite page

My dear Ruth Park this is a large sheet on which to write a little letter, & taken (& done) a-purpose.

You break my heart with your writing because you know the things I know; they are in your blood as they are in mine, and I never was able (too much work & too poor) to write them till I was old. Memory stirred in the ashes, but the fire—the young fire— was dead.

But the fire is not dead, only the hearth is changed. More than that, the world will never die while the Celt is alive.

and if your children don't carry on your torch—writing, science, art, or even shinty—in a hundred years time I'll get up out of my grave and wallop them— for the world is really worth saving.

May the thunder & the wonder of life's sea stay in your heart.—Mary Gilmore

addendum.
2 Claremont
99 D'hurst Rd.
King's Cross
21.5.47
Your letter just came—and P.S. you needn't answer this. It is already answered by your letter.

My dear Ruth Park this is a
large sheet on which to write-a
little letter, & taken (x above)
a-purpose.

  You break my heart with
your writing because you know
the things I know; they are in
your blood as they are in mine,
and I never was able (too much
work & too poor) to write them till
I was old. Somehow stirred in the
ashes, but the fire — the young
fire —, was dead.

    But the fire is not dead. Only
the hearth is changed. Some think
that, the world will never die while
the Celt is alive.

        and if your children don't-
carry on your torch — writing, science,
art, or even shirting — in a hundred
years time I'll get up out of my
grave and wallop them — for the
world is really worth having; of life;

addendum.
2 Claremont.
99 Darst. Rd.
Kings Cross.
21.5.47,
your letter
just-come.
and P.S.
you made it
answer this
it is already
answered
my letter —

stay in your heart — Mary Gilmore

Copy of letter written in 1947 by
Mary Gilmore to Ruth Park

Shunryu Suzuki, the old man with one sad eye and one merry eye

Zen Center, Page St, San Francisco

Remains of convict settlement at Kingston, Norfolk Island. Nepean Island to left, Phillip Island at centre. Drawing by Cedric Emanuel

Quality Row, Norfolk Island. Officers' houses of the Second Settlement, now mostly restored. Drawing by Cedric Emanuel

Ruined house on Quality Row, still to be restored to former elegance.
Drawing by Cedric Emanuel

5

Sitting in a taxi, one freezing July day in 1959, I looked at my shoes and realised I had never seen them before. This seemed a mild curiosity, and I stared at them for some time before I became aware that I did not know who I was, where I was going, whence I had come.

So many years later, I still quake when I remember the horror of that moment. It was plain panic, I suppose, my mind as disabled as my body.

In such an experience, all the boundaries of one's little life are gone. One is standing on nothing in the middle of nothing.

Somewhere in my mind was a stock of general, but non-allied knowledge. The objects that covered my cold hands were gloves, the landscape that rushed past belonged to a city. If I looked in the rear-vision mirror I would see my face. After a long time I looked; the face, which belonged to a woman in her late thirties, was unfamiliar.

'You did say the Manly ferry wharf?' asked the driver.

'Yes.'

The words meant not a thing, but a faint stirring of good sense indicated that if this unknown ferry wharf were part of my normal life, the sight of it might make me remember. I shrank from telling the taxi driver of my predicament. In addition to my terror I experienced a hideous embarrassment; I thought the driver might take me for a madwoman and drive me to a police station. Somehow I knew about police stations, it seemed. I also knew about money and where it was kept, because as we drew up on busy Circular Quay, I looked into the totally unknown handbag to see if there was any.

How cold it was! I walked up and down the Quay shivering as well as sweating, not knowing what to do, recoiling from letting anyone know I was lost in my head as well as in time and place. Then I thought, 'If I asked to go to the Manly ferry, maybe I live at Manly.'

Somehow I got through the turnstile, for I did not know what coin to put in the slot, and boarded the enormous old steamer *South Steyne*. It seemed sturdy enough to go to sea. Was Manly so far away? I sat behind one of the funnels which bore a plate stating that the vessel had been built in a Clyde shipyard. For a fantastic moment I thought I must be in Scotland.

'But the people speak differently. How do I know that?'

I made up my mind that if I did not recall my identity when the ferry reached Manly I would ask where the police station was, and find help. The decision calmed me; I sat quietly until the vessel began to lift on the swell crossing the Heads, and all in a moment, I knew who I was, I knew where I had been.

I was on my way home from a hospital where I had left my husband in an intensive-care ward. He had had a severe coronary occlusion and was in danger of another. By the time I reached home the phone might ring to tell us he was dead.

In the meantime I had to get home quickly, because our young children, who had, in the emergency, been picked up from school by a kind neighbour, might be alone. Not in any circumstances did we leave the young ones alone in the house. In all situations the children were our common priority.

Never again did I experience amnesia. Still, that dreadful hour or so, the consequence of shock and stress, left a legacy. Part of my memory never returned. The years between 1957 and 1959 are largely a blank. Certainly I know what happened at that time; lost years are fairly easily reconstructed from photographs, other people's memories, and one's own journals if such are kept, and they are.

Memory, hold the door, I entreat the goddess of recollection who is also the mother of the Muses. But she moves not a finger. The shoes I had first noticed as unfamiliar, remained that way, and I never wore them again. I felt they belonged to someone else.

'How sick is Dad?' asked our children.

I remembered my own childhood, my mother being taken off to hospital, delirious, close to death, and no one telling me anything at all. It was the way of adults then; don't worry the children, poor little souls. I did not know even if my mother were alive, an ignorance that inflicted so deep a wound of anxiety and grief that my personality changed for ever.

So I told my children plainly what the matter was, what the prognosis was. And our older boy, thirteen and studious, asked, 'Is it the same thing that makes him grab his chest sometimes when we're kicking a football about, or fooling around on the beach? But he said it was a pulled muscle.'

Other details, other stories. That night, sleepless, waiting all the time for the phone to ring, I came to the conclusion that D'Arcy had had other heart attacks, slight tremors following on exertion, which he kept to himself, refusing to acknowledge that they meant anything significant.

Heart attacks amongst men are commonplace. By the hundred thousand wives lie awake, dumbfounded as much as frightened. How did this happen to him, they ask, so strong, so decisive, only forty, thirty-five, fifty years of age?

D'Arcy was never ill; often he worked half the night and never felt the strain. He could lift great weights; walk a hundred kilometres in wild country with a swag on his back. How did this man of the calm presence, my holdfast, stray into the precincts of death?

In my head all was clamour, dislocated thoughts, fears.

It was true that he had had a terrible, stressful two or three years. But I had had them too, and I was not ill.

We had had many stressful years that had not visibly affected him. Why now?

'I can't bear this,' I thought, panic-stricken because I had to bear it. I had scarcely survived the death of my father two years before, though he, careful as always of those he loved, had shown me there was nothing to grieve about. Still, I grieved; I was a slow healer.

In the cobwebby dark I see someone standing in the doorway, the nine year old. A prickly little article, full of worries and loving-kindness, he is awkwardly placed between the profoundly bonded twins and the teenagers, who carelessly lump him in with 'the bubs'.

'I just want to know, is Dad going to die?'

'He'll try not to. He won't want to leave us. And you know he's very determined.'

'Are you sure?'

'Pretty sure. Here, get under the blankets and warm me.'

In a moment he is asleep, whimpering and restless. I wonder if he believes, as children often do, that something he has done has caused this crisis. He is always in trouble; always repentant about something. But his presence in the bed calms me; I know that although I shall not want to survive if my husband dies, I will. I seem to be divided arbitrarily into two people, one a mindless assemblage of differing terrors, the other chill and quiet, surveying the transitoriness of human life. Had I really thought that love and care guarded anyone, anything?

We are rag and bone, rag and bone, nothing beyond, and regardless of the value of an individual life, to such we must be reduced at last.

It was a long time before I could acknowledge that. For many years my bold rule of life had been: 'He who climbs the cliff may perish on the cliff, so what?'

But it is easier to say 'so what?' to death than to a damaged life.

At that time I was a faithful Catholic, though in fact I was not one at all, as my mother had never had me baptised. But whatever I felt about religion, it was as nothing to D'Arcy's archaic but ardent devotion, an Irish peasant's leaning upon God. He found God everywhere, even in people whom I could see were duplicitous and envious.

'Ah, he's really a decent fella,' he used to say, seeing some divine nub in a human-shaped bundle of meanness, savage secrets, horrid fragilities, defending him against my sharper eye and unkinder spirit.

For him the divine force was defined as it was by Hermes Trimegistus: 'an infinite sphere whose centre is everywhere, whose circumference is nowhere.'

This is obvious in his work, even the slightest.

So, being a faithful Catholic, I prayed for his continued life, asking the assistance of my friends in the next, undefined world. I did not ask for his continued health; I had no hope of that.

My fear of recurrent amnesia dogged me; in my handbag I kept a reminder card: My name is . . . I live at . . . my children are . . . But would I even think to look into a handbag become unfamiliar and find such information?

252

I spent hours each day sitting beside my husband's bed, first in intensive care, then in a quiet room where he was the only occupant. He dozed a great deal.

And I tried to work out how our life had come to this, D'Arcy deadly ill, myself confused, hesitant, my vision of the way ahead obscured. Somehow we had lost the plot.

For a long time now I had been uneasy about our life, its rush and fret, its chasing after deadlines, the pressing responsibilities of the children as they grew older. But I had thought only that it was fatiguing, not that it was fatal.

Nevertheless, I had longed to change it. I saw our youth vanishing with little to show for it.

'Aw, come on, Tiger, we have five good healthy children. And this nice house. What more do you want?'

'Life for ourselves, leisure to think. Study. Travel.'

But he couldn't see it. Writing was his mainspring. Time spent at the typewriter was time spent doing exactly what he was born for. But I was born for many other things.

Still, he tried to understand.

'The film will make everything easier for us,' he said confidently, and if things had gone as they should have gone, this hope would have been realised.

If the film company had ever paid for the property. Within six months of the release of *The Shiralee* it became obvious that Ealing Films had no intention of doing so. Letters, cables, representations by a London solicitor were ignored. Ealing was going to make the writer sue for his money. We, as well as they, were aware that no individual who sues a powerful film company is going to get far before he runs out of funds for legal costs.

The original film of *The Shiralee*, starring Peter Finch, is still showing all over the world. All D'Arcy ever received was £1,100 sterling, which quickly went in solicitor's fees. His publishers, who had skimmed off 20 per cent of the sale, saw the hopelessness of the situation and abandoned him.

'We have decided to make no further claim on proceeds,' they wrote. This translates: 'Don't count on us for any help, either consultative or financial.'

After many months of struggle it was plain that Ealing Films were in an unassailable position, and without honour they sat upon it. It was a killing blow to D'Arcy, who had characteristically trusted everyone connected with the sale of the property.

'I shall have to give up,' he admitted at last, 'and it's bitter, I can tell you. Well, they'll get no luck for it.'

Still Ealing did. They made a fortune. At the company's eventual demise they made another one by selling all the properties, including those like *The Shiralee*, whose contracts had become void by default of payment.

The lesson from this piece of highway robbery is one for all writers. Have the best agent possible; never let the publisher negotiate a film contract. Do not trust a solicitor's advice on the contract. Most solicitors know little about copyright and its intricacies. Never sell all audial or visual rights outright. Always include a clause that prohibits sequels, spinoffs and use of characters in other works or contexts. If possible get an upfront payment, as much as possible, and run for your life.

*

As far as I knew, D'Arcy had put the bitter blow of *The Shiralee* film debacle behind him. He did not refer to it again, and set to work to finish *Call Me When the Cross Turns Over*, the final title of what had hitherto been known as the Barbie Casabon Story. Once again this novel was a great success, and was published by William Morrow in the United States as *Woman of the Country* in 1959. Morrow's were delightful people, already publishing several Australian writers. Like all American publishers they wrote warm and charming letters, and I was able to read these to D'Arcy in the hospital. They stimulated him greatly, for he had been fretting that he could not even think creatively.

'It's as if I'm a fountain, and the water has died down to a trickle.'

'It'll come back. Don't you worry.'

It was fortunate, I know, that not for some weeks were we to learn that Angus & Robertson, in London, and William Morrow had between them botched the copyright registration of this new novel, and it was now in the public domain.

When he returned from hospital, D'Arcy spoke to us as a family group. The doctor had been frank about the strong probability of his having another coronary, which his damaged heart could not survive. He had been franker with me.

'Any time, any time,' he said.

But D'Arcy felt reasonably well, and his optimism had returned.

'I'll do all the sensible things,' he said. 'Keep to a fat-free diet, have regular long walks, try to keep away from stress. But I don't want to be an invalid, or be treated like one. I'm going to keep on writing, because that's what I am, a writer. I'd rather die at the typewriter than anywhere else. Understand?'

One thing he did not give up was smoking. He was warned by his doctor and the specialist, though this was before general alarm at the connection between smoking and vascular disease was publicised. He said he couldn't believe that smoking could really affect the heart.

But I think he was truly addicted. He was not a man who would wilfully throw away family, career and the exercise of his talent just for the sake of tobacco. The truth was that he could not give up smoking. There are some like that, I know.

Life resumed, but now there was a subtext. It is nothing unusual; millions experience it, the subtext of dread that underlies the life of those who live with a doomed person. (And whatever their affliction, how can it compare with that of the parent of a doomed child?)

My husband had almost eight more years to live, but as far as I knew he had three days or five weeks. Ground had gone from under my feet; insupportable anxiety consumed my days and nights. It was as though my quotidian life was smothered, extinguished by a great dark wing. In shame and confusion I told myself that many had lived through this pain and handled it well. But that made my own condition not one whit better.

Now I awakened with a start twenty times a night instead of eight or nine, and every time I awoke I put my hand on D'Arcy to see if he were still breathing. Then one night out of the darkness he whispered, 'Just cut it out. I know why you're doing it, and it's no good for you, or me either.'

Helpless rage at him, at myself, at the entire situation made me say, 'Oh, go to hell!'

'That's the stuff,' he said, chuckling, and gave me a hug.

He had, it seems, come to terms with his fate during his six weeks in hospital. No doubt he had felt fear, panic even, amazement that it had happened to him, as we all feel when sudden illness strikes, anxiety for me and the children . . . Who knows? He never spoke of what must have been many days of cogitation, reflection, and prayer. How much I would have appreciated hearing of the stages of his reasoning, his reconciliation with the knowledge of death. It might have helped me. But I was never told.

Yet I know from his completely natural, tranquil and even joyful demeanour that some reconciliation had taken place. To have his life cut short, maybe even at less than forty years of age, was no big deal. Not for many years was I to learn that the words 'nothing special' applied to almost anything in human experience, was a treasured Zen saying, so subtle, so life-encompassing that books were written about it.

I can only conclude that this awareness of an enormous truth was either D'Arcy's by birthright, or his Christian beliefs and practice had led him to it. It was not so with myself. For years I made my way through brambles and briars and never came out into any clear space.

*

In this story little is said about our children. Yet they were the unarguable priority of both our lives. As the children and I grew older together, they became my dear friends rather than offspring, but while they were young I was as fierce as a bitch with a litter.

Once I wrote that in an article, but the editor recoiled, saying, 'We can't have that.' As he had a bale of clichés ready to hand, he changed it to 'as fierce as a tigress'. But I haven't seen a tigress with cubs, and I have seen a bitch with a litter. And I recall a tiny bitch I once had, an angel in poodle form, who, knowing that her puppies were too young to be picked up, had no other defence but to gather them all under her chin and look up beseechingly with watering eyes.

But I was fierce, another kind of bitch altogether, and, although a committed pacifist and one who tried sincerely to love her neighbour, would have killed anyone who laid a hand on my children.

But children are people, and people are conundrums who never want strangers to know the answer. Children hate being dug up to have their roots examined, and I have never done that, even in my head. When I was young, children had their privacy violated almost by tradition. Where have you been? Why did you do that? Why don't you think this? Teachers, parents, aunts, neighbours, all felt they could tramp around at will in that flighty, extravagant landscape where children keep their daydreams and yearnings. The little ones, their sensitivities 'more tender than are the horns of cockled snails', have those sensitivities so often bruised and defiled.

'About time that youngster learned what life is all about!' the adults used to say. And still say.

So I don't write about our children. Suffice it to say that they all grew up level-headed, healthy and largely gifted. They turned out to be a librarian, a physicist, two book illustrators, and a musician who also works in the healing profession.

But at the close of the 1950s they were children, confused and frightened because their father had been ill.

One day he said, 'The kids bother me. Every time I look up there are blue eyes taking surreptitious peeps at me as if I'm going to drop dead or blow up.'

'Well, they worry about you.'

'Tell them not to.'

'I think you should do that.'

'Oh, God, I can't. You do it.'

From then on, it seemed to me, though nothing was said, he withdrew a little from the children, distancing himself. Did he have the feeling that they loved him too much, would be irreparably damaged when he died? That if he withdrew a little they wouldn't miss him so much? I don't know. It was the kind of Irish way of looking at things that had prompted his father, though with deep concern fortunately obvious to the boy, to jeer at his writing ambitions, because he knew that there was no chance of a superior education for his son.

But of course it was far too late for D'Arcy to stop his children loving him.

*

'Writing is a peaceful business, I fancy,' remarked the doctor.

'A blessing Mr Niland isn't doing anything worrisome and stressful, like law or medicine,' he said in his kindly way.

I nodded civilly, thinking of the twelve-centimetre-high file relating to *Call Me When the Cross Turns Over*, its inexcusably bungled copyright and the solicitors' letters to the three film companies that had seized upon it as an accessible property.

Few things aggravate a writer more than the ivory-tower legend, except perhaps the common idea that you peck away at the word processor for a week or so and a bestselling novel shoots out the top. But there's no use in explanations that the whole business is one of sweaty labour, endless rewriting, as day by day the strangers in your head reveal level after level of themselves. And they—your characters—*are* strangers, even if you have created them yourself. You have some idea of what they are going to do, but their motivation shows itself of its own accord. This is what makes a memorable character, 'a real person', as readers often say—motivation deeply and acutely observed by the writer. Which sometimes takes months, or even years, of intense concentration.

The world is full of books in which the characters simply *say* and *do*. There are certainly legitimate genres in which this is sufficient. But in real and lasting writing the character *is*.

I was terrified of telling D'Arcy that there was every chance of the film, and indeed every other proprietorial right in his new novel going off to rapacious strangers. In his absence I had done what I could—put the book in the hands of the London agency, Curtis Brown Ltd, at that time not the oldest literary and dramatic agency in Great Britain but certainly the most ferocious. They had engaged a solicitor to act on the writer's behalf.

Of the three film companies that had seized upon the unguarded movie rights, one, inconsiderable and probably poorly funded, quickly dropped out. The second, Twentieth-Century Fox, said at once that they appreciated the extreme injustice of the situation, and were prepared to buy at normal rates as soon as the copyright was properly established. The third, the British company, I shall call Parachute, said they were going ahead with production regardless. Parachute were a fine company. They had produced several superb, indeed classic, films. Under other circumstances their interest would have been most acceptable.

This was the confused and troubling situation I had to present to a man just recovered from a near-fatal heart attack. On my own authority I could go no further.

Remembering his frustrated fury at the behaviour of Ealing Films, I waited for him to drop down dead. But he lit a cigarette and said calmly, 'What else can you expect from film companies?'

This costly and endlessly involved dispute went on for nearly three years. It was impossible to allow it to dominate our lives. D'Arcy's novel, *The Big Smoke*, which had won another literary prize while he was still in hospital, was published by Angus & Robertson, neither party tactlessly reminding the other that the book had previously been rejected out of hand. *The Big Smoke* did very well in the States, despite the ingenuous astonishment of some reviewers that there were any large cities Down Under. This novel was optioned for film several times, though I imagine that if a movie had been made the location would have been shifted to Pittsburgh or Chicago.

Most established writers with a track record of good or even moderately selling books derive some income from film options, the majority of which do not result in films. As a beginner, I had a romantic idea of story scouts, swivelling eager noses, reading every new book, rushing to the producers to argue the property's desirability. When, however, I began to do treatments and plot breakdowns for a film company, I realised that most properties are bought simply to prevent any other company getting them. For a fleabite, possibly also claimable as a bad debt, the film company then has that property tied up for a year or two, or until others have lost interest. Most film companies have incredible morgues of purchased but unmade cinematic material.

My novel, *Serpent's Delight* (marketed as *The Good Looking Women* in Australia), was a Catholic Book Club Choice in America, and attracted five film options in ten years, helping to keep our family going during the difficult and stressful decade of the 1960s. During those bad years, when I had so little time all I could write were a few children's books—by no means easier but so much shorter—and my ABC scripts, everything seemed to go wrong, beginning with the trouble over *The Cross*.

For Parachute were adamant. The *Cross* file shows many civil and well-reasoned letters from both the writer of the novel and the solicitor his agent had retained. Answers are either abrupt and rude or do not appear at all.

Suddenly, representatives of Parachute appeared in Sydney on a reconnaissance trip. Horrified, D'Arcy came out of his workroom and told me, 'You're not going to believe this. Those two bastards actually expect me to help them find good locations. The man who just phoned said he wants to pick my brains. Would you believe such brazen cheek?'

'Ignore them,' I urged, not liking the look of him, short-breathed and pallid.

'No fear I won't. I'm going in to front them.'

'Please, please, think again. You're not really fit enough for a blazing row.'

'Back off, Tiger.'

No argument on my part prevailed. I was permitted to go with him, but only to North Sydney, where it was his custom to leave the car, rather than stravage around trying to find a parking station on the metropolitan side of the Harbour Bridge.

'You stay here. Don't worry. Aside from breaking both their noses, I shall be as quiet as a lamb.'

'Oh, God, don't.'

But he had jumped on a bus and was gone. I prowled around the old green Holden, knowing a brutal argument could be fatal for him. Let him break their noses, dear God, I implored, but don't let him have another coronary.

The quietest of men, D'Arcy rarely lost his temper. He was, however, immensely strong. I once saw him take by the nose a noted bisexual writer, much heavier and taller than himself, who had been regaling a dinner party with scurrilous remarks about Beatrice Davis. Without a word he led that clown down three flights of stairs, out into the street, and put him into a taxi. He then returned without comment and sat down to finish his dinner.

After I had spent two wretched, terrified hours, he turned up looking grim.

'What happened, what happened?'

'Later.'

He started the car and my head almost snapped off. That ride was more like a television police chase than anything I have seen in real life. We came out of North Sydney like an enraged wasp, narrowly missing several cars and a bus, side swiping so closely at parked vehicles that we must have blown the dust off their duco. Never had I so longed to see a police car on the Holden's tail. Twice my forehead hit the windscreen—it was before the days of seatbelts—and my chin came a bruising crack on the glovebox.

'You're going to kill us both!'

No answer. I had never seen my husband in a rage so blind, so heedless, and never did again. If I had had the chance I might have looked at his knuckles to see if they were skinned, thus giving some clue to the fate of the Parachute representatives, but I had no chance. Down the Spit Hill like a drag-race contestant, across the bridge, up the winding road on the northern side, dangerous at the best of times, into Seaforth, the car's tyres squealing.

'Please stop and let me out! The kids have to keep at least one parent!'

He overshot the turn into Woodland Street where we lived, swore, and braked at the lights at Condamine Street. I whisked open the door and shot out across the road, heedless of honking horns and shouts of indignation. At that stage I didn't care if he did kill himself. All I wanted was to get home alive.

Halfway down Woodland Street the Holden gently drew up beside me.

'Get in, you melodramatic rat.'

'You can talk about melodrama!'

'Ah, but *I* have reason.'

The tidal wave of passion seemed to have passed, for he was grinning.

Just the same, he had another heart attack that night, not a coronary, what the doctor called a cardiac episode, but enough to put him into hospital for a few days.

'I can't stand much more of this,' I thought late at night, sitting up writing *Muddleheaded Wombats*, waiting for someone to call from the hospital. 'I'm going to go to pieces.'

By the same token I knew I *would* stand it until the strain of apprehension and incessant vigilance terminated in the only way it could, with my husband setting out for the Styx. And at the very thought of that I stopped being young, often seeing my mother looking out of my face, with the expression she had had as she watched Mera dwindle, grow silent, and turn away from life.

I never had the full story of D'Arcy Niland's meeting with the men representing the company that had grabbed his novel. I knew they were patronising in the extreme, implying that he should be gratified and flattered that a famous film company thought his work worth stealing.

'Only they didn't say stealing, of course, they said using, developing, *promoting*. Promoting, mind you. One of them, the podgy one, even said that if I stopped kicking up a fuss Parachute might even throw me a few thousand quid.'

'A bone to keep the dog quiet?'

'They were so dumb, so full of themselves, I don't think they even knew they were insulting me. That's when I got so mad.'

'You didn't . . . Not noses? Teeth?'

'Of course not. Violence is foreign to me, as you know. No, I just picked up the podgy one in the Italian suit, and deposited him on top of the bar, and wouldn't let him get down. Nothing really.'

'And then?'

'Well, the bar was full, and the patrons pretty full too. They were most helpful. So he slithered around a bit, smashing glasses, the barman yelling. *You* know. I shook hands with the other bloke, though. He was the scriptwriter, a fairly decent fellow. He felt bad about doing down another writer, I think. And then I left.'

'A pleasant afternoon, in fact.'

But a meeting which provoked the fury demonstrated by that hazardous drive had not been pleasant or even tolerable. For a long time he looked grey and wrung-out, so that I cursed films and everyone connected with them.

Cables must have flown out of Sydney, because a day or so afterwards Parachute cabled an offer of £5,000 for purchase of film rights.

'No,' ruled the post office at Balgowlah, 'you cannot send a cable saying "Sod you."'

God help me, I almost wished he had taken the offer, contemptible as it was. I wanted the fight to be over, the risks to his health minimised, our family life closer and warmer, himself to be free sometimes to help with the tetchy problems of the children, two of whom were adolescent and the other three itching to be adolescent. Overworked, unable to sleep more than three or four hours, and never at a stretch, it was no marvel that I dreamed of mountains and reedy lakes, beautiful enough, except that the mountains were to fall off and the lakes to drown in. I was no longer a warrior woman, indeed had I ever been one? I was a person worn to shreds.

'I'm tired,' I said. 'I'm anxious. I'm frightened.'

'Well, you needn't be,' he said. 'We'll get Parachute in the end, you'll see.'

'Don't dodge the issue, damn it. Why can't I talk about the way I feel?'

'Because I'm scared. I need you calm and matter-of-fact. Otherwise I'm afraid I might not be able to hang on.'

I saw then, or thought I saw, that his serenity and good humour might not be as wellfounded as it looked. Certainly the encounter with the men from Parachute had stressed him beyond bearing. But I should not have gone away determined to keep my torment to myself, to endure silently. Every person is owed his own sorrow, and the expression of it, too.

*

After all the problems centred on *Call Me When the Cross Turns Over* the dènouement of the affair came suddenly and quietly. Curtis Brown Ltd and the American publisher, William Morrow, between them contrived to have the copyright correctly registered and backdated. Parachute was caught on the simple issue of literary plagiarism, for their script was written after registration.

They settled out of court, the damages not great, but sufficient to discharge the legal and other debts incurred in this affair, with a reasonable sum remaining.

The British Society of Authors were valuable consultants in this dispute, not the first of this kind brought to their notice. Subsequently they and their United States counterpart more vigorously pursued the issue of *inherent copyright*, which is that a literary work does not require to be legally registered, as copyright inalienably resides in the work itself. Nevertheless, it would be a reckless writer or publisher who did not register correct copyright. This registration, or patent, creates definitude. It establishes the existence of the work at a specific date, and the name of the person claiming authorship.

Copyright law, and the International Copyright Convention not withstanding, there are still many countries, even signatories to the Convention, which permit their own entrepreneurs to ignore the copyright of foreign authors, publish books without permission or acknowledgement, exploit subsidiary rights, and pay nothing. There is, effectively, no redress for the writer.

However, no injustice to writers in the field of copyright equals the ongoing, iniquitous law of public domain which decrees that copyright becomes void fifty years after the author's death. When this happens the work is up for grabs by anyone and for any purpose. The time of lapse differs according to the country; in the United States it is very much briefer.

Here we have the extraordinary situation of specific and personally created material, thus *sui generis*, never to be exactly replicated, thrown to the commercial world fifty years after the death of the creator, without whom it would not have existed at all. This happens to nothing else on earth except artistic creations. From real estate down to the most trifling personal bibelot, what is legally owned is owned. It remains the inalienable possession of the owner, and through him, his heirs or assigns.

The egregious argument is that Art (beware when the capital letter enters discussions of this nature) belongs to humankind, and that allowing a writer's family to enjoy any fruits of his work for as long as fifty years is, if anything, a concession. This I shall believe when I read that one of the publishers standing on the edge of the grave of some famous writer, waiting for the starting pistol's report, publishes his public-domain edition for free, just as a donation to humankind.

'See this money left over? We'll take an overseas trip with it. England, Ireland, Rome. You know you've always longed to travel. Don't argue. Shut up. That's it.'

I went to our family doctor, a kind, commonsensible man, to ask if this would mean increased risk.

'Yes, but there's always risk. Your husband's decision must be, does he want the risk here or there?'

269

6

'You're sure, now?' I asked. 'You wouldn't rather go to Memphis in the States to do that research on Les Darcy you've always wanted to do?'

I knew he was torn between Ireland, which he hankered to see, and Tennessee. Every writer has something which he wishes to write most of all, and for D'Arcy Niland it was the biography of one of Australia's heroes—the young boxer whose brief but blazingly successful life ended in Memphis in 1917. His was a character of astonishing integrity, yet his main interest for me as a closet historian was that he had been the centre of a violent political upheaval, crucial to the future of his country as a nation.

All his professional life D'Arcy Niland had collected material about this boy, interviewing his friends, trainers, supporters and enemies. But no one had ever done the American research. The last few months of Darcy's life were a half-glimpsed landscape, obscured by legends, suspicions and fantastic speculations.

'No, I'll have to relinquish that dream. We can't afford to do both, so Ireland it is.'

'But Rome first, and then London, for you to meet the Curtis Brown boys, and me to visit Michael Joseph's, in Bloomsbury.'

'And me to spend absolutely *days* in the Victoria and Albert Museum,' said Anne, who, besides being a librarian-ship student, was something of an antiquarian.

Unlike our previous ill-fated departure for England, when my every doomsaying instinct had indicated that we were doing the wrong thing, this second and grander venture was organised with ease. The twins agreed to spend two terms at a Blue Mountains boarding school; Anne was to come with us; and my mother and sister with the latter's two children, to cross the Tasman to look after the boys and the assorted dogs, cats and other household pensioners.

Leaving the little girls was a fearful wrench. Their father's face was as woebegone as theirs. Driving home-wards he muttered, 'What made us think that going to Europe would be worth this?'

Flying westward, though they say you get badly jetlagged that way, is very satisfying. There's the mighty curve of the planet, plain as a pikestaff in front of you. The faster you fly the more steadily does the sun appear to sit on the horizon; it is sunset for ever. But the time comes when your aircraft descends for fuel at Singapore or Bangkok or somewhere, and the night immediately rushes in like an occupying army, losing you that lasting day.

Night flights are uneasy and hallucinatory, especially when the lights are turned out and the curtains drawn between you and the service areas. The engines speed up and the plane begins a new, urgent vibration. They're in a hurry to get to Rome. We all are, except my husband, who vacated his seat an hour ago and hasn't returned.

'He's sick,' I think. 'He's collapsed in the toilet and they can't get the door open!'

But when I go aft to investigate, there he is sitting on the floor with two stewards, playing two-up.

'This is Dilip,' he says, 'and this is Krishna.'

'Come in, spinner!' adds Krishna.

No, he doesn't want to get to Rome in a hurry; he's having a great time where he is. And fortunately this is how the entire five months go, without illness, without anxiety, but with unexpected benefits.

But Rome was the city I wanted to see above all. Perhaps it was my love of Latin that had persuaded me to read Roman history so intensively I felt I had lived there. I wanted to see everything, experience things that could only happen in Rome.

Peripeteia is a word one might hear but twice in a lifetime. Nevertheless it is a good and useful word which means a sudden change of fortune, not only without warning, but of a type beyond conjecture. It is mostly applied to events such as St Paul's conversion on the road to Damascus, because of the word's root being *fall*.

All the same, in a fall, even Paul's crash from his horse, there is a static moment between losing balance and hitting the ground. One has time to realise: 'I'm falling!'

With me, and with John Milton and Martin Luther, who had the same experience in the same place, there was none of that. My peripeteia occurred in St Peter's Basilica, in Rome, and in the twinkling of an eye. I have no explanation. I entered those imperial portals an uncommonly devout Catholic, full of solemn bliss that, in spite of all obstacles, I had got there at last. Within five minutes something had happened. Between one split second and the next, without any shift in consciousness, I knew I was a Catholic no longer.

It seemed best to go outside to think about it, so I did. Past Bernini's preposterous marble monsters, the Swiss Guards with their bad-boy faces and Michaelangelo bloomers, and into the colonnade. The sky was like the Queensland sky, immaculate and as deep as forever. Swifts or swallows, small scissor-tailed birds, flicked like bats into the crannies of St Peter's stupendous façade. Like dark moss they clung to curly beards, scrolled gowns, croziers and palms and open martyred mouths.

I knew something significant had happened. Yet my mind was a space seemingly filled with nothing. The velocity of thought was so great there was total stillness. I was aware, however, that I was an observer, and content with that.

I sat in the sunshine beside a seminarian, a large potato-faced boy in soutane and black bedpan hat. In rapture he gazed at St Peter's, eyes full of tears, rumbling something in what was possibly High Dutch. His face, if not the words, was fully translatable: How marvellous that God has allowed me to come and see this wonder for myself!

273

His artless joy delighted me; his was the figure of a million, million pilgrims. It was easy to imagine a phantom staff, stout wallet, and a band of cockleshells on his foolish hat. I entered fully into his awe, his happy gratitude, and was conscious that what he felt and what I felt were parallels, and would continue as parallels. We came from the same place and would go on through life to the same place.

'I suppose you feel very upset and guilty,' said my husband when I told him later.

'Not a bit of it,' and I tried to explain that I hadn't given Catholicism away, it had given me away, I didn't know why. But there seemed no reason why I should be sad about it.

'I don't think we should tell Anne,' he said soberly, as if I'd spent the afternoon gallivanting with a lover, and although he'd forgiven me, the children mustn't know.

However, my feeling of total and benevolent freedom surprised me. Always I had taken for granted that almost unbearable guilt accompanied loss of faith. Certainly sometimes it must. Too many times have I been the recipient of confidences from lapsed Catholics, laicised priests, and nuns who have fled convents. She's a listener, they think, and off they go, mostly tedious tales of remorse and ruination, so that one wants hard-heartedly to cry with Meister Eckhardt: 'For the love of God do not yelp about Him!'

Nevertheless I am profoundly grateful I have a Catholic background. Not being a baptised Christian I unwittingly thieved it, but that makes me all the luckier. Catholicism introduced me to literature, fine art and a continuous range of historical drama that no other human establishment is venerable enough to give. What a mirror of humankind it is! Brave, corrupt, brilliant, opinionated, staggering along on basic instabilities, human indeed.

It is true that in later years I did get baptised. My mother was extremely ill and, wanting to right what she now viewed as a wrong, asked me if I would undergo the ceremony. I entered into this with all wholeheartedness; I think no one can afford to lose the chance of gaining grace, no matter whence it comes. Eunice Gardner, the pianist, was my godmother and Frank Sheed, the famous Catholic apologist, my godfather. I told him that the baptism probably wouldn't take.

'Not for you to say,' he said. 'But at least it will save me worrying about you.'

Frank was a genial, gregarious, amusing man, but every now and then one had a disturbing feeling. Whoo! We've got something pretty saintly here, I'd better watch my step.

His wife, Maisie Ward, *was* a saint, an adorable woman. An aristocratic English lady of refined education, she could not say 'to hell with it' without a perceptible pause before and after 'hell' as though the word was in quotation marks. I loved her. Her charity was boundless; she poured out her life's energy in the service of others, and when a problem came her way she went after it like a terrier until it was solved.

My christening, archaic and solemn, was followed by unexpected happenings, momentous or not according to one's frame of mind. First, beloved Maisie died. Frank sent me a memorable cable: 'Joy in heaven. Maisie went home today.'

Our good friend in the Order which had arranged for my baptism had a heart attack, and two of his colleagues fled, one to marry and the other, a conservative scapular-wearing Irishman, to become one of those unsettling Californian priests who consecrate cake or Sao biscuits and conduct the Mass in mime with groups of amateur actors in wigs and greasepaint. That also is a peripeteia of a sort, I expect.

But that was in the future, and we were still in Rome. Because of D'Arcy's friendship with many priests we were taken to interesting places not open to the public. These men, lonely perhaps for ordinary male conversation, sought him out, never the reverse. This was not devotional or reverential friendship, my husband blanching at the thought of calling one of our black-socked visitors Father Joe. It was Joe or nothing. All enjoyed arguing about sport, literature and politics. Still, D'Arcy sometimes shook his head ruefully over the pitiful ignorance of the world that he found in these good men.

'They go into the seminary too early,' he said. 'Tucked away in a pod. I'd like to see old Bob with a swag up, on the road out of Marree. Six months with empty pockets and no hope of a regular job would make his soul grow. And poor woeful Damien, full of devout fairy floss! But crikey, what could anyone do with Damien?'

Nevertheless, our hospitality had been repaid with fifteen or twenty letters of introduction to Rome-based members of their Orders.

The American Capuchins led us to archeologists, haunters of subterranea, who grumpily led us around floodlit fragments of old, old Rome, up bits of rutted streets, into a fallen-in grog shop, around the mosaic floor of a bathhouse. There is a pensive familiarity about these cities beneath cities. Inevitably one ponders: is this how my city will be one day, two thousand years away from the blue sky? But, though grumpy, these dedicated archeologists were kind. I was allowed to paddle in the Cloaca Maxima and when I wished to be shut into the deaf-and-dumb cell in the Mamertine Prison to see how St Paul or the notorious Jewish patriot, Simon Son of the Star, felt before they were led out to be beheaded, our lavishly whiskered guide obligingly clanged the iron door on me.

One Irish Augustinian was directed to be our guide for a week; a jolly jabberer he was, ardent about food. I see him sitting eternally in a trattoria, poking cherries into his mouth with one hand while ten or twelve workmen file past, each kneeling reverently and kissing his other hand. It is this sort of thing that unnerves stern types like Presbyterians when they visit Rome. But one mustn't take it seriously. Such little courtesies are traditional and graceful; no race could be more sophisticated and streetwise about their religion than the Italians. Or, if it comes to that, more sincere.

This Irishman did his best to arrange for us to visit the famous stigmatic, Padre Pio, but the trip fell through.

'Ah, never fret,' he comforted. 'Who's to know if it isn't a lot of holy blather anyway? What about seeing *Il Babbo* instead?'

It was endearing how the ordinary populace of Rome referred to the Pope in familiar ways, not only *Babbo* (Daddy) but SS (Suo Santissimo) and plain Giovanni. But from the vast crowd of pilgrims that jammed the concourse in front of St Peter's every time John XXIII appeared at his balcony, there rose such a fantastic outpouring of respect and love I felt he should stagger before it.

We did have a semi-private audience with the Pope, along with hundreds of other people, and I'm glad I did. I much approved of the impatient way he nipped out of his carrying chair, hitched up his petticoats and trotted up the steps. He was a brisk, affectionate, wise old Italian *Babbo* and I would have liked to give him a hug. He looked ill, and probably was—very sallow, dark stains about his eyes.

We were sitting in the front row of seats—our Augustinian must have had some clout—and as the Pope passed on his way out, he gave us a grin, and raised his hand in blessing. As he lifted his hand, light from the high windows shot directly through the prodigious stone in his ring, in a ray so richly golden I gasped. I thought, 'That's a topaz in that ring, an enormous one.'

But everyone tells me the Papal ring is amethyst. However, that's how I saw it.

Eventually we reached Ireland.

'And would you be carrying any tinned salmon, sir?'

All three of us looked narrowly at the Customs Officer. Was this an Irish legpull? He sighed.

'For the love of God *why* would people like yerselves be carrying tinned salmon? But it's a question they make us ask.'

'Who?'

'Them.'

'Ah, them.' We were on familiar ground. The Establishment, bureaucracy, the faceless ones. Australia jumped with people fulminating against Them. We nodded sympathetically, shook our heads with the correct ruefulness. Them! The injustices, the idiocies we good ordinary people had to endure from Them!

'I can see from your name you're one of us, sir. Come home at last, then?'

'God willing.'

So we passed out into early morning Dublin, a mist rising from the River Liffey and soiled swans sailing on its indolent brown stream.

Our time in London had been frenetic beyond imagining. I felt as if I had spent a fortnight in a cake-mixer, so frequent had been the hospitality, so many the enthusiastic offers of future work. But everyone who offered, added, 'You're crazy not to live right here, on the spot. Australia is so far away.'

'But it isn't,' I'd say. 'Only twenty-four hours by air. And the airmail takes a couple of days at most. And there are telephones . . .'

'Oh, I don't know,' they'd reply. 'It just seems on the edge of nowhere. It's so *out there*.'

And indeed English people do commonly speak of travelling *out* to Australasia, though you never hear an Australasian say he's going *in* to the United Kingdom. I presume this curious anomaly is a leftover from the days of 'outward bound' sailing ships, or when London was the centre of an empire. Many people speak this way still, though no place in the world is now very far from any other place, and Australians living in Australia have little trouble getting work at long range from Europe.

We had met film directors and producers, sat in on the sets of films then being shot, and passed within the orbits of famous actors and actresses, some of whom mechanically glittered at every chance-met stranger, but others who were unpretentious craftspeople. These level-headed ones were supported in their levelheadedness by the admirable attitude of Londoners, whom I never saw flock around and gape. I daresay they did peek at much loved stars, but secretly. Once my literary agent and I lunched in a hole-in-the-wall restaurant in Soho (then not so sleazy as it is now). She said casually, 'Have you met Roger Moore yet?'

Mr Moore and Harry Corbett were chatting away at a nearby table, though one would never have guessed it from the demeanour of waiters or other patrons. When my agent caught Mr Moore's eye, she invited him and Harry Corbett to finish their coffee at our table. They were pleasant men, both amateur painters, who had visited an art exhibition that day.

Harry Corbett was a largish goodlooking man, very different from the persecuted romantic Harold of *Steptoe and Son*. He preferred stage work, and said in his unaccented voice that he would never do another *Steptoe* if he could help it.

In real life Roger Moore did not have the watercolour good looks he had on the screen. Film must have flattened out or made pallid the strongly masculine character of this man's handsomeness. His colouring was striking, his eyes the richest blue, his hair the blond of good whisky. He moved with flexible grace.

'Bloody fellow sounds as if he has everything,' grumbled my husband as I described him.

'And he's friendly and good mannered as well.'

'Not losing his hair at all?'

'Thick and shiny.'

'Well, anyway, Sean's losing *his* hair.'

But Sean Connery didn't care. He wouldn't wear a toupee except under pressure; he went out without it and didn't mind at all if his fans saw his bald patch.

He seemed to me very much his own man, disregarding others' opinions of him or his acting abilities. Physically he was—and is—impressive to a degree, tall, athletic, like an idealised portrait of an aristocratic Highlander. In fact, he came from a Lowland working-class background, and brought with him all its hard humour and hardheadedness.

He told me casually, 'I reckon I have about five more years' work in my face.'

As we know, Connery has gone on to far better film work than he ever did in his youth. However, this random remark illustrates how little he thought of his striking good looks except as a business asset.

He was funny, too, in the dry Scots manner. Speaking of being paid off from the Navy and given a civilian suit too long in the arms, too short in the legs, tight here and baggy there, he concluded his story, 'After I sold this suit to my father . . .'

At that time he was being considered for the role of Fascinatin' in the Twentieth-Century Fox version of

281

Call Me When the Cross Turns Over. In spite of his looks, his fame, his reasonable, if not outstanding, abilities, I didn't find him fascinating at all. In my experience fascinating men are mostly homely, if not downright ugly, and history supports me. Such men work on their personalities; some become charming, others well nigh irresistible. Handsome men don't bother. I don't say this was true of Sean Connery, but I was not sorry when through contractual and loan difficulties he dropped from the prospective cast.

Our hotel in Dublin is small and Jane Austen-ish, once the town house of a member of the Quality. Foursquare, Georgian, built of raspberry brick, it has half-moon fanlights and a wrought-iron fence with brackets for holding torches, and tall extinguishers where the linkboys doused them.

The hotel looks straight across at the Dail, the Parliament, which is housed in a wing of the magnificent palace of the Earls of Kildare.

What a city this is, still half possessed by the ghost of England's eighteenth-century glory, cynical, elegant, superbly tasteful. Yet the dead leaves blow up and down the streets and pile against exquisite Georgian doors; here and there the cold wind pounces through broken glass in the fanlights. The great pillars of the Courts, the Customhouse and Trinity College are velvet black with soot. The Liffey loiters beneath a cargo of slow-moving rubbish.

'Oh, God, I love it,' says D'Arcy, and for a moment the grey fades from his face. For he's had two or three little turns—griping pains in the chest and jaw, enough to remind him that he must go more slowly. He enjoyed the joyful turmoil of London, meeting all those stunning people, though he didn't know the names of half of them. One day, I recall, he came back to the hotel full of the great conversation he'd had with a little pink bloke called Dickie, who later turned out to be Richard Attenborough.

'Oh, God, I love it,' he says, looking out the window at a baker's boy on a bike. There's a shabby little shrine to Our Lady stuck in a corner of the wall, and the boy is having a feast of trouble balancing his tray of cakes in one hand and snatching off his white cap with the other. But he even manages to make the sign of the Cross as well.

While Anne and I explore, D'Arcy rests. When we return we find him sitting up like Jacky in an armchair in the parlour, every sign of loving attention about him, a cup of tea at his elbow, an old lady's shawl over his knees, and every religious paper in the business laid ready to his hand.

'I'm the king of the castle,' he says complacently. 'All I had to do was to tell the mistress we'd seen His Holiness so close I could have cracked him one with a stick. They come in every three minutes and ask me to tell them all over again.'

A married couple named Dulihanty were the master and mistress of the little hotel. They had an ongoing legpull that Mrs Dulihanty had gone after the master like a ferret after a rabbit. Mr Dulihanty expressed it this way: 'She was following me everywhere and tormenting the soul from me, so I married her just to get rid of her.'

They were assisted by innumerable aunts and nephews whose yells of hilarity could be heard from the service areas any hour of the day or night. But most of the work seemed to be done by a thickheaded useful called Michael, incessantly called for by both guests and staff.

'Mee-hawl! Mee-hawl!' wailed the voices, in the bar, out of the bar, in the cobbled courtyard where we kept our hired car, on the steps where he sat to rub up the brass or set the mousetraps, for which there was plenty of use.

'Mee-hawl, my treasure, you've brought me good news,' said D'Arcy one day, as the lumbering young man delivered a cable. 'And so I have a little something for yourself.'

Michael had eyes with a light in the iris, like blue glass in the sun. They almost fell out of his head.

'Oh, holy Jesus, me pocket won't know itself!' and he rushed off down the passage shouting, 'Uncle, Uncle, the Yank give me a punt!'

The sight of the cable had put me into a sweat for fear it was from Australia with bad news, but it was the best of news. Months earlier we had airmailed an entry in a television-play competition run by the powerful Lew Grade Organisation, and forgotten all about it, as usual. We had won first prize, a handsome prize, and in pounds sterling, too.

'Do you realise what this means to us?' I asked.

'Could we really?' he asked, reading my mind.

'Yes, and we shall. We'll go to Memphis, and do that research on Les Darcy you've always wanted to do.'

'Oh, God,' he said. 'Where's a church? I have to give thanks.'

For him it was not a happy coincidence; one of his friends in heaven had pulled the strings.

Leaving Anne at the hotel, we flew across to London and were presented with the cheque. Second and third prizes were won by another Australian and a New Zealander respectively, which pleased us greatly, for the competition had been open to the entire Commonwealth.

We flew back to Dublin, rented a more comfortable car, and drove off through the gauzy rain into an antique landscape. The hills wore swansdown caps of cloud; a wasp nest of a ruined castle was stuck on the side of a steep; larks tossed around in a gentle sad sky.

That is a bewitching land; you can fall into it and be lost willingly, with nothing to mark your vanishing, not even one of those strange Irish tombstones, inscribed with mystic circles, cups and mazes, or the lichened images of thoughtful crowned saints.

Like so many pilgrims to Ireland we looked for ancestors, mine from Derry and Clare, D'Arcy's from Kilkenny and Offaly, once called King's County. We travelled almost five thousand kilometres on that first exploration of Ireland. (Twice we returned, and once in later years I went back by myself.) And five thousand kilometres, in a country the size of Tasmania, or the State of Maine in the United States, is detailed travelling.

If ever there was a leaky land, it's that one, oozing water in every direction—puddles, lakes, bogs and countless streams two metres wide that spout down mountains and try to hurdle the road in one jump.

Our hire car stuck in one of these once, and was pulled out by a tinker's thin horse, its white hocks painted red.

Meantime the car was swarmed over by children, fat as butter and thick with dirt, who moaned for alms while their mother aimed swipes at them with a coal-black petticoat and screeched, 'Get out of there, ye ginger rateens! Ah, mister, if you could give them just the smell of a penny, they'd fall off like fleas!'

We escaped at the price of all our loose change, a packet of mints and two Qantas kangaroo pins, which went off to awed cries of 'Gould! Pure gould!'

The tinkers were on their way to Puck Fair at Killorglin, a Kerry market town which since the thirteenth century has annually been the scene for a ceremony of the frankest paganism.

The casual onlooker marvels that the Church has not come down upon this three-day hullabaloo like a ton of bricks, but no.

'It takes the sting out of them,' a parish priest cosily says of the revellers. 'And it's not considered a success until there is a knock down and drag out fight or two.'

The Puck is a splendid mountainy billy goat, swathed in a magenta cloak, brought into the town on the back of a red truck. He hates everyone, scorching the crowd with his split-yellow eyes, trying to butt the silver-garlanded girl who attempts to crown him with gold. But this is all to the good. A docile Puck is thought little of. He's hoisted with block and tackle to the top of a sixteen-metre-high pedestal, and left there for three days and three nights (though not without food and water.) Forecasts for the ensuing year based on his demeanour during the 'honouring' are freely made and bet on.

People come from as far away as Glasgow and other parts of the Irish diaspora for The Gathering, as the fair is also known. The pubs remain open all night; the travellin' people get married, drink, fight and play the pipes; news is exchanged and fought over; cattle and pigs are sold.

'The ceremonial came to Ireland with the Normans,' says the priest. 'I daresay the Puck represents the devil. But the Ould Boy isn't such a bad fella in Ireland, thanks be to God.'

Our hunt for my ancestors had gone very well, as I have described elsewhere. My grandmother had left Ballindrum much later in the nineteenth century than D'Arcy's forbears had left Galway and Dublin.

He was fortunate however, in that he had a surname unusual even for Ireland, and so whenever we found a Niland in the telephone book he rang it up. Without fail he found that the person at the other hand was confident he was a third cousin or some such, greeting him with hospitable yelps of 'Come on over and have a jar.'

One set of namesakes lived many kilometres out of Galway city, and so were not on the phone. As it was Easter Sunday, I felt sheepish about calling on them unannounced.

'They're all so devout, they'll probably be saying the family Rosary.'

'We'll be sweet, then. They'll be filled with the holy spirit and fall on our necks.'

I persuaded him to put off the venture until the afternoon, when we wouldn't clash with the ceremonial midday dinner. Thus, by the time we'd been misdirected down many green velvet lanes and passed through many villages bent like wishbones, it was four o'clock and I felt reassuringly late.

The namesakes lived in a flatfaced eighteenth-century farmhouse, set amongst stone walls topped by shaggy golden grass upon which two goats were grazing.

A flock of lilywhite geese preceded us slowly up a drive lined with holly bushes; at the end stood a drenched madonna with a broken nose and rain running like blessings off her outstretched hands. There were also several cars. A tremendous smell of roast pork, and a fearful row, emanated from the house. It obviously wasn't Rosary time, and I took instant fright.

Too late. D'Arcy gave the door one clout with the door knocker, it whisked open and a woman seized him by the scarf and jerked him inside.

'God be praised that you're here, Doctor,' she yelled, 'and poor Uncle Martin gasping for the priest this half hour back.'

'What's the matter with the poor man?'

'And didn't Dan say when he brought you the message? It's a pig's toe caught in his throttle and him half strangulated with the coughing and barking, poor Martin.'

At this point she drew back, crying aghast, 'Holy mother, it's not you after all, Doctor!'

There was no hope of explanation; the hall seethed with people. Over-excited children jumped up and down shouting; someone was waving around a carving knife and fork. In the midst of this hubbub we were borne towards a handsome dining room, where a mild, neolithic-looking old man wearing a large bib lolled in an armchair making genteel hooting sounds. An immensely old lady with a green marble cross weighing down her neck tossed a drop of Lourdes water on the sufferer from time to time.

As far as I could see the old man looked quite bright, not in the slightest purple, in fact, rather fancying being the centre of such uproar. The family party had arranged itself in two divisions. There were the practical, who wanted to stand Uncle Martin on his head, and the resigned, who had already given him up to the mercy of God. The noise was terrific.

Will someone take off the man's bib? Declan, will you take off Uncle Martin's bib? If the man's going to snuff it, there's no reverence in a bib.

Put away the holy water, Granny, there's a girl. Say a decade for him, that'll keep you busy.

Ah, poor Martin, and him making such headway with that pig's foot. He always did love a pig's trotter, God bless him. Who'd have guessed it'd come against him like this?

It's the toes that did it, Declan, the toes.

'Let's have a go,' said D'Arcy with great briskness, and he gave Uncle Martin a shake as if he were a half-filled bag of chaff. 'Come on, spit it out!'

Uncle Martin shut his lips tightly and glared up at him defensively.

'Open your gob and let me get my fist in!'

Uncle Martin coughed like a seal. The moment his mouth opened he was a gone man. After some frenzied gluggings and struggles out popped the small white bone.

Ah, you have a way with you, whoever you are!

'Blessed be God, when the family fails, He sends the stranger!

Just then in bustled the doctor with his black bag. Uncle Martin subsided dramatically and began to snore like a steam engine on a grade, but the doctor took in the situation at a glance.

'Sorry I wasn't here earlier, Norah. Doesn't look much wrong with the old devil. What a day I've had, seventeen cases of the blind staggers. I'll be thankful when the holy season is over. Now, that's enough of that, Martin. Sit up like the grand man and Norah will pour you a short one. And I'll have a sip with you. Now, then who are you? Ah, I've got it, you're the Yanks who've been eating at the Green Flag Tearooms. I've heard about you.'

'Saved my life,' began Uncle Martin, determined to get back into the limelight. From the corner of the room Granny's voice rose as she huffily began the second decade. Someone brought me a cup of Irish coffee that tore off something at the back of my nose. I settled back to listen.

'My name's Niland and my grandfather came from around here . . .'

Niland! Wouldn't it be the glory of the world if we were all third cousins! Aren't I always saying that Easter is the best time of the year, Declan? Be quiet, Uncle Martin. Aren't I now, Declan?

We had no luck in Offaly, whence D'Arcy's maternal grandfather, the brutal farrier William Egan, had emigrated long before.

'Not worth tuppence he was,' says his grandson, 'and hard as nails with my mother and her sisters, but it's a sad thing that a man should vanish into the ground like a raindrop the way he has.'

Nothing remains of William Egan but a story that he was a victim of the great evictions, when the landlords changed over from agriculture to cattle-raising. His entire family starved in a ditch, it is said. Otherwise nothing is known except that he 'had hair like a young bull', presumably thick and tightly curled.

'God rest the old rip, nevertheless,' says D'Arcy, whose son Rory has the same hair.

We came to Offaly from Athlone, through hesitant rain, pink blackberry bloom, peat cuttings the deep colour of cooking chocolate, shattered stone walls growing topknots of thick and livid grass.

'The flowers here don't close when it's raining,' observed Anne. 'In Australia they wrap up tight.'

'Not worth their while in Ireland,' agreed her father, driving through sudden sunlight.

Offaly's bogs grew flowers like a garden, as far as the eye could see—daisies, red poppies, meadowsweet like rags of cream lace stretched out on bushes to dry. On a thatched roof bloomed ragwort, and to my dismay, gorse being such an invincible noxious weed in New Zealand, a gorse bush in a cottage garden, trimmed and pampered.

We are on our way to Clonmacnois. In my young days, when I had no books, and if I wanted to 'own' a poem or piece of text I had to learn it by heart, I had committed the T.W. Rolleston poem to memory, and often spoke it or parts of it to D'Arcy when he became ill and couldn't sleep—'In a quiet watered land, a land of roses' and 'many a blue eye of Clan Colman the earth covers, many a swan-white breast.'

Thus we come through the mist to a land we know well, St Kieran's city fair, not a soul to be seen, the ruins sketched in grey against the steely Shannon, a young shallow river lipping the slopes like nothing more than a big puddle of rainwater. The bulrushes shuffle and sigh; there is no other movement or sound.

This is a long-gone city. Only two topless towers; crumbled pyramided walls; tombstones standing or tilting in the grass, or lying like stepping stones amongst the daisies speak of centuries past. Tall Celtic crosses, incised with mysterious dumpy figures still in high relief, state that here was Faith, and here it is still.

Clonmacnois is only one of such sites, but there is something here so tender, so patinated by the long reverence of pilgrims that more than any other place it speaks of the five 'extraordinary and radiant centuries' when Ireland's scholastic fame influenced the known world. For here was a university, a collegiate town of churches and schools, which could handle six or seven thousand students at a time.

'Here is heard only the cry of an otter, or the sharp creak of turning vellum page,' wrote a physician from Crete who had already studied at the University of Alexandria. Indeed, many of his tutors at Clonmacnois had their education at Alexandria. In those days there was great come and go between Ireland and Egypt.

In 548 A.D., not so long after St Patrick's death, this site was deeded to St Kieran by the High King of Ireland.

Like most monastic seats of learning, Clonmacnois was placed near a stream, up which foreign students could conveniently travel. This tradition was to lead to the downfall of such universities all over western Europe. The Vikings brought their longships up the rivers, and the Dark Ages fell like a wintry night.

The ancient Irish schools were free to scholars. They were supported by endowments from rich, pious or princely people, and had their own fishery, quarry and farming privileges.

'I wonder did they have a library,' says Anne, the dedicated apprentice librarian. Yes, a celebrated one, and a school devoted to copying, the finest scriptorium in Ireland.

Time has taken away the fame, the ornaments of the world, from Clonmacnois but left undisturbed its grace.

'I'm going to come and blow about here when I'm dead,' says my husband, and I wonder whether this is what he meant, consciously or unconsciously, when the Customs man at the airport asked him if he had come home at last, and he answered, 'God willing.'

So we went to the United States, and in California, New York and Memphis followed the near fifty-year-old trail of Les Darcy, finding him in yellowed newspaper files, old men's stories and official records of all kinds. Mostly D'Arcy did the interviews, and Anne and I did library research, peering through viewers in libraries and repositories until our sight fogged.

'Ah, man, he was a lovely fella,' said one old man, who'd been at Les Darcy's bedside when he died. 'I think

293

of him still; he had such a smile even when he could no longer utter a word.'

For months, years after we returned to Sydney, parcels of old letters, notes, photographs and scrapbooks came to us, legacies from the old men of Memphis who had known Les Darcy, wanted D'Arcy Niland to write that book.

But he never did. Perhaps the magnitude of the task daunted him especially when he knew his life might end any tick of the clock.

'Come on,' I would say. 'I'll catalogue all this material for you. Act as your researcher, get things in order.'

'That'd be great, Tiger. But first I'll write this story, this article, clear my desk. You know how it is.'

Yes, I knew how it was, except that I still wrote on the kitchen table between household tasks. Work kept me from worrying. And there was a practical reason, too; I had to keep busy, hang on to my regular assignments, grab all the new ones, just in case anything happened, an anything undefined even to myself. I broke into a sweat of terror at the thought I might become ill. What would happen to the children then? At this time Anne was working and as nearly independent as anyone could be on a young girl's wage, Rory was at Sydney University, and the three younger ones still in secondary school. They all needed support of every kind.

My habitual insomnia became worse; I roamed the house at night, distraught, afraid that if I lost hold of my composure for a moment I'd never get it back. There was not one whose advice I could ask. The doctor, a kind thoughtful man, was concerned about his patient. When I consulted him about D'Arcy's refusal to give up smoking, or even smoke less, he cautioned me not to bother him further.

'He's stuck with the habit. No use now. But you mustn't pester him. Never get him upset over anything.'

I believe this advice should have been qualified. The well people of the household have their rights, too. The children had the right to challenge their father's withdrawal from them, in a time when they felt hurt and frightened. Their companionship and confidences would have been mutually rewarding. And what did he think of my calm efficiency? That I didn't care? I longed to tell him otherwise but every time I spoke of his illness he brushed me off.

'Don't bother your head about that! Now, off you go, I have to work.'

It would have been much better, much wiser, if we had wept together, but in those days I didn't know that.

There were also periods of tranquil achievement as though he were going through a remission. Every time that happened I thought, 'The coronary must have been an anomaly, a one-off thing. He'll never have another.' And this was in face of the small 'cardiac disturbances', blackouts, frequent deathly exhaustion, the way his looks had altered! The loving heart will, I suppose, lie to itself until the end.

I noticed every change in his appearance.

'He's getting older,' I chided myself, 'Only seven, six, five years away from fifty.'

And I was encouraged in this folly when I observed that I seemed different, too. More than ever, I saw my mother, as she was when younger, peeping out of my face. There you are. Getting older, just as he is.

D'Arcy Niland was a good-looking man. Now that he was changing he did not resemble either his father or mother. He came to look like somebody else, similar and yet not the same. An elder brother, perhaps.

Only in the last ten years, since I've been able to find photographs of earlier Nilands, closer to Original Thomas, do I see that he was beginning to look like—in fact, became almost a replica of—kinsmen who died at the end of the nineteenth century. How he would have enjoyed this affirmation of the continuity of life.

Almost every day he wrote as much as he had ever written; sometimes he went out to visit the more elderly friends in his vast circle of 'good mates'—Charles Laseron the geologist; Griffith Taylor, the geographer, who had gone with Captain Scott on the epic expedition to the South Pole in 1912; Cyril Hume, the ship modeller, and the many old seamen who frequented Cyril's world. D'Arcy wrote about them all.

'I've an awful fear, Tiger, that men like that, real men, are becoming extinct. I want to make sure they'll not be forgotten.'

During this time we returned to London for three months while he wrote the script for Twentieth-Century Fox's film of *Call Me When the Cross Turns Over*. I was terrified, feeling that the long hours, the incessant contradictory yap about the script always indulged in by everyone connected with a film—in short, the false hysteria of the movie business—would affect his health adversely. Still, he finished the script, a fruitless business, as shortly afterwards the film was shelved indefinitely. During this time we had a meeting with the head of Fox in Europe, Darryl Zanuck, then declining, I believe, but still immensely powerful. He was a strange man, very small, with a two-storey forehead and many, many teeth. Throughout the interview he jumped up every few minutes to chin himself on gym bars that stood beside his immense Mussolini-style desk. It was unsettling, though probably a necessary brag from an insecure person. I may be small, but by God, I'm strong! Mr Zanuck had begun professional life as a scriptwriter and was brilliantly informed about scripts. Just by listening (I was invisible to him), I learned much that I was later able to put to good use.

'But he's a dead man running,' said D'Arcy on the way home. 'If you walked around the back of him you'd see nothing but air.'

It took him a long time to recover from that frenetic time in London, but he rallied once more and began mapping out a long, substantial novel set in the middle years of World War I, when Australia at last cut loose from colonialism and became a nation.

'I'm calling it *Dead Men Running*. It's about a mercenary soldier, and they're always dead men running.'

He worked at the book for a year, finished it in March 1967.

'Crikey, I feel whacked. But I had something to say, and I've said it.'

Two days later he went to the doctor for his usual checkup, and was told he'd better go into hospital for some tests and a few days' rest.

I went to St Vincent's with him in the ambulance, Rory followed in the family car so he could drive me home. All was leisurely and unworried.

We waited outside the room while the nurse settled him in, and I was glad to see that the cardiologist, Dr Selden, had already arrived.

Rory and I were standing there idly talking when Dr Selden came out and told us D'Arcy had suffered a sudden cardiac arrest. He died ten or fifteen minutes later. We did not see him again.

Inscribed on the bronze plaque which marks his grave are the words: 'Sing No Sad Songs for Me.'

PART THREE

1

When my husband died I handled grief very badly. People remarked on my calm or the capable manner in which I handled the innumerable complexities that follow a sudden death. I was unlikely to embarrass or distress them by weeping or throwing myself in front of a truck, and though their desire to console was genuine, they were secretly relieved.

'You're being wonderful,' they said.

To be wonderful is to handle grief badly. And so I nearly died. In a way I did die, as one might die of shock after an amputation or a dreadful wound.

My own character and disposition made things worse for me, terribly worse. Reserve, independence, stoicism are not the qualities needed in grief. My sorrow when Mera my father died had taught me only one thing, that I could survive that sorrow. Not *how* one survived.

Our culture knows little about meeting grief head-on. It has come to be our most impregnable Tower of Babel, the very symbol of non-communication. We stand about in tears, wishing we could assuage the pain of persons dumb-founded by woe, but mostly we don't know what to say. Better to make no reference at all? Better, more tactful, to allow them to get over it in their own time?

It is all kindness, and no help. Thus, thrown entirely upon oneself in a comfortless darkness, one has the choice either of being wonderful or falling to pieces. And if you have children or others dependent upon you, you cannot afford to fall to pieces. So mourning is not done, and the tears that run down inside turn to acid that may corrode your soul for years.

I found myself in a strange country, where no one knew the way except my fellow bereaved. There was no one in those times to tell me anything. The doctor gave me tranquillisers, D'Arcy's priest friends 'religious consolation'. I looked at these genial or melancholy fellows and thought sadly that they were, as D'Arcy had said, tucked away in a pod, isolated from the bloodstained, blissful, bawdy life of what, somewhat slightingly, they called 'the world'. Had the sword of unbearable sorrow ever pierced their honest hearts?

You can't learn about bereavement; you can't teach anyone. It is like cold. You may inform a person who has never felt cold of every scientific fact—cause, consequence, attributes—but he will have no knowledge of cold until he experiences it.

So it is the fellow bereft who help. Tears were beyond me until an Italian shopkeeper, John Quattroville, who had suffered the loss of his baby daughter in a dreadful accident, took my hands and with speaking eyes gazed into my face. That was all. After that I was able to cry, but never where people could see me.

No one ever told me that the body grieves, slows down, its systems short circuit; that the immune system becomes so unstable you become a target for the so-called 'widow's syndrome'. All kinds of small illnesses occur, in a long chain of aggravation, not psychosomatic ailments but real ones. The red vanished from my hair; in three weeks I was ash blonde. My teeth began rapidly to show small specks of decay. I had so many bodily disorders that I expected any moment to hear two sharp snaps, as the arches of my feet gave way.

Today we know of the effect of extreme sorrow or shock on the hypothalamus, and how a stressed body can succumb to much graver diseases, such as cancer. But we didn't know then.

Our family's financial emergency was extreme. Because all our belongings, all our savings, were jointly owned, everything was frozen. For some months we existed only on what I could earn from the Australian Broadcasting Commission children's scripts. There was no insurance. The Niland family did not believe in insurance after poor Auntie Bid lost all her premiums in an insurance crash in 1928. The question was never examined; I think there was some superstition attached to it. Four or five days before D'Arcy died, he came to me in the kitchen, and with a half shy, half wistful expression said, 'I suppose I really ought to get insured.'

303

It did not seem to have occurred to him that no company would insure him. I said gently, 'Oh, don't bother your head about that,' and he went off quite happily.

Perhaps illness had made him even less practical than usual. Or was he fully confident that I would manage somehow when he had gone? I don't know these things. I could not bring myself to think of them; certainly not to discuss them with him.

Perhaps he really thought I was a warrior woman.

It was a terrible time, robbing Peter to pay Paul in order to cope with bills, as I had done in earlier, poorer times—'if I pay the gas account now, and leave the rates until the second notice from the Council, maybe that magazine will pay for the short story before then . . .' Miserable subterfuges and ruses.

At this period I cashed in my own life insurance and those of the children, at considerable loss. For a long time it was a case of chin above water, and little else.

In those days we paid estate or probate tax, and I had the humiliating experience of going slowly through the house with a tax inspector, valuing all we owned. We had a thirteen-year-old refrigerator.

'Who bought this?'

'I did.'

'Where's your receipt?'

Any article for which I did not have a receipt—and most were so old receipts had vanished years before—was automatically attributed to D'Arcy's estate.

'But why?'

'The Department deems that the breadwinner purchased the item. So it is part of his estate.'

Over the years I had bought most domestic appliances, the car, the furniture. My husband, in our easy-going and practical manner, coped with council rates, accounts of all kinds. We had never had any disagreement over money. It was not his, not mine. All that came into the house belonged to the family. Now almost everything we owned was assessed as my husband's property.

Oh, my sisters, I lamented, never think of yourselves as contributors to assets, actual or potential. No matter how hard you have laboured to support the family, or build up your man's profession or business, your name is written in mud.

The little inspector was into power. How he bloomed when I revealed that I had bought the house, and it was registered in our joint names.

'But you're not going to say our home is part of my husband's estate?'

'Only half of it. I notice you did not pay gift tax.'

'But it wasn't a gift! It was our home! And besides, I've never heard of gift tax.'

'Ignorance is no excuse. You'll have to pay that now, and also be fined for not paying it when the purchase was made.'

In fact, however, after I had appealed to the latent humanity of the Taxation Department, the fine was waived. Still, I had to pay the gift tax. Would the same situation have existed if my husband had bought the house and registered it in our joint names? No. He is deemed the breadwinner, the natural purchaser of the family home, and if he wishes in his generosity to add his wife's name to the deed, who could construe that as gift-giving? I came to the conclusion that in the Department's eyes the wife is never the bread-winner, even when she is.

Presumably, with the abolition of probate and gift tax, many of the cruel absurdities confronting the widow in my time of trial have vanished. But you never can tell.

So life was hard, often bewildering. But avalanches of financial worries are only an exacerbation of what is essentially a time of bitterest depression. During such an experience some people fall into *accidie*—listlessness, torpor, sloth—a snail's withdrawal from the normal world. Some take to drugs, or drink, or comfort food. I continued writing scripts and anything else I could lay my hands on. Inside I was eaten up by sorrow, devoured.

'It'll be better when a year has passed,' said the doctor. Lies. For many years I was a castaway, isolated from the world at large, moving civilly through a professional life that scarcely impinged upon my inner world.

One of my children said to me in later years, 'I always feared you were going to knock yourself off.'

'Why didn't you say something?'

'Didn't know what to say. But I kept an eye on you.'

And I recalled how, when my family was marooned in a frigid and isolated mill valley in New Zealand, my father was made so wretched (and I understood him so well) that every time he picked up his rifle and went out hunting, I went too, a gun-shy, silent girl, tense with terror, tagging along stubbornly in spite of his exasperation. Until at last he cried, 'All right, then. I won't do it. I give you my word! Yes! Go home, damn it!'

Because we have forgotten how astute is the observation of the children who love us, we do terrible things to them.

Nearly every night I had violent, perilous dreams, often of a blue sky, nothing but blue sky, a void. In it a gap would open, sometimes even a door. In a frenzy of longing I would rush towards it, knowing I could jump through it into oblivion. But I always awoke, sweating and shaking.

Then I'd get up, get the children's breakfast, send them off, and begin to write. A lifetime of literary practice had taught me that I no longer had to know delight, or humour, or energy in order to convey it. The woman and the writer were separate.

For six weeks the enormous heap of typescript that was D'Arcy's last novel, *Dead Men Running*, lay on his desk. I did not have the heart to touch it. He had left few things because he had so few possessions; this typescript, his old Olivetti portable (upon which I type these words today), his fountain pen, a thin gold chain with a cross and St Christopher medal which I had given him to replace Sister Roche's ragged scapular, a pair of nail clippers that he'd never learned to use successfully—'bloody thing took off a piece of thumb!'—and his library. He'd never been one for owning things; he didn't even have a car, but drove my unkillable Morris.

Still, he'd left many good things that could not be called possessions. And I remembered how, in the early morning after the night he died, I awakened from a distracted half-sleep to see two little pyjamaed figures standing beside the bed.

'We have made a solemn vow to make Dad proud of us,' said whichever twin was spokeswoman for that week.

So they have, as all his children have. That's something for a man to leave.

But it was necessary for me to edit *Dead Men Running*, have it typed, and get it published. Even to read the book was painful; the writer's voice was so clear in those sharp sentences. But there was really nothing to edit. I checked dates and events, for the novel is set in the tumultuous days of World War I, when Australia, still a new Federation, was torn apart over conscription and the nation's ambiguous loyalty to the old Empire. But he had done very concentrated research; there were no errors.

The novel was published simultaneously by Hodder & Stoughton in Australia and Michael Joseph in Great Britain, a little later in the United States. It also became a most successful television mini-series.

As soon as our funds were released I took the three young ones to England, the girls to further their art education, and Patrick to attend the Royal Academy of Music. He was an unusually talented pianist, and D'Arcy and I had long before decided we would stretch every financial sinew to give him his chance.

It was a quixotic decision; I couldn't afford to keep three students in London, and, as it turned out, the art tuition the girls got there was not as good as they had already been having in Sydney. Still, somehow we managed, and the experience was valuable to them.

It was 1968. Frank Sheed and Maisie Ward were in London, like other Catholics waiting for Pope Paul VI to release the encyclical *Humanae Vitae*, summing up the decisions of the endless deliberations of the Vatican Council, set in motion by old Pope John's desire for *aggiornamento* or updating. A group of us—I was still officially a Catholic—were in Rule's, a fascinating restaurant once frequented by Edwardian men about town and their light ladies but in the 1960s favoured by representatives of ancient English families which had remained loyal to the Faith during the bad centuries of persecution. Dungeons, fire and sword were part of their family histories. My friend, Frank Sheed, ran through rapid introductions—Peter, his ancestor the Venerable Gervase, copped it under Henry VIII, hanged, drawn and quartered. Christopher, collateral descendant of Blessed Margaret, burned under Elizabeth. And so on. I was just about to tell them about a collateral ancestor of my own, a Covenanter who for his loyalties was squashed to death at Paisley in the seventeenth century, when in hastened a pallid messenger from Westminster Cathedral.

'You're not going to believe this, but that absolutely blighted old wop has come down against contraception!'

This acerbic assessment of the Holy Father seemed a sad comedown when presented to men with martyrs and exiles on the family tree, but they nodded resignedly.

'Of course, you know what this means—the end of the Faith as we know it.'

As this more or less has come to pass, the moment was a historic one.

My agent had gathered up assignments for me, doing breakdowns of film properties for two or three London-based companies. In some cases, after I had broken down the novels to their bone structure, I also did the treatment. Many of the novels had little or eccentric bone structure, ribs where they shouldn't be, or backbones with kinks. In this circumstance I sometimes ventured to suggest orthopaedic adjustments.

This work is an invaluable exercise for any writer. It led me to the habit of graphing anything lengthy or significant that I wrote thereafter.

Some novels, of course, often charming, estimable ones, had no bone structure at all, but relied for their reader impact on character, atmosphere, and elegant text. Such are impossible to carry to the screen without drastic changes. They simply are not cinematic. Yet producers do, and frequently turn out bastardised versions of such novels, causing consternation in the writers and anguished protest from readers who loved the original novel.

This work, erratic as it was, was well paid and after I returned to Australia, provided a basic income.

However, I truly hit bottom in London. That city has had so many griefs of its own that mine seemed sharper, more isolated than before. The surpassing sorrow was not something I could discuss with the children; perhaps they experienced the same and could not discuss it with me.

I spent much leisure time wandering in old churches, over dimpled paving stones engraved with names of those who died three and four centuries ago. One bore the words 'The Past Seems to Mee Like a Dreeme', and all I could say was 'Oh, yes, yes!'

But those sad wanderings brought to me the realisation that death must be insignificant. The realisation, yes, but not the comprehension.

Bad, bad. Yet, what is the good way? Not, I think, with the attention of 'trauma counsellers', so often in their twenties, with no or little personal trauma in their life histories. My belief is that bereavement is the time to open your heart to people at large, not necessarily to only one person. John Quattroville knew what he was doing.

In this way I am opening my heart to readers who are, or have been, in that dark, roadless country.

Yet some people, simple people, too, know the good way to handle grief, as distinct from the murderous wonderful way.

Seven years after my husband's death, when I lived on Norfolk Island, I attended an Islander funeral. The Islanders are the descendants of the Pitcairn people who were 'given' Norfolk Island when their own little rock in the Pacific became too small for them. On Norfolk, where there is perhaps still no mortuary, people were buried very soon after death. Sometimes the family said goodbye to a loved child or mother in the morning and by sunset they were hidden from sight. Almost all the Pitcairn people are related; they have their feuds, scandals and battles, but so do all families. And so anyone who dies has many people come to say Godspeed.

How memorable was that burial! Until the last moment the grave remained open; the family was not anxious to say goodbye. Like their distant ancestors, the Tahitians, they carried green sprays of leaves. Some wore garlands of willow or hibiscus. They sang the very old Pitcairn hymns, taught to them, it is said, by pious whalers from Cape Cod and Boston. They wept in each other's arms, laughed often, for they were repeating one to another little anecdotes of the person who had left them. Now and then one or two wandered to the graveside to say something affectionate (or so it seemed from their expressions). And it seemed to me that this was not a parting ceremony at all, but a loving gathering.

There was a natural wisdom in these people. I knew from other residents, mainlanders as we were called, that this generous expression of grief, this comfort shared in the homeliest way, would go on for weeks until the bereaved were ready for normal life once more.

In significant ways this funeral was like the Maori tangis I had attended as a child, although there was a grand element to those if the deceased person were chiefly. My conviction is that this is the right way, the way dictated by our hearts. We know that even in paleolithic times the dead were laid tenderly to rest, food and drink accompanying them to speed them on their way; a cherished necklace, a favourite dagger laid upon the sleeping breast. Thus the dead are not depersonalised, as they come to be in modern civilisation. They are left space, and if they wish to, they will occupy that space.

*

My intention when I returned to Australia was to sell our house at Balgowlah Heights and buy a small one for my two older children to live in, if they wished. I was to go back to London as soon as possible. But by November of that year I was invited by the powerful *Reader's Digest* to consider a year's contract to do the text of one of the *Digest*'s special books. The *Digest* has always paid its contributors well; the sum offered me was far more than I could have earned by freelancing for two years. Though I was still doing children's scripts for the Australian Broadcasting Commission, I was nervous about the future of kids' radio programmes in face of the flood of television for children, so exciting, innovative, and although physically still black and white, psychologically brightly coloured.

It took many long discussions with all my children before I decided I could leave the three young ones alone in London for a year. This was probably a mistake. However, none of them has ever told me the history of those years (for the year stretched considerably) and I shall not ask questions. They survived well, and are three charming, affectionate, and productive people. So, whatever happened, and in my anxious imagination at the time everything happened, it did them no harm.

We sold our family house, and Anne, Rory, myself, the three dogs and a shifting number of cats moved to a small house further up the coast. There I wrote for the *Digest*, text as ritually ordered as a religious ceremonial, not my kind of thing at all. But the *Digest* has lasted for many decades; undoubtedly its management knows what it needs. So vanished 1968, with the spectacular splashdown

313

of Apollo 8, after orbiting the moon ten times, the first flight of its kind.

Politically it had been the most explosive, frightening year imaginable . . . the great Tet offensive in Vietnam; assassinations of Martin Luther King and Robert Kennedy; Czechoslovakia occupied by Soviet and other Warsaw Pact troops; strikes, student riots, conscription riots; massive police-student battles in Mexico City; Nixon elected President of the United States; the noise was deafening.

Nevertheless, I persevered with the *Reader's Digest* assignment, writing about mountain devils in springtime as 'small enamelled lovers', and having the *Digest* change the words to 'minor members of the iguana family'. My health was unreliable, my spirits deeply depressed. I missed my husband and younger children night and day.

Even when I felt better than that, it seemed I was at the bottom of the sea, mile-high water on top of me. Certainly I wrote a great deal, but it was all done from my head. Wherever I lived, in my heart or spirit, there was numbness and inertia.

None of my experiences of widowhood is peculiar to me; I suggest no uniqueness. It is because my experience is universal that I write as I do. Certainly, some people are more resilient; with others no profound affection has been present. People must be people, after all, as varied as blades of grass, alike only to the careless eye.

In hindsight I see that I might well have continued going on as I was, overworked, anxious, sleepless, lonely, on the verge of clinical depression, except for an unpredictable happening.

314

Having delivered my fortnightly quota of work to the *Digest* office, I returned to the city to spend an hour or so. For me, these stray hours always concerned bookshops.

I remember walking through the shop in absolute darkness of soul. Any reality of life was non-existent. Picking up a book I looked at the picture of the author on the back of the jacket. An old man, I thought, maybe a sick man, with one sad eye and one merry one.

I thought, 'I'm in the pits, and I could be there forever because I don't know the way out. I wonder what this man would say to me?'

Behind me a voice answered, 'He would say "Detach! Detach!"'

The person who spoke was a young man. I think he had a shaven head but I'm not sure now. He was a Pole, a student or novice at Diamond Zendo in Hawaii, a disciple of the well-known Buddhist teacher, Robert Aitken. All these names were strange to me then.

One might say with reason that this meeting was fortuitous. Nevertheless human life and behaviour are far too immense and full of enigmatic contradictions for anyone to say, this is sequential, that is not. My observation is that if grief, rage, terror—any of the primitive emotions—are experienced with enough furious intensity some unanalysable critical point is likely to be reached.

Then something occurs, it does not matter if it be fortuitous or not. It can be a glance, a word, a blow, an incident. The mind flips over, changes its 'set', and without the intervention of the will, perceives the possibility of a new direction.

315

This did not happen to me when I met the young man in the bookshop. Not then.

'I've been watching your face,' he explained. 'I could see you're in a heavy space. And that's what Suzuki-roshi always advised his students . . . detach, detach!'

He told me that he was the son of Polish migrants to Australia. In business in suburban Sydney, they had had some financial trouble, and his *zendo* had released him to travel home to help them. In his time he had studied Soto Zen with Suzuki, who had written the book I held, but found Soto too soft for his intractable nature.

'I need something fiercer,' he said. 'I find it in Rinzai.'

'But what is Zen?'

'It's about consciousness. A system for human life. A way. The less explanation the better.'

'But, this book?'

'You won't find Suzuki-roshi explaining anything. Zen isn't for learning, it's for living. Either you cotton on to it, or you don't.'

'Tell me about Suzuki.'

'Oh, he's dead. In a way.'

And with that the young man smiled and walked out of my life. In a way.

All the way home I gobbled up Suzuki's book, which was called *Zen Mind, Beginner's Mind*. Quickly I realised that Zen was some version of Buddhism, that Soto and Rinzai probably were the names of divergent sects, and *roshi* meant master. But Suzuki-roshi's lectures had originally been given to students who already had a working knowledge of Buddhism; they were not for gobbling by ignorant

316

people like me. Still, there were powerful sentences—the world is its own magic; to give is non-attachment; we actually are the true activity of the big existence, reality itself; our practice is not to gather something in your basket but to find something in your sleeve. Something within me echoed all these statements, and I could see how Suzuki-roshi was dead only in a way. His voice was clear, his words simple, except that I could understand them only here and there.

Something stood between him and me; it was that which inhibits most Westerners, and particularly Christians when they are confronted with Buddhism, most of all any of the branches of Zen. We are absolutely stuck with the idea that we *do* something, and are in due course *rewarded* with something. This pernicious fixation seems to be a human frailty. One must teach it, after all, to animals. In its severest form it rules authoritarian religions and political ideologies. A Zen master would say, 'Detach! Detach from this idea without roots.' He might even add, in the maddening Zen manner, 'Who is the person acting? Who the one rewarding?'

Certainly Suzuki-roshi informed his students that if they practised certain things, it was likely that there would be a satisfactory *consequence*. As a physio instructor might tell you that if you assiduously do specific exercises, the pain in your arm will probably cease.

The most liberating thing of all, though I did not recognise it until I actually studied in Zen centres, is that Suzuki-roshi and other Zen masters would not care a spit if you never did any of the mental exercises they recommended. Why should they be ambitious for you?

317

You do your own work, or you do not. They're not there to hold you up.

Many months passed before my mind pulled away from the reward-punishment syndrome. I saw that cause and effect rule the universe, and that my never-lifting grief was an effect.

'Well, I know the cause,' I said to myself. 'D'Arcy's death. I don't have to think about *that*.'

But even after a few months I was in the habit of querying everything. This process is so painful that one not only flinches but squirms. The illusion that our own value-patterns, whether familial or cultural, alone represent the truth is as strong as death. Indeed people do die for it. This is right and that is wrong, we say, for human beings have an irresistible urge towards polarity. Yet all spiritual wayfarers have observed that it is a dangerous thing to allow oneself to become rigidly aligned.

Buddha said, 'To see the truth, neither be for or against.'

I realised very clearly that I must examine the cause of my grievous depression, and not take it for granted that I already knew. But it was a threatening exercise. For months I asked myself how I could detach from my husband's character, life, death? Such seemed the vilest disloyalty. Wasn't the very fact that I mourned him so profoundly proof of my devotion?

What a shock to see ego in that last sentence, not newly sprung, but well-rooted, blooming! And, digging deeper into my motivation, I saw at last that in letting go of my husband I subconsciously believed I would be relinquishing twenty-five years of my own life.

318

There was a block in my head. I could not understand detachment. I believed it means indifference.

But detachment does not mean indifference to anything or anyone. It means only that there is no desire to possess these things or that person. In possessiveness lies all the pain—loss, anger, unbearable yearning. All the flies that bite.

How long it took me to allow my husband to go! I said many times, 'Go your way. Thank you for everything. Go, and be happy!' but had no feeling that somewhere his spirit flew off joyfully, nothing to hold it to earth.

I had not reached that point of which the Zen masters say: 'Have you climbed to the top of the ladder, to the last rung? Then step off.'

But years afterwards, on a sunny height in Norfolk Island, where he had never been, the lofty pines standing silent in the way they do, and the fairy terns flipping in and out the boughs like snowflakes or falling flowers, I felt him close, and then gone forever.

'Goodbye, darlen,' I said. 'See you molla!'

Which is the way Norfolk Islanders say goodbye, for they believe in tomorrow.

2

In 1972 the ABC *Children's Session* died, accompanied by cries of deprivation from country children, parents, and correspondence-school teachers. The session, in its declining years, had outlived its value to city kids, who now had films, television, and a rapidly increasing flow of visual and audio teaching aids. But those of us aware of the almost inconceivable isolation of inland children were sad.

There is no way to comprehend the boundless loneliness of the Australian outback until you fly over it and look down upon a cinnabar red emptiness that appears not to belong to familiar Earth. But there, amidst the fantastic tangle of dry rivers, aberrant rivers that run from the coast to the old salt sea that is not there any more, the eye catches the occasional dazzle from an iron roof, the small green blur of a few trees, the wink of a dying dam.

In places like these, with the nearest neighbour five

hundred kilometres down the track, I first saw Australian children, ruddy, shy, with homecut hair, rush in from their chores to listen to the ABC *Children's Session*, hoping to hear their own romantic Argonaut names.

So passed something both precious and historic. Also down a hole in the ground went our family's basic source of income for twenty-five years, and I was panic stricken. Such a basic income, even if it be minimal, is the writer's safety belt. By the same token it can be the writer's curse, for he tends to cling to it, often at the expense of more valuable work.

It was queer to find myself scraping carrots or washing my hair without thinking about a *Wombat* script at the same time. I had written scripts in trains and buses; sitting beside the beds of children with mumps; in the middle of the night when I couldn't sleep. Wombat, affectionate, bumbling, in a word muddleheaded, belonged in the family. He had originated there, too, when one of my daughters said in the tragic tones of a four-year-old confronted with the hopeless, 'I don't think there's anyone in the world I'm smarter than!'

It occurred to me then that many tiny children may feel like that. They are, after all, forever being corrected, taught, led this way and that, as though they are not, by any standard, all right just as they are. So I thought, I'll work out a character that any child is 'smarter than'. He turned out to be the muddleheaded wombat.

As it happened, I said goodbye to Wombat as a radio character, but not otherwise, as he has appeared in many books, picture books, as a puppet and in the theatre.

He has been translated into ten other languages as Vombat, Battino, Woo, El Wombo, Wombi, and Lille Ville Vimse.

During our long association Wombat and I have been through many trials together. I have answered thousands of brief, large-written letters addressed to Wombat's Mum, and perhaps a hundred long serious letters discussing the curious psychology revealed by the scripts. The writers did not think I knew, so they told me. I have fought off translators who desired to convert Wombat into a bear (for the Malays) and a resolute Indian who thought this burrowing animal would do better behaving as a monkey. I once managed to pacify an English editor who required him to live in a tree, and was happy to confirm to a Japanese publisher that Wombattu-san was indeed a cousin of the esteemed Koara-san.

Wombat and I, there is no denying, are close. We even share the same favourite Hans Andersen fairytale, the one about the ugly dumpling that grew up to be a beautiful scone.

Thus the loss of my radio assignment marked a significant turning point, only incidentally related to the disappearance of a small basic income. It was the kind of shake-up I needed.

For twenty-eight years I had been a necessary person to my family.

'And now what?' I asked myself.

The twins had returned to Australia in 1970, had their own flat and were earning a precarious living as illustrators. They were independently minded, and, as far as I could see, capable in all ways. The musician also had returned,

322

to be employed in the Music Department of the Australian Broadcasting Commission. The elder pair, though one still lived with me in the doll's house at Allambie Heights, had long since been supporting themselves.

'Then what am I here for?'

The answer was: Nothing. Except in the undefined supportive maternal area, I had outgrown my job. I was Mum Emeritus and that was all.

It was an astonishing thought that I had no more family responsibilities. For half a lifetime I had been the housekeeper, the carer, the person who got up in the night to attend to people sick in the froat or the bitch nervously having her first pups. I had wept bitter tears while endeavouring to fulfil a teacher's command: 'Please remember that in the school concert the twins will be *dressed as frogs*.' No one on earth can truly cope with that bit shaped like a double map of Africa that goes between a frog's back legs.

Thousands of ordinary Mum memories assailed me. The notes pushed under the loo door—'I definately want my cricket pants washed, they are hambugger all over.' Or: 'My brothers are pigs, why did you have them? You are truly mean.'

Those days of ceaseless demands had gone. Now I could cut my toenails in peace. I could have long hot baths instead of two-minute showers out of which I jumped at least twice to cope with crashes on the door and cries of: 'Mum, I left my school socks, paintbrush, baked-bean sandwich, textbook, hair brush in there, I know I did!'

I didn't have to do anything for anyone. It was an eerie sensation. For a week I felt run down like an old clock.

At the same time I was obscurely angry. My old friend, Cyril Hume, the ship modeller, knew the feeling.

'You're yawing,' he said. I was not at all pleased. After looking up the word in the dictionary I felt it did not apply; I was not zigzagging unsteadily, nor had I deviated from my course in a horizontal line. On the contrary I appeared to he standing still, like a liberated slave, not knowing which direction to go.

At that time I was unstable in my Zen practice, and still occasionally lapsed into superstitious customs left over from my youth. As a child I had been much impressed by a neighbour who, faced with a dilemma, closed her eyes and stabbed a finger at a page of the Bible, coming up with a text that inevitably proved to be the right advice.

My Auntie Rose, the one who read Marie Corelli, longed to emulate this wise neighbour, except that she had no Bible. Every time her husband drove her mad for one thing or another, she lamented this fact.

'Never mind, Rosie lovey, use your cookery book,' urged her sisters.

With what satisfaction one recalls the expression of simple pleasure on her face when her forefinger came up with, 'Beat to a stiff froth.'

Hoping for equal luck, I took my chances with Suzuki-roshi's book. What I drew was this: 'One thing flows into another and cannot be grasped. Before the rain stops, we hear a bird.'

By now I was sufficiently advanced in Zen kindergarten not to feel that everything a *roshi* said sounded as if he'd found it in a fortune cookie. I realised that Master Suzuki was drawing my attention to the vital Buddhist concept that nothing is static, all is evolving. Which included myself.

The thing for me to do was to stay tranquil, practise my meditation, put that bitumen stuff on the leaking roof gutter, clip the dogs, and wait quietly until I flowed from being a scriptwriter into being something else.

'How would you like to write a *big* book about Sydney?' asked William Collins's senior editor, Stephen Dearnley. 'One of our Companion Guide series? History, geography, information for visitors, stories, everything?'

I was familiar with Collins's Companion Guides to great cities. Designed for the authentic traveller as well as the armchair variety, they were more literate, more idio-syncratic than the invaluable Fodor handbooks, but just as practical. The reader received transport advice, gallery and museum-opening times, shopping suggestions, shortcuts to save time and feet, as well as hundreds of those playful and amusing anecdotes, scandalous as well as historical, that tell more about the intimate character of a city than a truckload of statistics.

'I would,' I replied. 'Except that . . .'

'What?'

'Are you aware that Sydney is being pulled down? Everywhere along the skyline I see scaffolding.'

'Well?'

'In no time this will be an out-of-date guidebook.'

'When that happens, it will be a history of the way Sydney was in the years before the mid-seventies. A research and reference book.'

Here was an unprofitable thesis for a publisher, not less so for a writer. Still, I could see the value of this curious assignment. The book would be a record, my own story of the Sydney I knew so well, a kind of farewell garland.

For now the idea had come, revolutionary, alarming, that if flowing operated so admirably with regard to work, it might well do the same with location. There was now nothing to stop me from flowing from place to place.

'Maybe it's time I went off and lived somewhere else,' I told my children. I expected pleasant smiles and a casual 'Good-O, Mum.' Not so.

'You've rocks in your head.'

'Mum's lost her marbles.'

'Kids opt out, not mothers.'

'What do you *mean*, you're giving us back to ourselves? Who *asked* you to?'

'Where are you going to live, anyway?'

'Maybe an island.'

'*An island*?'

'Shut up now. I won't be going for a while. I need about twelve months to do the guidebook.'

Islands, islands. An oneiric vision of islands shimmers before most inward eyes, and none of us quite knows why. They are towed into fiction as though they are ornamented rafts, with serpentine palms and savages of epicene beauty, dressed in evergreen leaves. Do we learn anything from savages so depicted, their girlish features, combed hair and bodies far removed from the utilitarian shape of the real people who tear their living from limited land or the indifferent sea?

Perhaps that life on an island, or so the dreamer thinks, is bountiful, and the inhabitants kindly?

'O, delectable isle!' cried Edmund Banfield, the Beachcomber, who in the last decade of the nineteenth century began a twenty-five-year love affair with Dunk Island of the Barrier Reef, and wrote his unforgettable *Confessions* about it. Can one imagine his passionately crying 'O delectable continent!' of Australia or any other? Indeed, of Australia, that other besotted islandman, Dr L.P. Jacks, says in his book *Among the Idol Makers*: 'It interested me not in the least. It was too big. No castaway twelve years old could be expected to manage such a place.'

Is it this, then? Is an island intimately connected with childhood, and the child's desire to get away from the damnable surveillance of adults? Perhaps this explains why *Robinson Crusoe*, *Treasure Island*, *Coral Island* and innumerable others in all languages remain basic literature—each one gives valuable pointers on how a twelve year old might manage.

We also, it seems, need our islands to be *round*. In Elizabeth Riddell's marvellous poem, the old seaman longs for an island like a big green apple he can hold in his hand. St Columba, coming at last to Lindisfarne, wished to find 'a little island like a plate, with a spring, birds, and the grace of God'.

Yet islands are most often long skinny bones; rags torn off coasts, crumbs of rock with but a handful of soil in which grows a thornbush. So many are but the tail-ends

327

of mountain ranges, as are the islands of the Whitsunday Passage, marching out to sea.

It seems to me that islands are symbols of something for which the human psyche longs—unity or completion.

On such things I pondered as I ran about Sydney doing research, and as the days and weeks in the braying, hooting, yowling city went on, I cannot deny that a golden haze of romanticism settled over the idea of islands. I began to yearn for peace, silence, even solitariness. For in those years when Sydney was beginning to pull itself to pieces, the air was full of fearful noise, the sky of dust. Everywhere were boarded-up doomed buildings, Victorian warehouses, colonial godowns, stone and sandstock cottages that had resolutely survived amongst shops, pubs and offices of a later age. And the terrible sound of the rock pick tirelessly pecking away at Sydney's sandstone foundations was over all.

There was such a sense of impulsive urgency about the obsession for demolition, as though no one had thought about any form of change except destruction. Tear down the old city that was, at base, a European city, full of ups and downs, dogleg lanes and cobbled dens; a narrow-streeted city, eccentric and crowded. Yet it had always been itself, a scallywag, joyfully arrayed in sun and sea, a city born of sorrow and exile but never ashamed of that.

I could see what they were after, the City Fathers and the town planners—something civilised, modern, conformist, the universal utilitarian city you see so often on television, damned by its own dullness.

328

'Oh, my poor old girl!' I used to cry, stepping aside to avoid trucks laden with enormous ironbark beams, black with age and pocked with axe marks. Or I stood behind the barrier and witnessed a stout-set old building collapse in a fury of dust, nothing left standing except the wrought-iron cage of a lift, and half a marble pediment inscribed with the face of Prince Albert.

Thus, in my way, I ran ahead of demolition, never knowing what next would be destined for destruction, but determined to record it.

Nothing replaces field research, even if you're writing fiction; the image that hits the eyeball is immeasurably more powerful than the one you read about in someone else's book. Readers recognise this at once. We might, for instance, be studying the Bible or some other classical text, perhaps with a touch of scepticism or cynicism. Suddenly there is some small detail, often irrelevant to the storyline, and we find ourself saying: 'The writer must have seen that with his own eyes. No one could invent that!'

Many writers build an entire career on the rewriting of other people's research. Though I resent those who, in this way, mine my own work, especially the *Companion Guide to Sydney*, I feel they have missed the pleasure of real contact with the human beings who lived the stories, and out of the blisses and tragedies of their own experience, developed the philosophy or the wit.

I cherish old men on park seats, drowsing in the sunlight, washed up on the shores of their lives but not fretting too much about that. They're most often glad to talk, and to activate their memory I often use a simple ploy.

'My grandfather used to live in Toxteth Street,' I say in Glebe; 'Johnston Street' in Annandale. (It must be a street with old houses.)

'Is that so?'

'His name was Thompson.' (The name must not be unusual.)

'You don't mean old Clarrie Thompson, the jockey?'

'It could have been.'

This is journalistic fly-fishing. You crack a lure across the water and though you may not come up with Clarrie Thompson, you may get some ribald stuff about going to the Randwick races in a horse buggy with two dozen light ales, a dozen pork pies, and a couple of high-steppers in feathered hats, and seeing the Premier of the time in similar company. Everything that deals with real events or real, preferably historical, people, has to be checked, of course. Old men usually have wonderful memories, but sometimes are shaky on dates.

Old ladies sitting at bus stops are less communicative, looking at you sideways and holding their little mossy purses very tightly in case you're a weirdie.

Two people assisted me greatly in this immense work of love, Collins's editor, Stephen Dearnley, English but an ardent lover of Sydney and consequently well-read in her tradition and history, always diffidently offering good suggestions not only of ideas but of places to find them. The other was a library reference officer, Shirley Denson, then of Manly Library, a person with a fantastic stock of Australiana, not on a computer program as such would be today, but in her head. I count such reference officers as people to be prized beyond rubies. But, alas, though professional writers use them constantly, they are rarely thrown a flower.

At last the book was done, and I was satisfied with it. I have always hoped that it is indeed a voice raised in praise of colonial and Victorian Sydney.

About this time I began to wonder what I was going to live on, when I removed to my island. I had never applied for a literary grant, and did not much like the idea, but after much cogitation I did so. For years I had had an idea for a novel floating around in the back of my head—a story about a dwarf and his attitudes towards a world monstrous in its dimensions, but never too big for him. So I applied for a grant and was given it. Grants diminish greatly after taxation, but a careful writer, with no ambition to live opulently, can manage.

'And besides,' I told the children, 'I can live very cheaply on Norfolk Island.'

'Surely you're not going to live on Norfolk?'

My decision was disappointing even to myself. I had considered so many islands, up and down the Australian coast, and even as far afield as the outliers of Fiji. The ocean, after all, is speckled with delectable dots of islands, ravishing, secluded and often inconvenient to the point of madness. My desire was for an island refuge both convenient and inconvenient, and so my mind had finally settled on Norfolk Island, only 1600 kilometres from the Queensland coast. A loved friend, long resident on Norfolk, had made a useful comment: 'If you're a visitor, the island is not remote,' she said. 'But it's a million miles from anywhere if you live here.'

I had often stayed with this friend, and so already knew the island fairly well. I liked the faded colonial splendours of its tragic early history, and the slow speech of the island women, like waves breaking on a still day. Even its shape pleased me, a soft triangle, little and compact. We knew it was the highest surviving peak of a monstrous volcano, submerged since the Dawn Ages. But any unsuitable protrusions, lava flows and the like, the sea had bitten off long before.

It was like a ship, all alone in the ocean, secure, well-found, never sunk yet, and its pines were ten thousand masts.

It was wonderful for me to know, as well, that only two hundred years before, Norfolk had been a true desert isle, no one living there, no sign of previous occupation, its forests silent as though in a dream. What was its name? Could the island have spoken, I imagine it saying, like God to Moses, 'I am what I am.'

Secure in selfhood, it did not require a name. Still, mapmakers cannot abide namelessness.

Captain Cook, in 1774, called it Norfolk Isle. Nevertheless, it remains what it is, and no name cast upon it by a wandering British Navy captain alters that.

I had visited Norfolk Island in summer and noted approvingly that it was nowhere near as hot as Sydney. And I had been there in the rainy season, a time of mushrooms, overflowing tanks, and plant growth deliriously green. In between slipping and sliding like a drunken cow on Pompeian red dirt roads, I crouched under hedges, raincoat pockets full of water, and thought how glamorous it was that Norfolk was a trade-wind island. Also I was impressed that this small isle was, after Sydney, the oldest British settlement in the South Pacific.

In sober fact, I was bemused; my reasons for living there had climbed into the realm of fiddle-faddle. I hadn't an inkling that water-shortage always threatened; or if the ship didn't arrive with gas cylinders you had nothing to cook with for weeks. That the gentle docile cows, which had the run of the island and the right of way on all roads, were capable of jumping your fence, or proceeding across your cattle stop on their knees and eating everything on the property, not only vegetables, but fruit trees, shrubs, *everything*—that the island had been, right from the First Settlement, the helpless victim of every imported insect and plant pest. Fortunately the animal pests had been confined to Norfolk's small companion islets, Nepean and Phillip, which, though once heavily wooded, were consequently as bald as Martian rocks and much the same colour.

More importantly, if my aim was to experience a season in solitary, to detach from the venal world, it would be difficult to realise. An island community cannot help but be a microcosm of humanity at large, neither better nor worse, though it often seems spectacularly worse because it is always under your eye.

Nevertheless I went there, having sold my collection of Australiana to finance the diabolically complicated move, lived on almost nothing for two years, wrote a great deal, stayed ten years and would be there still if it had not been for an unpredictable illness.

I still dream about it—the seamists drawing saltscapes on the windows; the ferny-tasting water, the rainbows that seemed to be everywhere, high arches, low arches, pillars and wisps. For like all islands this one had particularised showers, phantoms with low hesitant voices that marched across houses, roads, gardens, leaving clearly defined edges.

Now that I live in the locked-up, barred, suspicious city I dream most of all of the marvellous nights, with all the doors and windows open, the sky powdered with stars as with icing sugar, lapping almost to the edge of the verandah, so that after a while illusion took over and all turned upside down, the darkness of the bedroom now the sky, and the bed floating on a phosphorescent sea of immeasurable depth.

For when I could afford it, I built a house on a hill. The island people—Bounty people as the mainlanders call them, though they don't like it, having no good memories of *H.M.S. Bounty* and Captain Bligh—the island people said, 'No, no, you must build your house in the walley. Always!'

But I wanted a 360 degree view, the two little mountains and their rainforest to the west and north, and the ocean and hills and dales to the east. Madness. Who wants to build on a hill on an island? You want to live in a crow's nest on a mast, or maybe on the weathervane above the steeple? For all islands are in the roadway of the winds, and Norfolk Island perhaps more than most. Though my house was a lovely house, tightly built by a good Dutchman, the winds found every crack. Wide as a hair? No matter. All the better to go shree-shee through, day and night. The winds sang around windows, under doors, and through the footings. There were high airs and low airs, some spiral, some as undulating as the sea, and they all found me. For a while I had shelter. There was a huge pine to the east. We had built carefully so as not to disturb the roots of that tree, for it had been there first. It fenced off the wind outside my bedroom. Norfolk pines do not sough; they are noiseless creatures even in storms. But within three years that pine began to talk, tick-click, tick-click. It was not the tree itself; the tree, had it been able to talk, would have shrieked, for it was now infested with pine beetle, chewing out its heart. On the island they knew no cure; they advised that the pine be felled, lest it fall on the house and kill that too. So down it went, thirty metres tall, and the wind leaped in and began whispering and fluttering through invisible cracks, getting into the hall and shaking the lampshade into a cascade of tinkles.

Many things were written in that house, dozens of articles of one sort or another, some for the *Sydney Morning Herald* women's page where I seemed to have inherited in a modest way the mantles of the much-loved writers, Charmian Clift and Helen Frizell. There were also several Wombat books, and three books for teenagers, including *Come Danger, Come Darkness* and *Playing Beatie Bow*, which won prizes and became a film.

The novel about the dwarf, *Swords and Crowns and Rings*, was written, and won the Miles Franklin Award. Maybe Miles, who had so disliked my younger self, would have been furious; on the other hand she might have mellowed since departing this life in the early 1950s. The award varies in value according to the investment market, and in my year it was exceptionally small, just enough to cover airfares from the island and brief accommodation. Still, I was most pleased to have won it, feeling the event a kind of reconciliation with that salty little woman.

Though I regained my health within a year or two, feeling once again the buoyancy of physical life, I still could not sleep, and so developed the adventurous habit of night-wandering in my minute ex-hire car which bore all the wounds of its previous occupation—doors that either jammed or would not shut, permanently open windows, lights temperamental, bits forever dropping off. Still, it served. Not since my family lived at Tanekaha Valley in New Zealand had I had the opportunity to observe the true country darkness, so lacking in any form of refracted light that it is absolute, a positive presence rather than an absence.

In darkness, like all things, the island changed shape, becoming immense, gullies deeper, hillsides rearing up like the walls of skyscrapers. The tall red guava hedges leaned inwards; sometimes there was a sudden whispered alarm from green linnets or other small birds cosied amidst the foliage. Who's that at such an hour? A cat or a cow? No, one of Them.

How I hate being the enemy.

The cows were asleep, too, often in the middle of the road. But residents of the island did not have accidents; we all knew the obscured bend where one crept through on the wrong side of the road; the ruts that might swallow a wheel; the steep crumbling bank that was called Place Where Russian Sailors Went Over, referring in the common island way to an exciting incident of years before.

When I had visitors staying, and I often did, they sometimes accompanied me on these prowls, not liking it at all, astonished by the blind darkness, exclaiming with relief should they see the dim spark of an eremite farmhouse in a remote 'walley'. I often playfully drove them to a place on the western road, close to the cliff and called Ghost Corner, I think. There one might wait under the trees and hear eerie mumblings, whispers and shuffles, most uncanny in the stillness. But the ghost sounds came from muttonbirds, murmuring to their chicks in the burrows that ran from the cliff face under the road.

Still, there are real ghosts on the island, infrequently seen.

Though my house lay in the path of the winds, there were often mornings of entranced stillness. Then the island seems enclosed in a bubble or glassy dome. Time and space vanish; did they ever exist? It is as though stillness were a new dimension. Once, I remember, I stood outside, amazed that I could hear the tinkle of teacups in my neighbour's kitchen, across two paddocks. And while I stood there, I observed an event I fancy must be rare. I never met another resident who had seen such a thing, except the one I called that day.

Just beyond my boundary fence grew a prodigiously tall pine. The islanders round about called him Big Bob, and the name was warranted, for he could be seen from almost all over the island. Big Bob's boughs, as big as trees themselves, were welcomed over my fences, and his roots went under the house, immense and muscular. I had refused to have them cut.

Suddenly, from the corner of my eye, I saw the tree explode. There is no other word for it. Big Bob swelled to half his size again, a colossal arrowhead of gold. Again and again these explosions occurred, each time to a lesser degree, and all the time the astonishing cloud of fine yellow pollen drifted down the tree to the ground.

That morning many things had come together, the degree of warmth in the air, the windlessness, the fertility of the tree's two classes of cone—the small male and the large round female—and I had witnessed an apocalypse.

At the time, for the event lasted but four or five minutes, I had opportunity only to shout to the nurseryman, working in his garden down the road, but he too observed the last half minute of Big Bob's transcendence.

The islanders whose farmhouses were built along my road, each with a decent interval of eight or ten paddocks in between, told me that Big Bob had been there forever. Their great-grandfathers had recalled him as a mature tree. So he might well have been the 250 years of age that, it is said, Norfolk Island pines can live. They also told me that the trees set cones only two or three times in twenty years, and these were not always fertile.

As anyone who has read my previous book of auto-biography, *A Fence Around the Cuckoo*, will be aware, I began life as a seedling tree myself, or near enough, so both the rain forest and the ever-present pines on the island were esteemed and loved by me. My workroom window looked out on Big Bob, and for several years I had watched his vast boughs gather in the dawn light, then the ruddy sunrise, until he looked as though he had secret fire in his heart, turning his whole being not red but bronze and amber.

We had been through a cyclone together, a time of tremendous noise, when the guava wastelands and the forest disappeared in the rain, blown into visibility by this gust and out by that, an illusory leafy city. The rain forest gave out immense vowel sounds, urrrrr, ahhhhhhhh! and the white oaks, natives related to the hibiscus, creaked and squealed, swirling and lashing, shedding seed capsules by the ton. But the pines, and most royally Big Bob, made small sedate arcs with their crests, and a slow swimming movement with the long boughs, like a host of sea anemones.

These magnificent trees, *Aracauria heterophylla*, are not pines as we commonly use that word, but belong to a genus which also includes the splendid bunya-bunya, the hoop pine and the New Zealand kauri. They are endemic to this tiny island. But once when the land masses were differently disposed on the globe, they grew in many places. The coal seams of Antarctica are made of what was once Norfolk Island pine.

3

Thus my island years went past, some swiftly, some slowly, as years do. My older family in New Zealand seemed to need visits far more than my young people in Australia did, and so my children were able to make their way through their early mature years without my fussing around, a description usually given to maternal interest and solicitude. All the aunts, like my mother, had been widowed in middle age, and sadly I watched these erstwhile radiant creatures dim, become old, and draw even closer together for company and protection. Like birds in a cage they had their squabbles and fierce chirpings, coming together at nightfall with unsubdued murmurs of 'And don't you do that again!'

Both Wendela and Rosina were predeceased by their children, Stuart during the war, and Wendela's Helga with cancer in her middle years. As a girl Helga had been beautiful in her bright Norwegian way, a kind girl with whom all animals seemed to be in love. She had married late in life; her animal lovers dwindled down to one old cat. When she died her husband left the hospital, returned home and took the cat straight to the vet to be put down. He had been jealous, I suppose. Anyone in the family would have taken the cat, including my sister, who, in her habitual way, had been most practically supportive of her cousin Helga in the latter's painful illness, and cared for her mother for the rest of her life.

My sister in truth devoted much of her life to a selfless caring for old people growing older. Each one of them was welcome to come and live with me, but that drawing-in of the spirit had taken place as it does in most of the old, and they could not bring themselves to interrupt their protective routines.

'Live on an island? Oh, no, dear, I positively couldn't!'

'I couldn't leave my house. Someone might break in.'

'Wild horses wouldn't get me on to a plane, and that's all there is to it.'

'Joc doesn't mind giving us a hand now and then.'

So they leaned more and more heavily, creating an all too common situation, where a willing and loving young woman's life is chewed up in support of others with no future. But what is the answer to the problem of the old and frail?

All this time I assiduously practised Zen. It is best if the student has a teacher, or rather guide, but still possible to make some progress in understanding this interesting discipline if she has written guidance. Our elder son, a physicist, was doing postgraduate work at Berkeley in California, and often sent me books unobtainable in Australia. And few planes arrived on the island without bringing me a parcel of carefully chosen books from Anne, our librarian daughter.

'Don't want you reduced to reading the print on Weetbix packets,' she said. One might well have done. The local library was, at that time, a few hundred old and commonplace books housed in what appeared to be a disused fowlhouse in the middle of a paddock. Later several other book-starved residents and I got together and put enough pressure on the Administrator of the time—'Of course, Your Honour, a cultured and aware man like yourself will realise'—to attain better things. I believe that first reasonably housed and stocked library was the nucleus of what is now an admirable one for a small South Pacific island.

Although I studied Zen teachings in all earnestness, I was stuck in many areas. The *roshis* make no bones about the fact that you can learn till the cows come home, but that does not equate with experience. There was I, with Big Bob in front of my nose, completely understanding that it was because he was not resistant to the cyclonic winds, but allowed their furious energy to flow through his being, that he had been able to stand for centuries.

And yet I was not able to do likewise.

Having a damaged backbone, one of the many things I resisted was pain. I resented it because it prevented me from doing things, hated it because I felt it unfair. (What have I done to deserve this, and so on.) Every time I had a bout of back trouble I counter-attacked, stiffened up, raged at my inability to drive this devil out of my spine. But it was much stronger than I; I might have spent my life fighting it and I would not have won. The thing to do was stop being rigid and resistant, not to welcome the pain, but to allow it to flow through.

My predicament was a small one compared with many of the sad or deplorable hells into which people will themselves. Still, I created it myself by habitual reaction. We always do, at least until we awaken. This is all that enlightenment or awareness is. Waking up. Nothing special.

Here is a Zen story illustrating how heaven and hell, good and bad, and other bothersome human conditions are constructs of our own minds.

There was a *roshi* sitting calmly, minding his own business, which was to be calm. Along came a ferocious-looking samurai and barked, 'Tell me the nature of heaven and hell!'

The *roshi* looked up at this terrifying warrior and said, 'Why should I tell a disgusting great lump of nothing like you?'

The samurai nearly burst with rage, but the *roshi* continued, 'An ugly frog like you, a slug, a worm, why should I tell you anything?'

The samurai whisked out his sword and was just about to cut the *roshi* in half when the *roshi* murmured, 'That's hell.'

The samurai wasn't stupid; he was just used to behaving stupidly. He understood that his feelings of insult, anger and wounded ego had put him into such hell he was ready to slice this man in two.

Tears filled his eyes. He put his hands together in sorrow. The *roshi* said, 'That's heaven.'

*

343

When Beres, my brother-in-law and old playmate died of a heart attack in 1976, sadness remained with me for so long, that at last I realised loneliness and nostalgia for our shared youth had a great deal to do with it.

'Detach! Detach!' I told myself, but although I had at last been able to let my husband go, freely and with love, somehow I had a great struggle over Beres. He had been such a funny boy, so joyful, wanting to please.

Yet I knew more clearly than ever that it was time to detach from him and all he represented—not that these things should be forgotten or made lesser or greater, simply not possessed any more.

For a long time I had been in touch with the Zen Center in San Francisco, one of a complex of seven Soto Zen study venues effectively founded by Suzuki-roshi. I wrote to inquire if I could stay at the Center for a few weeks.

'Sure you can, Mrs South Pole,' they wrote back.

Mrs South Pole! I came from so far away they could not believe it. None of the sixty resident students at the Zen Center had heard of Norfolk Island or knew anything of my kingdom, the Pacific Ocean, except one, an older man, a lone sailor, who had seen Rapa-iti and even passed within hail of solitary Pitcairn. During recreation we talked of sperm whales, thundering through the water like great black wheels, dead on course for Antarctica. Once I had watched three off the north coast of Norfolk, though they were very rare at that time.

But the lone sailor had seen eight or nine in a pod, and although his little vessel had been a considerable distance away from the travellers, it had tossed about like a floating leaf in the turbulence of their passage.

'You can see divinity in the great whales,' he said.

I did not tell him that twice in its history Norfolk Island had been a whaling station.

I was much older than others there, but no distinction was made in any way, any more than it was made for gender or race. One was not commended for work well done, nor reproved when it was poor. It was taken for granted that we were there because of choice, and because we wanted to find what 'was in our sleeves'. Consequently everyone worked and meditated hard, for each one knew that life, in its innermost sense, was at stake.

The Center was in Page Street, running down to historic Market Street. Page Street was lined with Edwardian houses, seedy and tottering, but the Center itself was a calm, solid old building, originally built by wealthy merchants as a refuge for Jewish immigrant girls. So the Star of David was everywhere.

'So what? All the same difference.'

This was our timetable:

4.40 a.m.	*Wake up bell*
5.00	*Zazen (formal meditation)*
5.40	*Kinhin (walking meditation)*
5.50	*Zazen*
6.30	*Service*
7.05	*Work*
7.20	*Breakfast*
8.30	*Work*
12.00	*End Work*

The timetable operated similarly all day until the final meditation period at 8.30 p.m.

We slept on futons, but because of my back I was used to a mattress as hard as a brick. My roomie was a Canadian woman, Jeanne, both warm and reserved as are so many from that likeable nation. Like me, she was an ex-mother, a seeker, needing the full richness of spiritual life, but not quite sure where it was.

'Time and time again I've pointed, saying "There it is!" but I've been wrong. My kids think I'm crazy. They think my fulfilment should rest with them. But there's more, I know there is.'

I told her then of the island women and their huge enfoldment of life. And of one in particular, whom I didn't know very well, but who, on meeting me in the road, suddenly grabbed me in a hug that lifted me off my feet.

When I, laughing, said, 'Why did you do that?' she answered, 'Cos.'

Jeanne laughed. 'Isn't that pure Zen? No cogitation, no analysis, just being.'

She had been at the Center when Suzuki-roshi died there. He wanted to die where his students could be with him daily and hourly, so they could understand completely that death is nothing special. She told me that a few hours before he lapsed into unconsciousness someone asked, 'When shall we all meet again?' and a small wasted hand came out from under the blanket and described a circle in the air.

'Everything is one?'
'Yes.'

346

Still disorientated by jetlag, that first morning I shot off my futon wild-eyed. Yet the wake-up bell was a dulcet fairy tinkle that scooted through the many corridors at an inhuman speed, I imagined a tiny monk, a Tinkerbell monk twenty centimetres high, and was considering this mystery when Jeanne groaned, 'One of these mornings I'm going right out there to clap a flowerpot over him!'

Laggards were called to the *zendo*, the meditation hall, by a rapidly accelerating tattoo on the *han*, a thick wooden board, often made in the shape of a fish, hollowed in the middle, and giving forth a resonant, curiously exciting sound. As the beat increased, it was impossible to keep from breaking into a run.

'That guy sure plays a mean *han*!' I heard some sprinter mumble as we streamed into the *zendo*. I tried to hesitate on the threshold, to savour this moment of which I had often dreamed as I meditated alone on my island verandah. At last to be meditating with other people of the same mind! But there was no chance to hesitate. I was swept onwards, and in a moment was sitting on my black cushion, facing a dim wall, sinking into the familiar darkness of deep meditation. Down, down past the receding sounds, the visual illusions known as *makyo* which are often startling and beautiful but must be disregarded, into the silence where breath almost ceases, and the mind is completely at rest.

Buddhist meditation is so different from Christian meditation (which I had also done extensively in my Catholic days), that it would more correctly be called contemplation. In this practice there is no specific purpose or goal. It exists of itself and what comes from it exists of itself also. When pressed for a why and wherefore, questions which rise from irrepressible human curiosity, a great teacher of the past, Nangaku, said that everything we do is *zazen*, provided we do it singlemindedly. A rock or a plant does this all the time. But as our monkey minds have difficulty being concentrated, we must practice.

This is not news to any of us. Every sage who ever lived said the same thing. One thinks, for instance, of St Benedict's 'Work is prayer'. But Soto Zen, for me at least, was the simplest way.

Though in the following six years I was to travel to Japan four times, twice studying in monasteries, each time sitting *zazen* with other students, when I think of a *zendo* it is that vast shadowy room in Page Street, San Francisco. Once the basement of the Jewish hostel, it had become in all ways Japanese, empty, cold, with raised platforms around the walls, bearing the round, pleat-sided cushions used for meditation, placed in neat rows. With no difficulty I can bring before my inward eye the golden wood floor, the pale wheaten hue of the black-bound *tatami* on the platforms, the black cushions. I smell the air with its faint scent of incense and undisturbed chill. And always, no matter what country I am in, when I begin my daily meditation I return there.

Once a week we had a free half day, and one week I wandered along to the *Examiner* office, the newspaper that had offered me a job in the early years of the second World War. I was still grateful for that generous offer from the *San Francisco Examiner*, for although Pearl Harbour intervened, stopping dead all travel, and I was not able to take it up, the very knowledge that someone wanted me, young, female, and far away as I was, stiffened my spine and sent me forth to try my luck elsewhere.

But what if I had been able to accept that position, had set out for San Francisco, as I was all ready to do? If the Japanese attack on Pearl Harbour had occurred just a week or two later? I would have been marooned in the States for the duration of the war, and as I was at the prime marrying age, probably would have married an American. On such an unpredictable occurrence had the pivot of my life been poised.

I thought I'd walk down to the Bay, which, although located within eyeshot of Zen Center, had always been invisible in fog or smog. The streets were shabby, industrialised, rather like Sydney's dockland. Both cities had been born of the sea. As I watched, the smog broke up into smoky lacunae, and a tremulous wind rose, smelling of rusty ships and unfresh shores.

Had my life been lived in San Francisco would I have been a writer? As usual when I begin to ponder life's puzzles, my thoughts drifted also to the puzzle of writing, a passion I have never understood. Is it just a human instinct for storytelling, as universally we have a powerful instinct for story-hearing?

With me there had always been a confluence of two streams, literary and personal, and I had taken great risks for both. Yet that unappeasable thing within me that needed to write had never required fame or success. The writing was sufficient. Once a book had been published I never willingly looked at it again.

What had I always wanted to write? What kind of thing?

It seemed I didn't care. All I wanted was to write stories, short or long, fact or fiction, in which the reader could walk about, see a familiar reflection in the looking-glass, say, 'Oh, yes, I know! I've been here all the time but didn't realise it.'

The only thing you have to offer another human being is your own state of mind. And the state of my mind had been gladness, gladness about the world I was in, and the fact that I was in it.

Only the evening before, the teacher had spoken about enlightenment, how it does not change the person, merely his comprehension of the world and himself. He quoted the saying of a truly enlightened person: 'Where we were ice we are now water, of exactly the same substance but with different freedoms.'

With a rush of joy I felt that of late I was thawing a little. Surely I had realised some little thing here and there, about writing and myself? Before I knew it, the idea had sneaked up on me. I was preening.

Fortunately, after a while I was approached by one of San Francisco's many student beggars, beautiful, well-fed, clean, wearing those magnificently tooled leather Texan range boots that cost $US600.

Gently he asked, 'Would you give me fifty cents, ma'am, to help me buy a ticket to Santa Barbara?'

'What say you give me fifty cents instead?' I asked, teasing.

He looked at me in consternation. Probably he had never been asked for money in his life. He walked slowly away.

'Well, you shameless little fraud!' I thought. And then, 'Hey, hey! Watch it! If he's a fraud that's his problem. Yours is quite different, and there's no need to have it at all.'

So I went quickly after him and gave him the fifty cents.

Text Classics